Y COMPOSERS

György Ligeti

by Richard Toop

Φ

Phaidon Press Limited
Regent's Wharf
All Saints Street
London N1 9PA

First published 1999
© 1999 Phaidon Press Limited

ISBN 0 7148 3795 4

A CIP catalogue record for this book is
available from the British Library

Printed in Singapore

Frontispiece, a master of
stop-watch precision –
György Ligeti at a rehearsal
of the Ten Pieces for
wind quintet

Contents

Preface

The story of music's post-war avant garde, with all its attendant controversies, now stretches over half a century. Reputations have been won and lost, and great ideas have come and gone. Composers like Pierre Boulez, John Cage, Karlheinz Stockhausen and Iannis Xenakis have secured their place in history; but at the turn of the millennium, from all this brilliant constellation, the composer most firmly ensconced in the public ear is surely György Ligeti. When he first burst on to the international scene in the early 1960s, he was regarded as a provocative young ultra-modernist, standing alongside Boulez and Stockhausen at the head of the European avant garde, and pioneering a completely new style of music based on dense, labyrinthine but glistening textures. In the late 1960s, in contrast to the wild, often anarchic experimention of many of his fellow composers, Ligeti gained a reputation as a perfectionist, a master jeweller constantly whittling away at his chosen diamonds, and always finding new facets. Then suddenly, in the mid 1970s, his music branched out, embracing influences ranging from the Middle Ages to modern Africa, but always keeping its own voice. Since then Ligeti has established a unique reputation as a composer whose work reaches way beyond the confines of the avant garde: as a modernist who has gone beyond the old versions of modernism and found new, broader and more appealing possibilities.

This may sound like an easy path to success; it was not. Many composers of his generation were caught up in the horrors of World War II, but Ligeti's experiences were particularly traumatic. He sought to cauterize the personal wound left by those times, not by denying intense emotions in his music, but by stylizing them. This may well be one of the reasons why his work has had such universal appeal. Back in the late 1960s, the eerie qualities of his music were seized upon by Stanley Kubrick for the film *2001: A Space Odyssey*, bringing his work to a much wider audience; that audience has steadily grown, and nowadays Ligeti is frequently hailed as the saviour of modern music. Not that this is an epithet that he would care for: he is the least messianic member of the post-war avant garde, and distrusts all systems and ideologies. Yet in the context of the 1980s and beyond, there is something about Ligeti's constant search for new stimuli, whether from Africa or from fractal mathematics, which seems to embody a late-twentieth-century optimism – a conviction that, even without resorting to esoteric extremes, the age of new discoveries is far from over.

Ligeti is not an easy subject for the biographer. He now talks openly about his early years, but brings down a protective shield where the later decades are concerned: his recent life is not relevant to the music, he says, and for the most part he does not want to talk about it. I did not feel inclined to meddle with this desire for privacy; as a result, the reader will note that as the book proceeds, the biographical element recedes. In its place, increased attention is given to the world around Ligeti, and his own view of it.

In English, there has only been one Ligeti monograph to date, by Paul Griffiths (Robson, 1983, revised edition 1997), though others are in prospect. In German, on the other hand, the Ligeti literature is extensive: in addition to numerous interviews and essays by the composer himself, three important books have appeared in recent years, all by authors who have known Ligeti for many years. Ulrich Dibelius's *Ligeti: Eine Monographie in Essays* (Schott, 1994) sagely summarizes three decades of contact with the composer and his works; Wolfgang Burde's *György Ligeti: Eine Monographie* (Atlantis, 1993) provides a wealth of new information concerning the earlier years; and Constantin Floros's *György Ligeti: Jenseits von Avantgarde und Postmoderne* (Lafite, 1996) offers valuable insights into more recent works. All of these books were of enormous use to me; many other useful sources are listed in the Further Reading at the end of this book.

Ligeti's pressing schedule during 1996 meant that my contact with him was restricted to a single but treasured lunch between rehearsals with the Ensemble Modern in Frankfurt. However, like previous authors, I was able to benefit from the expertise, tireless help and advice of Dr Louise Duchesneau, Ligeti's personal assistant since 1983, to whom I extend my undying gratitude – if only all composers had such assistants! In addition, my thanks go to Peter Eötvös and members of Ensemble Modern for insights into their experiences with

Ligeti, to Dr Jürgen Hocker for information about his mechanical realizations of Ligeti's works, to Bernhard Pfau (Schott, Mainz) and Peter Grimshaw (Boosey & Hawkes, Sydney) for the supply of scores, to Annette Kehrs for access to Schott's photographic archive, to Yann Orlarey (GRAME – 'Centre National de Création musicale') for a transcript of Ligeti's comments at the *Rencontres pluridisciplinaires* and to Kathryn Hill for the loan of various materials. My thanks also to the University of Sydney for granting an extended period of study leave which assisted me in completing this and other projects.

Richard Toop
Sydney, 1999

I

Cluj has often been an inspiration for and a subject of his compositions in 1938

I remember that when I was very small, I was always imagining music. It was a sort of ritual when I got up or went to bed ... there was morning music and there was evening music. It was all in my mind ... I think that's how I became a composer. But back then I was unaware that this was something unusual.

György Ligeti, in conversation with
Reinhard Oehlschlägel

Childhood and Youth 1923-45

György Ligeti was born on 28 May 1923 in Dicsöszentmárton (now Tîrnăveni), a small town of about 5,000 inhabitants in Transylvania. At the end of World War I the town had been ceded to Romania, but previously it had been in Hungarian territory. Ligeti's parents, both Jewish, were very much products of the Budapest milieu, and did not speak Romanian; his mother Ilona was a doctor – an ophthalmologist – while his father Sándor, a bank employee, was an idealistic socialist and pacifist with no religious beliefs. Accordingly, though there was a synagogue just down the road, it remained unvisited by the Ligeti family. Ligeti himself has said that he became 'Jewish' only through persecution; his real cultural roots were Hungarian (and to this day, the verbal components of his composition sketches are mainly written in Hungarian). Yet one can doubt this: in both the man and his music, there is a mixture of boundless inquisitiveness (one is reminded of Kipling's 'Elephant's Child' with its 'insatiable curtiosity'), a passion for arguing non-confrontationally with almost any proposition and a fascination with paradox that seems quintessential to European Jewry's intelligentsia.

Though Sándor Ligeti would come to regard his elder son as a bit of a dreamer, he was not exempt from fantasies of his own: he had always wanted to study science – chemistry and medicine – and his great dream was to have his own biochemical laboratory on an island in the Adriatic. These fantasies came to an abrupt end when his own father, a painter of civic murals, fell to his death, leaving behind a pile of debts. Since Sándor had shown a pronounced gift for mathematics, he was apprenticed to the Anglo-Hungarian Bank and sent to university, where he graduated in national economy and political science.

Pacifist or not, he was enlisted in World War I, in which he was severely wounded, gained some medals and was promoted to lieutenant. It was while he was in hospital that he met his future wife Ilona. The reason he found himself in Dicsöszentmárton after the war was that his bank dispatched him there to direct the local branch. In

1929 he moved to Cluj (the largest town in Transylvania), where he became the manager of a small private bank. The next year, however, an economic crisis caused the closure of all private banks, and much to his chagrin, he found himself left in the same office, but now reduced to selling state lottery tickets, on half his previous salary. Perhaps by way of compensation, he turned to writing and produced, in Ligeti's words, 'several books on economics, from a radical socialist point of view', as well as a novel about a utopian society in which money was unnecessary.

One has a mixed picture of the young György Ligeti. On the one hand, there is the small boy playing with the local rabbi's children, and even with those of the local Romanian aristocracy, who would probably have preferred their offspring not to be playing with Jews, but at least were relieved that they were not playing with 'pure' Hungarians. On the other hand, there is evidence of the precocious development that is often characteristic of the subsequent 'loner'. By the age of three György could already read fluently: the first book he remembers is a children's version of *One Thousand and One Nights*, in which he was particularly entranced by the tales of Sinbad the Sailor (though it was another twenty-six years before he would see the sea – the Baltic – at first hand). Another vivid literary memory is of a book of short stories by Gyula Krudy, which he was given at the age of five. It was a totally inappropriate book for a small child, but there was one story which made a huge impression on him. Reading it up in the loft, on a hot summer's day, he remembers 'being overcome by a strange melancholy'; its central character is an old widow who lives alone in a house full of barometers, hygrometers and ticking clocks, her husband having been a physicist, mechanic and astronomer. The superimposition of many musical layers 'ticking' at different speeds was to become a central feature of Ligeti's music in the 1960s, and he traces it back to this childhood experience. Moreover, the mixture of home, machine room and observatory was eventually to provide the scenario for the bizarre second scene of his opera *Le Grand Macabre*.

There are also more traumatic memories from that period. As he recalls: 'When I was three years old, I stayed with my aunt at Csikszereda for three months, as construction work was going on at our house. She was a teacher at an elementary school and had the idea that children had to overcome their aversions. When she realized that I was afraid of spiders she made me collect cobwebs with bare hands. It terrified and disgusted me.' Ligeti remains an arachnophobe to this day, and one essential aspect of his early work – the web-like 'micropolyphony' that enters his work from the late 1950s onwards – arises, arguably, from the need to exorcize this persisting horror, or else to transmute it into artistic gold.

For a small child, his awareness and fear of death was unusually strong. He remembers that there was a gipsy dog-catcher who was employed to round up strays, and kill the ones without owners. One day the three-year-old followed a stray dog into a house, and wanted to keep it; when his father said no, he knew the dog was going to die, and was 'horribly afraid'. Perhaps the most arresting experience of small-town life, though, was the children's funerals, where little white coffins would be pulled on small white carts: 'what that meant for me was that death, my own, was in the realm of the possible.'

It was fairy tales that most attracted him in his early years, and for a sensitive child, at least, such tales can be a source of fear as well as pleasure. In those years, he says, he was often afraid; as an instance, he cites yet another experience from the age of three, in which he suddenly realized that the Romanian soldiers who were in town on manoeuvres all spoke a language he could not understand, and that he was barred from communicating with them. Still, it is not clear whether there was always a real external cause for this fear, or whether (as seems more likely) it was the product of a highly sensitive and introverted imagination. At any rate, his solution was to create his own imaginary inner world, and retreat into it. The discipline of school studies, as one can imagine, did not appeal to him. On the way to school he would sometimes give names to all the clouds, or imagine that he was an aeroplane flying over the paving stones which had become the skyscrapers in his imaginary domain, which he named Kylwiria.

Such fantasies are probably common enough among imaginative children, but with Ligeti they persisted well into his teens, to the point where his father certainly felt some concern. On the one hand he was pleased that his obviously intelligent but innately unscholarly son was at least doing well in subjects like maths and physics. But when the fictitious land of Kylwiria began to sprout not only detailed city plans, but its own language and grammar, he must have wondered where it would all end.

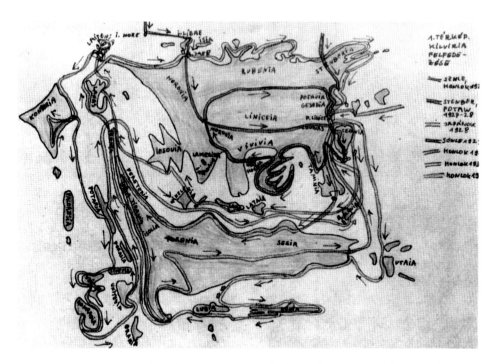

A map of Kylwiria, the imaginary land for which the teenage Ligeti not only drew up detailed civic plans, but invented a language

Ligeti's parents were music-lovers, but not practising musicians, though his father had learnt the violin. However, he had one distinguished musical ancestor: 'Ligeti' is an imprecise Hungarian translation of the German name Auer, and one of his great uncles was the great violinist Leopold Auer. As for the young György Ligeti, music – his own music – was part of his inner world from the start. At the age of three, he remembers, he already had an imaginary music for getting up and going to bed, which must have been something more involved than just a melody, or else he would have sung it. It never occurred to him that this was anything unusual: for many years he assumed that everyone heard their own music!

His early musical experience was both live and recorded – the family had a record player and a radio, but once they moved to Cluj they also went to concerts by the local symphony orchestra. By the age of eight or nine, significantly, he was making judgements of what he heard, and not just lapping it all up. He could sense that although the sound of a Beethoven symphony coming across the radio from Budapest was not as attractive as hearing it played live by the Cluj orchestra, the performance itself somehow seemed better.

Back in Dicsőszentmárton there had also been gipsy bands, but
their music did not appeal to the young Ligeti; overhearing fragments
of their music wafting into his bedroom at night, he had the
impression of 'huge, hard-winged cockroaches banging into a wall,
somewhere far away'. His mother sometimes sang gipsy songs, folk
songs and tunes from operetta after supper, but these too failed to
make a great impact.

One of the strongest impressions of these early years was his first
visit to the opera, to see Mussorgsky's *Boris Godunov*: 'It was a terrific
experience. I can still remember all the details, with a cousin, how it
was, where we sat, what sweets I got from her, how they tasted. I
would say that the visual impression was much greater than the aural
one, the musical impression didn't really stick ... I could describe the
basic impression like this: the sounds of bells, and the golden
splendour of all these kings, and priests and courtiers ... But
immediately after that I was at my first Verdi opera – I must have been
about seven – it was *La traviata*. And there I went into a sort of trance,
into this dreamlike state.' The cinema also made a great impact on
him: a non-musical highlight of his early years was seeing Charlie
Chaplin in *Modern Times*.

The transfer from junior to secondary school was a mixed experience. For a start, it involved a switch of language from the Hungarian
of his elementary school to Romanian. One curious consequence of
this, he says, is that even today he tends to associate elementary and
advanced maths (addition at one end of the scale, vector analysis at
the other) with Hungarian terminology, and the intermediate stages
(algebra, trigonometry etc.) with Romanian. As for music, he found
an elderly music master who, despite his eccentric appearance and
behaviour, managed to inspire students to read music and sing it at
sight. In the playground, on the other hand, the usual pre-pubescent
thuggery held sway. In the first two or three years he was bullied by
older children, and it was pointless to protest to teachers, partly
because this was 'bad form', but also because they were mainly anti-
Semitic, and highly unlikely to offer any help.

Rather than retreat into personal isolation, at the age of thirteen he
responded by joining Habonim, a recently founded, left-orientated
Zionist youth movement which is still active today. However, this
affiliation, which greatly displeased his anti-nationalist father, only

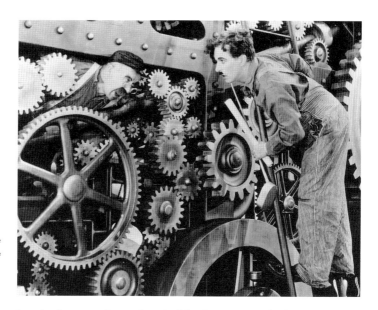

Ligeti's most vivid early memories of the cinema were of Charlie Chaplin, seen here in *Modern Times*. Complex mechanisms would always fascinate Ligeti.

lasted a few years. Just as later in life, the point at which group membership sought to impose obligations was the point at which he lost interest: 'The Zionist Left's collectivist ideas were alien to me, and as I advanced into puberty I could scarcely imagine myself working on the land in a kibbutz; I thought more in terms of becoming a scientist. So at the age of sixteen, after much hesitation, self-reproach and the fear of bad faith, I left.'

Ligeti did not learn to play an instrument until his teens, and even then, it was partly by accident. His persistent requests to have violin lessons had been turned down by his father, on the grounds that they had been no use to him and would be no use to his son either. But when a local music teacher discovered that his younger brother Gábor had perfect pitch and recommended that he should take up the violin, his parents agreed; within a few years his brother became a very able violinist and violist. After about a year, Ligeti protested that he too should be allowed to play an instrument (he was fourteen at the time), and since the family now already had a violinist, Ligeti was assigned to the piano. The family did not actually own one, but one of the neighbours in the same apartment block was a piano teacher, and she let György practise on a second grand piano, in a back room. (After a year of this his father relented, and got a piano.)

From then on, his attachment to the piano was obsessive – every day, after school, he would go straight to the teacher's flat and practise for six or seven hours, once again in a sort of trance. The results were impressive: within a few months he was attempting the easier Bach preludes, and then came some of Grieg's *Lyric Pieces*. In Ligeti's view, it was this first encounter with 'adult' works that made him determined to be a composer himself, and his first composition was a waltz in A minor in the style of Grieg (curiously, Grieg's music also made a great impression on the teenage John Cage). Moreover, the three-quarter-hour walk from school to the piano became a time in which he would compose in his head, evolving whole symphonies in a 'romantic-pathetic' style influenced above all by Beethoven and Schumann.

Though he never became a virtuoso performer, from his early teens he was fascinated by the notion of transcendental virtuosity: he particularly remembers Ignaz Friedmann's extraordinary recordings of the Chopin Etudes (asked why he played them so fast, Friedmann is supposed to have replied 'Because I can'). In retrospect, it seems significant that this passion for virtuosity roughly coincided with his first serious interest in composing – investigating the extremes of what is technically possible has always been one of his artistic obsessions. But it was not just solo virtuosity that intrigued him. Another of his favourite recordings was of Richard Strauss's tone poem *Don Quixote*; its notorious 'sheep' passage strikingly anticipates the dense, themeless textures that Ligeti was to pioneer in his own music of the early 1960s – indeed there is one passage in Ligeti's *Atmosphères* that sounds like a furtive homage to it. By this stage, his musical tastes were already partly at odds with his father's; for the latter, even Wagner 'wasn't really music'.

By the age of sixteen he had completed a string quartet, and though his school music master's reaction to it had been frankly disparaging, Ligeti now felt ready to attempt a major orchestral work – a symphony in A minor. It was not an entirely dilettantish undertaking: he had taught himself as much conventional harmony as seemed necessary, had read several books on orchestration, and had carefully studied scores by Mozart, Beethoven and Strauss. He had also joined a local amateur symphony orchestra (consisting mainly of Jewish doctors) as a timpanist, and was beginning to get some sense of the orchestra 'from inside'. He began work with enthusiasm: 'It was marvellous fun to write a proper score. I did it over the course of two summer holidays; we had gone to a small town, and I sat in the cemetery, with the big score paper spread out in front of me. I finished two movements. Stylistically, they were a mixture of Beethoven and Richard Strauss with a little bit of atonality, though only in the sense that Richard Strauss used it in his *Zarathustra*.' Among other things, it was going to feature a cannon shot – 'to impress the girls' (though a female co-student from those days remembers Ligeti as being rather remote: it was his brother Gábor, she says, who attracted the girls' attention).

That autumn, World War II broke out, and though Transylvania was not immediately involved, within a few months the increasingly unstable political situation in Europe was becoming apparent even in Cluj. In 1940 the boundaries were redrawn so that the town became part of Hungary (after the war, it would revert to Romania again). The next year the Hungarian government of Horthy made an alliance with Hitler, and the army was deployed to fight the Yugoslavs; later the same year the Hungarians declared war on the Soviet Union. Many of Ligeti's fellow students had joined the Iron Guard, virtually a Hungarian equivalent of the Hitler Youth, with a fanatical, quasi-mystical nationalistic basis, and a fair measure of 'blood and soil' thrown in. Ligeti would have wanted no part of this, even if he had not been barred from it on racial grounds: teenage membership of the Zionist Habonim had been his only foray into collectives, and once he left that, his history of ideological adherence was virtually over.

He matriculated from his secondary school in Cluj in 1941; by this stage he was almost sure that he wanted to be a composer, even if the sciences offered more attractive professional prospects, and indeed a song of his for mezzo-soprano and piano (*Kineret*) was published in Budapest that year, after winning first prize in a competition. Nevertheless, his musical studies had necessarily taken second place for a while. Anti-Semitism was now rampant in educational policy, and as a Jew, Ligeti could only hope to go to university (where he wanted to study physics) if he matriculated with distinction. This he achieved, but it still did not help; in the meantime a law had been brought in that allowed only one Jewish student to be admitted each semester.

In principle, the same law applied to the Cluj Conservatory. But here the director Viktor Vaszy took a more resistant approach, and once Ligeti had passed the entrance examination, he was allowed to enrol. So with his father's consent, he now took classes in harmony and counterpoint with the composer Ferenc Farkas (a former pupil of Respighi), and also studied piano, organ and cello. The organ gained particular attention, since there was a small instrument at the conservatory that was almost always available for him to practise on. But at the same time, he was also unofficially attending classes in mathematics and physics, in the hope of a quick end to the war, and more favourable conditions for study and employment. It was a gruelling schedule – too gruelling, as it turned out. After a few months of getting up every morning at five, after only four hours sleep, he suffered a severe nervous breakdown. This potential catastrophe had two positive outcomes. Up to then, Farkas had followed Zoltan Kodály's dictum that students should not be praised; but now he did begin to encourage Ligeti, to suggest that he might indeed be talented. In addition, since he had to go to Budapest for psychiatric treatment in the wake of his breakdown, Ligeti took the opportunity to have private lessons with Pál Kádosa, a more progressive composer than Farkas, and one who had established a solid reputation in the pre-war years. Kádosa placed great emphasis on analysis, and much of his tuition was devoted to rigorous formal analysis of the masterpieces of the classical repertory.

'Not a great composer, but a terrifically well-versed technician': Ligeti's teacher Ferenc Farkas

It was at this time that Ligeti had his first real exposure to 'modern music'. He already knew Béla Bartók's collection *For Children*, but now he encountered some of the major works of Bartók's last years – the *Divertimento* (a much more substantial work than its title suggests) and the Second Violin Concerto – and not just through scores or recordings, but in live performances directed by Vaszy. The real revelation, however, came from the Waldbauer Quartet's performance of an earlier work, the Second String Quartet of 1917, which so impressed Ligeti that for the next decade Bartók, and his string quartets in particular, came to represent a standard of perfection that became the yardstick for his own work. Stravinsky's work also attracted him, as did Hindemith's: he spent some time working through Hindemith's textbook on composition, *Unterweisung im Tonsatz* ('The Craft of Musical Composition').

A few pieces from this period survive, notably some for piano duet. The Bartók-Kodály influence is audible, as one might expect, but there are also traces of Stravinsky, especially of his early piano duet pieces. Perhaps the most curious aspect of this, as Ligeti points out, is that the strongest allusions often seem to be to pieces that he did not know at the time, such as the March from Bartók's *Mikrokosmos*, or more bizarrely, to Stravinsky's Symphony in Three Movements, which was not even completed until a couple of years later.

Up to the end of 1943, Ligeti had little real sense of the war raging around him, though on one occasion he was caught in an air raid on Budapest, and he was aware that of the many contemporaries being sent off to the Ukrainian front, few came back. His own situation changed radically in early 1944, when he was drafted into an (unarmed) Jewish forced labour unit, and composing became a thing of the past. From this point on, Ligeti's survival was a matter of pure chance. He cites a typical instance: 'First I went to Szeged, a big agrarian centre in the Hungarian Low Plains, and worked carrying sacks in army grain silos. The work parties were constantly dissolved, regrouped and transferred to other areas, as is entirely normal with military bureaucracy. So in March 1944 I and some other comrades were transferred to Fortress Grosswardein, and later it turned out that this saved my life: the Szeged work party was sent to the copper mines in Serbian Bor, and after gruelling work in the mines, on returning to Yugoslavia, they were shot to the last man by the SS.'

Romanian soldiers and civilians
under siege from the advancing
Soviet troops, September 1944

Wolfgang Burde suggests that the group's virtual internment in
Grosswardein was actually a calculated move by the Hungarian armed
forces minister to protect them from the Ministry of the Interior police
– the local gestapo. This protection came to an end after Soviet troops
crossed the Romanian border, surrounding Budapest by December.
The work party was now transferred to just behind the front line,
supplying ammunition. Though the danger from Soviet raids on the
munitions dumps was enormous, Ligeti says: 'We didn't feel it was
dangerous – we weren't living in the real world; once our relatives had
been dragged off, life and death became a matter of relative indifference.
If you died, you died; if you happened to stay alive, you stayed alive.'
It was probably a widespread reaction: Stockhausen, whose father died
on the Hungarian front, and who was drafted as a teenager to work in
a German front-line hospital corps, also recalls that life or death came
to seem like a non-issue.

Nevertheless, in October 1944 Ligeti decided to take a risk which,
if successful, would markedly improve his chances of survival. As the
Russian forces drew close, he hid in a wood – which left him in the
midst of fairly randomly aimed crossfire – and was eventually picked
up by the Russian forces, who detained him briefly, but then let him
go. He spent the next two weeks walking back to Transylvania, 'as if
in a trance'.

The rest of his family was not so fortunate. His father was taken first
to Auschwitz, then to Buchenwald, and was finally killed in Bergen-
Belsen. His younger brother had been taken away to the Mauthausen
concentration camp at the age of sixteen, and was killed a year later.
Only his mother survived; she too had been taken to Auschwitz, but
her medical training saved her: she proved useful as a camp doctor.
Ligeti describes the experience of these years as a wound that cannot be
healed, and the source of an undying hatred of those (but only those)
who were directly responsible. Until the day he dies, he says, he will
harbour fantasies of revenge, however incomprehensible these seem to
his colleagues at a distance of fifty years. One looks in vain for direct
traces of this in his music, but perhaps one can see precisely the shying
away from a 'confessional' style, and the obsessive fascination with
presenting innately extreme emotions 'in inverted commas', as a kind
of cauterizing response to personal trauma. Above all, it seems to be a
particularly potent source for his enduring distrust of all messianic
ideologies, whether political or artistic.

2

A city in ruins, hollow, and
full of logic. Budapest after
the end of the war.

As the start of the 1950s I came to realize that
what was possible for Bartók in the concerned
1930s was no longer possible for a composer of
radical avant-garde in the 1950s.

György Ligeti, in conversation with
Ursula Stürzbecher

First Encounters 1945–56

With the war over, Ligeti set his heart on further composition studies. In September 1945 he travelled to Budapest to take the entrance examination to the Ferenc Liszt Academy of Music, which was not only the leading music institution in Hungary, but one of the most prestigious in Europe. The main incentive, though, had been the prospect of Béla Bartók, one of the greatest of living composers, coming back from the USA to lead the composition classes. Alas, it was not to be. Within days a black flag was raised over the academy: news had just come through from New York that Bartók had died.

Waiting nervously for half an hour in the academy's art nouveau corridors before being admitted to the entrance examination, Ligeti struck up a conversation with another aspiring young composer who was to become a lifetime friend: György Kurtág. They had much in common: both came from Transylvania, both were Jewish (in Kurtág's case, half-Jewish), and both had taken a considerable risk to get to Budapest, crossing the Romanian-Hungarian border illegally, without papers. But their immediate personal rapport had more to do with the fact that they each found the other's timidity appealing and reassuring. Ligeti was impressed by the younger man's 'introverted attitude, and his total lack of vanity and presumption. He was intelligent and sincere, with a complex simplicity.' Kurtág, much to Ligeti's later amusement, interpreted the latter's timidity as religious severity – he assumed he was a Protestant theology student. (Clearly, there were some undecipherable personality traits among the budding avant garde: when the young Karlheinz Stockhausen first visited Herbert Eimert in Cologne, Eimert's first question was 'Are you a medical student?')

Ligeti and Kurtág turned out to have similar political convictions: both were convinced leftists, though without adhering to communism as such (Ligeti resisted various exhortations to join the party). Naturally, there were shared musical convictions too. Both young men saw Bartók's blending of chromatic and modal styles as the virtual salvation of new music in Eastern Europe, which made the sudden news of his death all the harder to cope with.

Ligeti describes post-war Budapest as a town without windows. The glass blown out by bombs was replaced by paper, and as winter drew in, the over-population of each available room was often the only source of heat. Even beds were hard to come by, while luxuries like one's own study, or a piano, were out of the question. Ligeti had a 'sub-let apartment' out in the suburbs: it consisted of a worn-out mattress, perched on the flagstones of a grubby kitchen smelling of gas, and overrun by cockroaches. Yet at the same time, he emphasizes, it was a time of enormous intellectual excitement and optimism. Even though the Jewish intelligentsia of the pre-war period had been virtually wiped out, the town had a younger population bubbling with ideas, and a fairly idealistic view of the leftist regime that had ousted the fascists.

The composition class at the academy was taken by Sándor Veress, who turned out, in many respects, to be a worthy substitute for Bartók, offering the same sort of left-wing idealism and moral leadership, and a commitment to the same writers that his students admired. In this class Ligeti learned harmony and counterpoint

Left, Hungary's greatest composer, Béla Bartók (1881–1945), who died in exile in New York

Right, Sándor Veress, Bartók's successor as composition teacher at the Liszt Academy. Within a few years, his opposition to communism would force him to emigrate.

(building on what he had already done with Farkas), as a necessary disciplined preparation for 'free composition', which was in fact not so free at all, but permitted the budding composer more scope than purely technical exercises.

Counterpoint was not just a matter of Baroque fugues. In seeking to raise the standards of choral singing in Hungary, Kodály had insisted that Renaissance polyphony be part of the repertoire, alongside folk-based works. It was thanks to this insistence that Ligeti not only found himself singing madrigals – a genre he would return to as composer many decades later – but also gained a sound knowledge of Renaissance sacred polyphony. Similarly, at Kodály's insistence, a cornerstone of counterpoint studies at the academy was to be the study of Palestrina's music, with Knud Jeppesen's classic *Palestrinastil med saerligt henblik paa dissonansbehandlingen* ('Palestrina and the Treatment of the Dissonance') as the core textbook. Whereas many young composers of the period would have baulked at such traditionalist prescriptions, Ligeti has always expressed his gratitude at receiving this rigorous training, even though he personally found Palestrina's style too 'smooth' for his taste: much less attractive than that of earlier, more arcane and labyrinthine composers such as Obrecht and above all Ockeghem, who was to provide a particular inspiration for his own work in the 1960s.

By this stage, he was already producing the first compositions that he still acknowledges today. Most of them are choral works; although Ligeti claims to have had 'a very poor voice', he was a good sight-reader, and regularly sang in small student groups from his Cluj schooldays onwards, so he was familiar with choirs 'from inside'. The choral works from his Hungarian years fall fairly clearly into three groups, each separated by breaks of a few years, and these groupings mirror the changing cultural conditions in Hungary: in particular, the way in which an initial sense of artistic freedom was restricted, and then completely repressed, by Stalinist cultural politics.

The first group dates from 1945 to 1947, that is, Ligeti's student period, and certainly seems mainly intended for amateur use; it comes to a halt with (or in fact, just before) the Soviet intervention. The pieces from the second period, 1950–53, are mostly more adventurous in style, and certainly assume choirs with a high level of technical proficiency. As we shall see, some of these pieces were considered 'unacceptable' in official circles, and since Ligeti wished to pursue precisely those 'unacceptable' aspects, in 1953–4 he turned to the string quartet medium, and worked on the *Métamorphoses nocturnes*, which stood no chance of public performance. The third group of pieces followed in 1955; some (though not all) show the same disregard for the 'party line' as the string quartet. Perhaps more significantly, a couple of these pieces offer the first clear anticipation of the avant-garde note clusters that Ligeti would explore a few years later.

It is always tempting, when listening to a composer's earliest works, to look for pointers to the later style, as if this were somehow a matter of predestination. In Ligeti's case it seems a little futile, since it was to be another decade before the first really characteristic work was begun, namely the orchestral *Visiók* that subsequently turned into the first movement of *Apparitions*. Though relatively few of the first group of choral pieces are arrangements of actual folk music, most of them are written in the style of Bartók and Kodály's folk arrangements; at times, too, the harmony is not so remote from Szymanowski's late works based on the folk music of the Tatras region. That is, the pieces *sound* as if they are folksong arrangements, even when the material is actually Ligeti's own. The pieces show ability, but no particular originality. In the 1980s, Ligeti came to take a rather critical view of this genre, and especially of those works which adapted genuine folk material. For him, the process of harmonization involves a distortion, a pseudo-sophisticated 'alienation' of the original music, which usually consisted of melodies with little or no accompaniment. But at the time, he concedes, that was the fashion, and when you are young, you like to do what is fashionable …

The one piece which stands out in this early group is *Magány* ('Solitude'), an exquisite and in some respects audacious piece for three-part choir composed in 1946; this is the first of many settings of texts by Sándor Weöres, a young poet (albeit ten years older than Ligeti) whose work was beginning to appear in progressive literary journals. At the time, Ligeti did not know him personally; the next year, after setting three further poems, he was able to meet him at a friend's house, and show him his work. Subsequently he got to know Weöres well – he says he was too overawed by him to become a 'friend' – and came to rate his poetry extraordinarily highly: he has referred to him as one of the greatest figures in contemporary literature, the equal of Hölderlin and Rimbaud. As if to prove this contention, when he finally came to set three poems by Hölderlin in the early 1980s, he worked almost simultaneously on three settings of Weöres.

Alongside the choral works, Ligeti was writing short pieces for his own main instrument, the piano. As titles like *Capriccio* and *Invention* suggest, these are not mood pieces, but explorations of musical material, pieces in which Ligeti teaches himself to compose. They arose from Veress's classes: initially, the students would produce 'exercises in form' in the style of Haydn and Mozart, and then go on to produce related works 'in their own style'. For example, Ligeti's *Invention* came about after he had produced a suitable number of Bachian inventions and fugues (thanks to his talent in this area, he soon became known in the class as the 'Doctor'), and Veress suggested that he should now write a 'half-Bach' invention. Nevertheless, Ligeti was essentially on his own; following the general convention of the period, Veress was not in the habit of commenting on student works. He would look briefly at them, and if he actually bothered to leaf through to the end (as happened with Ligeti), this was as much sign of approval as one could hope for. The style of these pieces, with their winding chromatic lines, is still 'progressive Bartókian', lying at the edges of tonality, but when one listens to them it is easy to forget that they are literally student works, for they show an entirely professional level of competence, coupled with superior invention. They also call for a more professional pianistic technique than Ligeti had at his disposal: the first performances of the *Invention* and the two capriccios were given at a student concert in the academy by György Kurtág and his wife Márta.

Another work from this period which suggests a very talented Bartók-Kodály adherent is an Adagio for solo cello, which five years later became the first movement of a sonata. Here, there was an extra-musical motivation: Ligeti was very taken with a young cellist, Anouss Virány, so he wrote her a slow *Dialogue* involving a sort of conversation between a man and a woman – the upper part melodious and beautiful, the lower part suitably yearning. Alas, when he handed the unsolicited work to the cellist, who was quite unaware of her role in bringing it about, she merely thanked him; she never played it.

In writing the piece, Ligeti had been making some conscious decisions about style. While some of the works he had written in the two previous years had been enthusiastically 'modern', his sincere socialist inclinations led him to feel that he should perhaps make a little more effort to write in an accessible manner, and this outlook is already reflected in some of the choral works of these years, as well as the cello piece (it may also be that the object of his desires was no devoted modernist …). At this stage, there was no official pressure on him to adopt such an approach; however, the political and artistic climate was about to change dramatically, and for the worse.

By 1948, Ligeti was already regarded as a highly gifted student. Veress now thought so much of him that, quite at odds with his normal practice, he was giving him one-to-one 'masterclasses'. Along with Erzébet Szönyi, who was Kodály's personal favourite, he had been given a grant to spend his final year of study with Milhaud at the Paris Conservatoire, the idea being that he would go first, and she

The Liszt Academy of Music in Budapest, from which Ligeti graduated in 1949, still one of the great European conservatoires

would go the year after. But his former teacher Ferenc Farkas had just joined the academy staff; in Ligeti's opinion he was 'no great composer, God knows, but a terrifically well-versed technician', and Ligeti felt there was still much to be learned from him, especially in terms of orchestration. So he suggested that Szönyi (who had already graduated) should go first. Thanks to the sudden descent of the Iron Curtain, Ligeti never got to Paris. In terms of Milhaud's tuition, this may have been no great loss (three years later, Karlheinz Stockhausen went to his classes, and was utterly scathing about them: 'extremely boring', 'mindless chit-chat' and 'slovenly' were typical responses). Still, one can only wonder what would have happened if Ligeti had encountered Pierre Boulez and the group around Olivier Messiaen in 1948–9.

As 1948 proceeded, several ominous events took place. The social democrats and communists in government institutions were forcibly united into a single party, and the Soviet occupation troops took to arresting officials who did not comply. Denunciations of 'Western decadence' became increasingly strident, and extended to the arts, following the pattern established in the Soviet Union. Official attacks on modernist tendencies had already started in Soviet Russia in 1936, when Shostakovich's opera *Lady Macbeth of Mtsensk* was denounced in *Pravda* as 'muddle instead of music'. Pressure was immediately placed on composers to write readily accessible works, preferably based on folk music, and with a clear and positive relationship to the aspirations of the Soviet state. Any kind of purely instrumental music ran the risk of being considered 'formalist', overly concerned with intellectual preoccupations irrelevant to the proletariat.

During World War II, the situation changed: Russia and the USA were allies, cultural exchange took place, and it was clear that modern, tragic-heroic Soviet symphonies and sonatas had much more potential prestige than cantatas about reafforestation. But once the war was over, the attacks on modernism resumed. Early in 1948 there was a congress of the Soviet Composers' Union at which Communist Party spokesman Andrey Zhdanov denounced all the leading Soviet composers – Prokofiev, Shostakovich and Khachaturian. The new climate of artistic oppression rapidly spread to all the Eastern European countries which now fell under Soviet control. Modernism was out, and folk music was the required model.

Though the extent of state intervention was not immediately apparent to Ligeti, by the end of the year he was left in little doubt that the experience of the Hitler years was about to be repeated, albeit with different victims. At the time he was the president of an independent student union, and one day he and other senior union members were called to a meeting which turned out to have been mounted by the ÁVÓ – the infamous state security organisation. The Roman Catholic Cardinal Jószef Mindszenty had just been arrested, and the students were now informed that he had been leading the church in a conspiracy against the state. It was therefore essential to weed out all Catholic students at the academy; as a first step, nine students should be identified, denounced, expelled and arrested. It was expected that Ligeti, as president, would collaborate fully. He did no such thing: he turned white as a sheet and walked out of the meeting. The first thing he did was warn all his Catholic friends, then he resigned from the presidency, fully expecting to be arrested himself. Fortunately, nothing happened: it turned out that Kodály had spoken out on behalf of the students, and still enjoyed sufficient authority to carry the day.

Earlier that year, noting that there was going to be a summer 'Festival of World Youth' in Budapest in 1949, and that the academy choir and orchestra wanted to present a cantata there, Ligeti had decided to write one as his graduation piece. It did not occur to him that the 'festival' would simply be a shop-window for communist ideology. He describes the piece as being resolutely diatonic, in places rather like Benjamin Britten, and partly a pastiche in Baroque style, with Handelian fugues. As for the text, 'The poet Kuczka (who was just as naïve, and just as disenchanted with the communism dictatorship) wrote an "enthusiastic", left-orientated text, extolling freedom, youth, and the coming independence for colonial populations etc.'

But after the events of December, the idea of offering any kind of support to the prevailing regime, however equivocal, appalled Ligeti. He desperately wanted to cancel the performance of his cantata, but this proved impossible (in the following months, having to work on the orchestration became so distasteful to him that he contracted severe gastritis). So the performance went ahead, and the outcome was disastrous. Party officials organizing the festival were incensed by the implicit anti-communism of the text; and even the music, which must

have been innately harmless enough, was regarded as dangerously
allied to 'reactionary clericalism' in its use of forms such as chorale and
fugue (the sacred works of Bach and Handel had been banned). Once
again, Kodály came to the rescue, but Ligeti had learned his lesson,
and resolved to stick to folksong-based works in future, at least for
public purposes. In the meantime Veress, who also had no time for
Soviet-style communism, had left the academy (he subsequently
became a highly respected teacher in Switzerland, where his students
included Heinz Holliger). His place was taken by Pál Járdányi.
Another defection at this time had more lasting consequences for
Ligeti. Kurtág's main partner in the chamber music classes had been a
highly talented violinist, Stefan Romanesco. In 1948, Romanesco
qualified as a finalist in the prestigious Geneva competition, and
seized the opportunity to stay on in Switzerland. Ligeti moved into
Romanesco's lodgings, and found that his landlady had a very
attractive daughter named Vera. Before long, the two fell in love, and
Vera would later become his wife.

As for composition, working with folk music was not necessarily
too great a restriction, for Ligeti was genuinely interested in the
Transylvanian folk music with which he had grown up. So after

Ligeti with his future wife,
Vera, photographed in
Budapest c. 1949. Vera
was a fellow-student at the
Liszt Academy.

graduating, he gained a grant to spend some months there collecting folk music, and at the same time, he engaged in musicological-theoretical work. Some of his colleagues at the academy had made notated versions of the improvised polyphony performed by Romanian village bands, and he wrote a paper analysing the basic features of this repertoire.

Coming back to Budapest, Ligeti again had reason to be grateful to Kodály. Ligeti's feelings about him were mixed: as a person, he did not like him much, but Kodály had already done a lot for him, and helped to protect him from subsequent politically motivated attacks on his music. By this stage, Kodály had retired as a composition teacher, but still had a professorship in Hungarian folksong. He was also engaged in overseeing a scholarly edition of Hungarian folk music, and tried to interest Ligeti in joining the project. By way of orientation, the young composer spent a few weeks working (without pay) in the Museum of Ethnography. One of the main tasks was to transcribe the music on the historic wax cylinders that Bartók had recorded early in the century. Ligeti was fascinated but intimidated: the cylinders were fragile, and after one had played them about ten times, they were unusable, and the information was lost for ever.

So he tried to back out, but Kodály was not taking no for an answer. The senior composer summoned Ligeti for an interview: 'he received me in a completely darkened room, a huge studio amidst three grand pianos, just wearing some little silk pants. It was an incredibly hot day in July. I was given a coffee, probably the worst in Budapest. He asked me if I would accept a paid position in this project.' According to Wolfgang Burde, Ligeti made every excuse imaginable: his ear was not well enough trained, he lacked perseverance (particularly hard to believe), and anyway, he was no 'insect collector': he wanted to compose, and a theory position was what he was after. Kodály retorted that he would never come to anything as a composer if he was not capable of this sort of painstaking work. But in the end, Ligeti's obstinacy won the day; moreover, within a month Kodály had actually secured a theory-teaching post for him, despite the young man's bad reputation with the communist authorities.

One might imagine Ligeti would have preferred a junior composition post. Not so, however: given the communist regulations

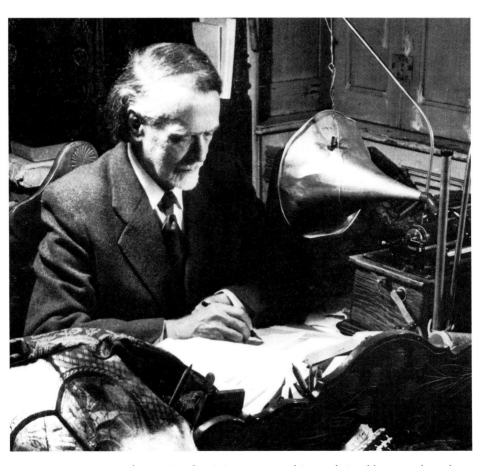

Zoltán Kodály (1882–1967), composer, educationalist, nationalist and patriarch, listening to a wax-cylinder recording of folk music

that restricted artistic output, teaching traditional harmony kept the composer of the controversial youth cantata away from official scrutiny. Moreover, Ligeti had a genuine interest in this kind of disciplined study, and in theoretical studies as a whole; during his years as a teacher at the academy, he produced a couple of text books on classical harmony which were still in use several decades later. He took his teaching seriously, as he would do throughout his life, and insisted on adequate standards. This sometimes had unforeseeable consequences; the pupils he felt obliged to fail included three of the four string players who went on to form the Bartók Quartet. When asked, a couple of decades later, whether they would consider playing Ligeti's quartets, their response was firmly in the negative.

He also startled some of his colleagues by sitting in on the analysis classes of Lajos Bárdos; they apparently considered that it was beneath one's dignity to show students there was something one did not know. But though Bárdos did not analyse contemporary music, Ligeti found the classes fascinating, and feels they had a vital influence on his own analyses of Webern and Boulez a few years later. Here again, one sees two basic Ligeti traits in action: a complete lack of concern for protocol, and a constant desire to learn new things and pursue them to the highest level.

Since harmony and counterpoint were considered a part of – or at least a prelude to – composition studies, some kind of public output was desirable, even from a young tutor. So Ligeti now produced a number of further choral works based on Hungarian folk materials, both arrangements and free compositions, as well as an orchestral *Romanian Concerto*. He once dismissed this piece as 'embodying the height of my compositional misconceptions' (referring once again to the idea that folk music needed to be 'civilized' through sophisticated arrangements à la Kodaly), though now, having revised it in the mid 1990s, he allows it to be performed. He also produced at least one piece that enabled him to thumb his nose at authority, even if it had to be a private gesture. In 1951, his friend Melles, who had conducted the ill-fated youth cantata, asked him to write something for a band of Budapest postmen, and he responded with a *Grand Symphonie militaire Op. 69*, an unashamedly 'formalist' neo-classical piece whose satirical spirit even extends to the spurious opus number, which refers to the most popular (or at least, best-known) of exotic sexual positions.

What is most obviously different about the new choral works is the sharp increase in virtuoso demands, most evident in the very rapid repetitions of notes in a piece like *Pletykázó asszonyok* ('Gossiping Women'). Ligeti says that by this time, he already felt that 'music should not be normal, well-bred, with its tie neatly tied'. In some of these works, even when they are based on folk materials, one can sense that he is pushing the boundaries of what was permissible, and in some cases he overstepped them. *Haj, ifjúság!* ('Hail, Youth!') was prohibited for 'adolescent recalcitrance' – presumably the authorities thought that the folk text describing a fairly weakly-resisted seduction, was an incitement to wholesale teenage promiscuity – while *Pápainé* ('Widow Pápai') was considered too dissonant. Sometimes, however, official endorsement was even more embarrassing than rejection. On one occasion Ligeti was asked by József Gát, a highly regarded pianist and choirmaster, to provide a folksong arrangement for his choir; however, he did not specify what choir this was. Ligeti complied with *Kállai kettös* ('Double Dance from Kálló'). A few weeks later, Ligeti was summoned without explanation to the headquarters of the ÁVÓ: the kind of invitation that no one wanted, but that no one could refuse. Turning up at the prescribed time, no doubt in considerable trepidation, he was led into a hall where fifty men and women in border-guard uniforms sang the première of his new piece. Needless to say, this piece was fully approved for subsequent public performance.

Paradoxically, the restrictive artistic conditions in which Ligeti was working may also have encouraged him to move in new directions. After all, in a situation where virtually all instrumental music not directly based on folk music was viewed with official suspicion, once he had decided to go on composing such pieces in secret, there were no external circumstances causing him to hold back stylistically. At any rate, it was around this time that he began to imagine the possibility of a quite different kind of music – a music without harmony or melody in the conventional sense. Needless to say, he had very little idea how to realize it, not least because he knew so little 'radical' music from the previous fifty years, apart from some of Bartók's. Early Stravinsky and Debussy had been played in the years preceding the communist takeover, but apart from scores of Berg's *Lyric Suite* and Schoenberg's Second String Quartet, Ligeti knew next to nothing about the Second Viennese School: for the most part, Schoenberg and Webern were just names in books. And while he had been struck by Stravinsky's orchestration, the music of Debussy – and especially his approach to form – had made much less of an impression, not least because until then Ligeti had been committed to the dynamic, thematically based forms developed by Beethoven and Bartók. The nearest approach he could find to what he now imagined was Wagner's prelude to *Das Rheingold*.

His first objective involved a sort of Oedipal rebellion: he had to try to move beyond the influence of Bartók. Two works in particular reflect this attempt, a set of eleven short piano pieces called *Musica ricercata*, written between 1951 and 1953, and the string quartet *Métamorphoses nocturnes* (1953–4), which likewise consists of a number

Folk music in practice: a gypsy fiddler surrounded by a group of Eastern Carpathian villagers about to dance

of short sections. One could regard the piano pieces as a series of preliminary studies, and the quartet as a first drawing up of accounts, a summary of what had been achieved to date.

At exactly the same time as Ligeti was working on his piano pieces, a group of young composers in Western Europe were founding a so-called 'serial' school of composition in which every aspect of the composition was subjected to strict arithmetical organization. A quarter-century earlier, Schoenberg and his school (primarily Berg and Webern) had inaugurated 'twelve-note composition', in which a single ordering of the twelve notes of the chromatic scale (which may be transposed, inverted and sometimes presented in retrograde) serves as the basis for a whole piece. The younger composers, intent on sweeping away every vestige of musical tradition, now sought to apply similar principles to rhythm, and even to such components as loudness and tone colour. While much less 'radical' than these works, the *Musica ricercata* pieces represent a similar expression of 'Cartesian doubt'. Ligeti says: 'I started to experiment with simple structures of rhythms and sounds, in order to evolve a new music from nothing, so to speak. I regarded all the music I had known and loved up to then as something I couldn't use. I asked myself: what can I do with a single note, what can I do with the octave, or with an interval, or two intervals, or specific rhythmic situations.' In practical terms, this means that the number of notes used in each piece increases: the first has just two (but doubled, also, at the octave), the second has three notes, until the eleventh uses all twelve. This last, actually written a couple of years earlier as an organ piece for a friend, is not a strict 'twelve-note' composition, though it uses a twelve-note theme. Here, as the title *Omaggio a Frescobaldi* ('Homage to Frescobaldi') suggests, the starting point is not so much the Second Viennese School as the highly chromatic *ricercare* style of the early seventeenth-century composer from Ferrara; in fact, the theme is extrapolated from the *Ricercare cromatico* of Frescobaldi's *Messa degli Apostoli*. However, the 'homage' is also a little tongue in cheek; with its remorselessly even tread, and its obsessively descending scales, the piece seems, in Schumann's phrase, 'fast zu ernst' (almost too serious). This is partly confirmed by Ligeti's later description of it as 'a severe, almost noble piece, hovering between academic orthodoxy and deep reflection: between gravity and caricature'; yet at the same time, he says, he would not necessarily discourage a more 'traumatic' reading in which the rhythmic 'emptiness' was interpreted as an emblem of life under Stalinist rule, as in much of Shostakovich's later work.

The musical outcome of *Musica ricercata* is, for the most part, much less iconoclastic than its intentions: Bartók is by no means left behind, and several pieces inhabit a world very close to that of his *Mikrokosmos* (which also has a didactic aim, though a somewhat different one). Even the final twelve-note 'omaggio' does not stray too far in style from the fugue in the *Music for Strings, Percussion and Celesta*. Though the pieces were not released for public scrutiny at the time, in 1953 Ligeti did arrange six of them for wind quintet, and five were eventually performed in Hungary; the final one, however, was considered to be 'too dissonant', even in the relatively relaxed cultural conditions that preceded the 1956 uprising. Although they had to wait a long time for their Western première, the resulting *Six Bagatelles* have since become a 'party piece' in the quintet repertoire.

In the same year, Ligeti came back to the cello piece he had written five years earlier, this time without romantic connotations. A well-known cellist, Vera Dénes, asked him for a piece, and he suggested adding a new, fast piece to the existing *Dialogue* to form a two-movement sonata. The new piece, *Capriccio*, was markedly different to its predecessor. Not only more 'modern', but also strikingly virtuoso, it was a first application of Ligeti's fascination with Paganini's string writing. Here, inevitably, difficulties arose with the authorities. Before the work could be performed, and before Ligeti could get any commission fee (his teaching salary was not enough to live on), the piece had to be accepted by the Composers' Union. Dénes learned the piece, and played it for a CU official who also turned out to be a KGB member. Not surprisingly, the piece was not approved for performance or publication. Dénes was permitted to make a radio recording, but it was never broadcast; the first public performance was to come thirty years later, in 1983.

The string quartet was a more major undertaking, from many points of view. Even in trying to move beyond Bartók, Ligeti naturally took the older composer's quartets as a standard – especially the third and fourth quartets, of which he had seen the scores, even though they were banned from performance. Yet here, even if there are many passages which are clearly influenced by his models (for example, the final Prestissimo, which is directly reminiscent of the end of Bartók's Third Quartet), there is also considerable evidence of the desire to do something different. This is already apparent in the work's subtitle, *Métamorphoses nocturnes*: if the 'nocturnal' aspect plays homage to the 'night musics' which are a recurrent feature of Bartók's work (and also seems rather appropriate to the clandestine circumstance in which the quartet was composed), the 'metamorphoses' signal a departure from the sonata structures and arch forms typical of Bartók. Here Ligeti sets out to compose a music which has no overt themes: only tiny motives which are gradually transformed, 'discursively' on a small scale, and by expansion of intervals on the larger scale.

As Ligeti says, the work can be regarded either as a single-movement piece, or as a number of shorter linked sections. Commentators disagree as to the number of major subsections – if one were to take every shift of tempo and texture into account, there would be dozens. Since the underlying procedure of the piece is to start with a basic four-note motive (two major seconds, a minor second apart), and gradually expand the intervals of the motive as the work proceeds, it seems logical to take the points at which the intervals expand as signalling the main divisions (so long as there is also a clearly audible change of tempo and texture), in which case one comes up with a nine-part form: an exposition, seven transformations and a finale.

Even though the style of Ligeti's *Métamorphoses nocturnes* is still far removed from that of the avant-garde works he would be writing a few years later, it contains, for the first time, some real premonitions of what was to follow. The deliberately 'neutral' harmony created by the parallel seconds at the beginning seems to mark a first step towards cluster composition, and the rising chromatic sequence which leads to the final Prestissimo even more so. A little more fancifully, one could say that the rhythmic neutrality of the opening bars, where one really does not sense any metre, is similarly prophetic. More telling, though, is the presence of three musical gestures which Ligeti used constantly in his works of the 1960s: a sudden wild, leaping figure (probably influenced by the Presto delirando of Berg's *Lyric Suite*), found here at the start of the second section ('Vivace, capriccioso'); a tendency for music which seems to be rising to a climax to be suddenly 'torn off', here in the course of the Adagio mesto; and the insistent, 'mechanical' reiteration of a single note – the clearest instance is the series of snap pizzicatos on the cello, towards the end of the work, but the Prestissimo also starts with the significant marking 'very evenly, like a precision mechanism: the bars do not signify an accentuation'.

Two other possible 'anticipations' deserve a mention. One is the occasional deviation from normal intonation: a quarter-tone quasi-trill in the cello at the end of the 'major thirds' section, and deliberately 'messy' octaves and unisons in the Prestissimo, caused, for example, by asking two instruments to play an A sharp, and the other two to play a B flat. The Prestissimo ends with an early indication of Ligeti's love of paradox: without any surface change of tempo, it suddenly turns into a 'senza misura' (unmeasured) passage, in which the instruments swish up and down the natural harmonics in the manner of Stravinsky's *Firebird*. In effect the music has become so fast that it suddenly seems to stand still.

For the rest, it is hard to get an overall view of this period, since many of the 'closet' pieces Ligeti was working on were left behind when he fled Hungary at the end of 1956. A few scores (including the *Métamorphoses nocturnes*) were sent on to him subsequently, and many others have shown up over the years, but much still seems to have been lost. Some of the most striking surviving evidence of his new direction is found in two choral pieces, *Éjszaka* ('Night') and *Reggel* ('Morning'), both composed in 1955; once again, the choice of texts by Sándor Weöres stimulates a special effort. *Éjszaka* uses just a handful of words to evoke a huge, labyrinthine forest, and then to cast a spell of midnight silence on it. Ligeti's first section uses the conventional device of canon to build up a huge diatonic, 'white-note' cluster, which suddenly shifts to the black notes, and drops drastically in both register and dynamic, with folk-like fragments in the sopranos, and a token C major triad at the end. *Reggel* is likewise in two parts, and evokes mechanical and natural ways of waking: a ticking clock (an image which will recur in drastic form in the works of the 1960s) and a cockerel. In the 'clock' section, Ligeti gives each of the four parts its own pentatonic scale, while the farmyard bustle (crowned by cock-crows reminiscent of Stravinsky's *Renard*) is portrayed at lightning pace (prestissimo), and demands considerable virtuosity.

In the early 1950s, information about what was happening in the West was particularly restricted. Virtually all modernist art was denounced as decadent, and even though an artist like Picasso was officially praised for his pro-communist views, his actual paintings were just as subject to prohibition as anyone else's. With the Cold War at its height, Western broadcasts were usually jammed in Eastern European countries. Above all, this applied to news and anything that could be construed as capitalist propaganda, including cultural broadcasts. But Ligeti was able to pick up the occasional German broadcast; for the first time, he heard the music of the post-war European avant garde – of composers like Messiaen and his pupils Boulez and Stockhausen – a new, abstract style in which there was almost no trace of conventional melody or harmony. Hearing it, he realized that there already existed a new musical world, light years away from Kodály and even Bartók, something he previously knew of only by hearsay, if at all.

Much of this music was closely associated with the summer courses held every year since 1946 at Darmstadt, a central German city just south of Frankfurt which was also famous for its Jugendstil architecture. The courses had been designed as a way of reconstituting new German music in the wake of the Nazi years of prohibition, but they also had a cosmopolitan policy, attracting artists and students from all over Europe, and subsequently from much further afield. In retrospect, the Darmstadt courses in the early 1950s have often been portrayed as hotbeds of avant-gardism. This is not entirely true: all kinds of contemporary music were performed there, and as late as 1956, the 'highlight' of the course was a performance of Honegger's oratorio *Le Roi David*, which represented the 'moderate modern' style of 1921, influenced by Stravinsky rather than Schoenberg! Still, from 1950 onwards, it did acquire a radical fringe, a group of young composers whose highly organized yet fragmentary music (inspired in part by Webern) set out to distance itself from every possible tradition. At first it was Boulez and Luigi Nono who attracted most attention, and, shortly after, Stockhausen. For some years, audience reaction was almost uniformly hostile: boos and catcalls were the order of the day; but gradually, these young composers gained influence, and started to move towards centre stage. Producers at the radio stations were much more supportive, and began to cultivate the young rebels, even if their works tended to be broadcast very late in the evening.

Darmstadt in central Germany, notable for its exotic Jugendstil architecture; the city was host from 1947 to International Summer Courses in New Music and soon became a Mecca of the avant garde.

These late-night broadcasts from Cologne, Hamburg and elsewhere were also regularly jammed by the Communist authorities and, as a result, it was only the high frequencies – the piccolos, and the high metal percussion that is such a feature of the early 'Darmstadt' style – that came through clearly. It is tempting to speculate that Ligeti's own fascination with extreme registers from *Apparitions* onwards may partly reflect this early experience.

However, in the months preceding the Hungarian uprising, the political situation had thawed to the point where broadcasts from the West were not necessarily blocked, and even some postal communication was permitted. As a result of hearing broadcasts from West German Radio in Cologne, Ligeti had written to Dr Herbert Eimert, the director of the electronic studios, to Karlheinz Stockhausen, who was clearly the driving force among the young composers, and to Dr Otto Tomek at Universal Edition in Vienna (Universal Edition had not only published the composers of the Second Viennese School, but was intensely engaged in fostering the new avant garde). In response to his request for study materials, Ligeti received parcels containing scores and articles. They were a revelation. As he puts it: 'It was a huge shock for me – perhaps the best of my whole life – to suddenly be able to study and hear things I had previously only dreamed of, or had caught in scraps listening to the radio secretly at night: it was like being set free.'

It was in this context that he began work on *Visiók*, an orchestral piece in which he tried for the first time to realize the kind of themeless textural music that he had long been dreaming of. Perhaps, more than any other before or since, this was *the* turning-point in his creative life, the moment at which he resolutely set out to find and enter a Promised Land. At this early stage, he was still groping for solutions: there was almost no music that offered even a partial model for what he was seeking. Xenakis's *Metastasis*, composed a couple of years earlier, might well have been useful, but he did not get to know it until years later. Despite the information filtering (and sometimes flooding) through from the West, he was basically still on his own. The fragmentary textures of post-Webern serialism, though fascinating as an indication of how radically other young composers were breaking with tradition, pursued an aim very different to his. In some respects, his best models lay two or three decades in the past: in the opening fugue of Bartók's *Music for Strings, Percussion and Celesta* (1936), where the counterpoint sometimes becomes so dense, and so rhythmically multi-layered, that one can scarcely follow the individual parts, and in the Allegro Misterioso from Berg's *Lyric Suite*, where the whirling chromatic figures, especially when played *sul ponticello*, interlock to a point where single pitches seem to be subsumed into a flickering, mercurial texture.

The score of *Visiók* was one of those left behind when Ligeti fled Hungary, though it was partly reconstructed in *Apparitions*. The last extant piece from the Hungarian period is the brief *Chromatische Phantasie* for piano. Here the impact of hearing pieces from the West is clearly audible, not so much in the chromatic clusters, which can be found in Bartók too, as in the fragmentary gestures which spring all over the keyboard: it may not quite be the Darmstadt style of Stockhausen's first *Klavierstücke*, but it alludes to it. Clearly, a major change was under way.

3

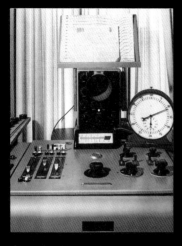

The new look of composition:
an assemblage desk in the
Cologne Studio for Electronic
Music, photographed in
1955, with sound banks
and sliders, a stopwatch,
and diagrams of acoustic
wave forms.

*One does not even need to look beyond the
mountain-tops of our own culture, to know
that we habitually assume that we are on
the right track.*

Karlheinz Stockhausen, "Die Situation
des Metiers," *Texte 1* (1963, 70)

Revolutions 1956-60

The Hungarian Revolution erupted on October 23rd 1956. There was hand-to-hand fighting in the streets for a week, after which the Soviet forces appeared to withdraw – it looked as if the uprising had succeeded. Ligeti and his friends were in an elated mood, looking forward to what they would do the next year. As he poignantly recalls, 'On the night of the 3rd–4th November we were incredibly happy: tomorrow a new life would begin … We were going to found a little music theatre, and the first thing we would play would be Stravinsky's *The Soldier's Tale*, which was previously forbidden. That's what we thought … And early the next morning – no-one slept during this night – at about four in the morning, one heard cannon fire from a long way away … The new Soviet troops had completely surrounded Budapest …'

So the fighting resumed. It was in the midst of all this that Ligeti finally got to hear some of Stockhausen's latest work. The circumstances could scarcely have been more dramatic. Stockhausen had written to say that *Kontra-Punkte* and *Gesang der Jünglinge* would be broadcast late at night on 7 November. In general, Western radio transmissions were jammed, but on this particular day, at 11 p.m., the WDR signal came through uninterrupted. However, listening was a perilous, potentially fatal business. There was a battle raging in the street outside; stray bullets were coming into the house, and everyone else had retreated down to the cellar. But you could not hear the radio in the cellar, so in a typical display of stubborn obstinacy, Ligeti stayed upstairs. He was determined to hear the pieces, and so he did.

By this stage, there was little doubt in his mind that he had to leave Budapest, and attempt flight to the West. However, this was certainly no easy decision to make, despite the external circumstances. Quite apart from the physical danger involved, he was leaving behind his cultural roots. The Hungarian literature that was precious to him would mean nothing in Austria or Germany – there were no translations to speak of, and the whole way of thinking was different. He also thought he was giving up a secure position at the Liszt Academy,

A moment of hope: in the midst of the Hungarian Uprising (2 November 1956), a group of freedom fighters raise the Hungarian flag over a captured Soviet tank.

though in retrospect this proved naïve: having already been identified as 'culturally subversive', he would almost certainly have been sacked within a matter of weeks.

Ligeti's attempt to leave had a bizarre beginning. He took a tram to say goodbye to his mother, but the tram was full, so he had to stand outside on the running board. An equally full tram came the other way, and one of the passengers on its running board was carrying a large rucksack, which struck Ligeti. The impact knocked him off the tram, and he broke two ribs. To have attempted flight when heavily bandaged would have been asking for trouble – he would have been immediately suspected of involvement in the street fighting – so he spent the next month convalescing.

During this period, the number of people attempting to reach the Austrian border was immense – about 200,000 within weeks – and

Hungarian officialdom made little more than token efforts to stem the flow. On 10 December, after a farewell visit to the Kurtágs, Ligeti, together with his girlfriend Vera, got on a train, which took them without incident to Sárvár, a station about sixty kilometres south of the border. After that, it was not so easy. Normally, every time the train stopped at a station, people would phone the next one to see if Russian forces were there. But this time, something had gone wrong: at Sárvár Russian troops surrounded the front coaches. Luckily, however, Ligeti and Vera were in one of the rear coaches, and were able to slip away with several others and find shelter in a postal depot. The next day they were among a dozen who still felt like going on, so they were put in a mail van, hiding under the mail sacks. Here the main threat to their safety was a three-year-old child, who had to be given a hefty dose of tablets to send him to sleep. They survived at least one check, and were transported to a location within a few kilometres of the border, where they were taken in by a farmer's wife.

There was another heart-stopping moment to come, which Ligeti describes as 'like a scene out of *Boris Godunov*'. They were sitting at table when there was a bang on the door, and in came a couple of Hungarian border guards with machine guns slung over their shoulders. They looked at the refugees, grinned broadly, and said, 'Well, well, our relatives from Budapest have made it here at last!' Later that night the farmer's wife took them a few kilometres further through marshland, ominously lit up by Russian Very lights (flares). Then they were on their own; they stumbled on through ditches, got through the minefields on the border without accident (mercifully, most of the mines had been removed in response to an Austrian trade embargo), and finally saw a light ahead of them. It was an illuminated Christmas tree outside the village church at Lutzmannsdorf; they were exhausted and covered in filth, but they had reached Austria. Next day, friends collected them and took them to Vienna.

Here the composer Hanns Jelinek, who had previously sent Ligeti his textbook on twelve-note composition, *Anleitung zur Zwölftonkomposition* ('Introduction to Twelve-Note Composition'), took him under his wing. Although the composers of the Second Viennese School – Berg, Schoenberg and Webern – were all dead, many of their former students and acquaintances were still in Vienna, and on one occasion, after a contemporary music concert tucked away in the innards of the academy there, Jelinek took a somewhat intimidated Ligeti to meet the inner circle. There was Erwin Ratz, who had been involved in the organization of Schoenberg's Society for the Private Performance of New Music, the soprano Ilona Steingruber and senior composers Wildgans, Schiske and Apostel. As Ligeti recalls, 'The prevailing Viennese atmosphere was as deep as the ocean: Erwin Ratz, red-faced, was raging about some contretemps of the musical world incomprehensible to me at the time, and Apostel, a glass of red wine in hand, lamented the state of the whole world, his varicose veins, and the ban on his drinking alcohol.'

However, this was not just a gathering of the elderly and intemperate. Also present was a young composer of about the same age as Ligeti, Friedrich Cerha. These days Cerha is best known (outside Austria, at any rate) for his brilliant completion of Alban Berg's opera *Lulu*, but at that time he was emerging as one of the main figures in Austria's post-Webern avant garde. Cerha was also a violinist, and a couple of recent pieces – *Deux Éclats en reflexion* and *Formation et solution* – used a novel kind of 'buzzing' pizzicato which so intrigued Ligeti that he later used it in his orchestral piece *Apparitions*. During these few weeks, Ligeti was able to gain a little money as a proofreader for Universal Edition – this was one task that did not require any great knowledge of

The composers Ligeti met in Vienna immediately after fleeing from Hungary were mostly from older generations. An exception was Friedrich Cerha (b. 1926), whose innovative aspirations were close to his own.

German. More significantly, it gave him more direct contact with what was to be his first publisher in the West.

Vienna was never meant to be more than a resting-point. Universal Edition notwithstanding, it was not a major centre for the new avant garde; the real action, clearly, was in Cologne. Ligeti arrived there on 1 February 1957, while Vera remained in Vienna with friends. According to Karl Wörner's classic account, derived from interviews with Stockhausen, 'Immediately after his arrival Ligeti had lost consciousness. He was taken first to hospital and then to Stockhausen's house [a slip of paper with Stockhausen's address had been found in his overcoat], where he slept for 24 hours and refused all food. On waking he broke into a four-hour-long conversation about new music and electronic music, then he went back to sleep for another day and another night.'

It is a beautifully romantic story, but Ligeti dismisses it as yet another 'new music myth', pointing out that he had, after all, spent some weeks recuperating in Vienna, and in any case, he was taken to Eimert's house first, not Stockhausen's. Nevertheless, he confirms that Stockhausen, with whom he stayed for six weeks, was an exemplary host. Within a couple of days he had been given a crash course in the latest musical developments, and in the following weeks, fully recovered from his journey, he was precipitated into a new artistic world. He listened to tapes of Boulez's controversial *Polyphonie X* and to *Le Marteau sans maître*, which was gaining 'classic' status even though it was still brand new. He also heard pieces from the Cologne electronic studio, as well as discovering the music of Webern and Schoenberg.

Conversations at meal times were often revelatory. After all, this was not just a new generation adding to the achievements of the past, but one convinced that it was recreating music from the roots upwards, inventing and discovering a new musical universe that would ultimately make the past – even the radical fragmentation of Webern's works – irrelevant. In this new world, construction was the name of the game. Composers devised huge abstract schemes in which every conceivable element of composition was subject to arithmetical organization. The abstraction of the music was reflected in its titles – *Cross-Play, Polyphony X, Composition No. 1* and *Music in Two Dimensions* are typical examples.

For a while, at least, electronic music was the standard-bearer of this new world. It completely bypassed the traditional performer, being created directly on tape with the use of various electronic sound generators which created everything from sine tones ('pure' wave-forms with no overtones) to the densest noise-bands ('white noise'). There was no need to stick to the chromatic scales of contemporary instrumental music, since any kind of scale could be produced. Indeed, there was no real need for scales at all: there was an infinite range of unpitched sounds and novel timbres and textures waiting to be explored. And everything could be controlled by the composer to the minutest degree! Talking to a studio technician in the mid 1950s, Stockhausen said: 'In twenty years time, no-one will listen to Bach and the classics any more.'

By 1957, at the age of twenty-eight (five years younger than Ligeti), Stockhausen was already convinced that he was the most important living composer; and not without reason, because it was he above all who was spearheading the group, not just at a theoretical and ideological level, but by producing works such as *Gruppen* for three orchestras and the electronic *Gesang der Jünglinge*, which are still regarded as classics of the 1950s avant garde. He would discuss, theorize and prophesy for hours; these were not mere empty words, but the ideas that were producing masterpieces. In the early months of 1957, Ligeti was able to watch Stockhausen completing *Gruppen*.

Stockhausen was not, however, the only star in the Cologne constellation. His principal assistant in the electronic studios was the composer Gottfried Michael Koenig, who had joined the studio staff three years earlier. Koenig had recently completed a ten-minute piece, *Klangfiguren II*, which is generally reckoned to have been the only work from that period that in any way matched up to *Gesang der Jünglinge*. But Koenig's approach was very different to Stockhausen's: he saw electronic music as an area of research, rather than the messianic path to a new era. His objective, relatively scientific attitude was very much to Ligeti's taste. In addition, there was the hard-line Italian avant-gardist Franco Evangelisti, who constantly sported a leather jacket and dark glasses. Evangelisti was one of the first composers to introduce chance elements into a highly structured context, and went on to abandon composition altogether in favour of 'free improvisation', forming a group – Nuova Consonanza – whose

'Already convinced that he was the most important living composer': the young Karlheinz Stockhausen (photographed in 1960)

members included Ennio Morricone, better known for his enormously successful 'Spaghetti Western' film scores.

There was a literary wing too. The experimental poet hans g helms (the lower-case spelling was presumably inspired by e.e. cummings, rather than the proto-fascist stefan george) introduced the group to Joyce's *Finnegans Wake*, leading them through sessions which reminded Ligeti (whose English was scarcely up to Joyce!) of arcane interpretations of the Talmud. There was also Heinz-Klaus Metzger, one of the most brilliant pupils of the philosopher Theodor Wiesendgrund-Adorno, who acted as polemicist for the group.

Though undoubtedly an exceptional group, it had its unsavoury aspects. For a start, it was entirely sectarian and intolerant. Earle Brown, a member of the musical avant garde that had crystallized around John Cage in New York in the early 1950s, and who spent some time in Cologne in the 1960s, recalls that he tended to show up a few minutes late for concerts, and as often as not, he would encounter

Young Turks at the 1957
Darmstadt Summer Course:
(left to right) *musique concrète*
pioneer Luc Ferrari, Franco
Evangelisti, Ligeti, Yoritsune
Matsudaira (a prominent
member of the newly
emerging Japanese avant
garde) and Luigi Nono

Evangelisti walking out! It was also fiercely competitive (Stockhausen
most of all, and Koenig least), and a hotbed of intrigues and changing
alliances. So Ligeti's position was understandably equivocal; the
intellectual stimulus was enormous, but the internal politics were of a
kind he was all too familiar with from communist rule – at least in
Cologne no one got imprisoned or shot. Besides, within a few months
he had a fellow 'refugee outsider' when Mauricio Kagel arrived in
Cologne from Argentina; Kagel too would approach the Cologne
group with a mixture of fascination and scepticism.

   As one can imagine, it was a situation that created few friendships.
But there was one member of the group with whom Ligeti did establish
a deep and lasting friendship, the composer and conductor Bruno
Maderna. Born in 1920, he was a few years older than the others, and
whereas most of them were struggling to establish their importance,
Maderna already had a prodigious early career behind him. At the age
of twelve, he had conducted 120 musicians from La Scala, Milan; in
his teens he had studied composition with leading Italian composers

such as Pizzetti and Malipiero, and in 1942, shortly before being enlisted, he had been entrusted with the first Italian performance of Webern's recent Orchestral Variations (which, incidentally, shows that cultural conditions in Italy were a good deal more tolerant of modernism than those in Germany). After the war, Maderna had soon taken up twelve-note composition himself, and had gone to the Darmstadt courses in 1949, a couple of years earlier than Stockhausen.

By the mid 1950s Maderna was heavily engaged with the new avant garde, extracting more lyrical consequences from serialism than Stockhausen (though also, apparently, taking greater delight in its mathematical aspects), and along with Luciano Berio he had founded an electronic music studio at Italian Radio in Milan. However, he never used his seniority to 'pull rank'. On the contrary, he was constantly encouraging his colleagues, and putting his abilities at their disposal. In later years he would be particularly associated with performances of Ligeti's *Aventures* and *Nouvelles Aventures*.

If the main intellectual stimulus came from Stockhausen and his contemporaries, it was Herbert Eimert whom Ligeti regarded as his benefactor. It was Eimert who had encouraged Stockhausen to go to Darmstadt in 1951, and had secured him a position at the electronic

Herbert Eimert (1897–1972), founder of the Cologne Electronic Music Studio, and tireless supporter of younger composers

studios in Cologne. But by this stage, Stockhausen had long since come to see Eimert as an old man standing in the way of his ambitions (a little like Siegfried's attitude when he encounters Wotan in Act III of Wagner's *Siegfried*). For Ligeti, on the other hand, Eimert was the perfect gentleman, the benign patriarch who, without having any particular financial resources of his own, managed to conjure up all kinds of institutional support for the young composers.

Almost immediately, Eimert was able to secure a small monthly stipend for Ligeti. Since Eimert did not know any of his music, this was an act of pure charity, which Ligeti repaid as best he could by dedicating his first major work, *Apparitions*, to him. The stipend paid the rent, and left a little over for food, but on the whole the next eighteen months were to be a hungry period in which dinner invitations were much appreciated. For the rest, Ligeti's basic diet was herrings in aspic at a stand-up food stall in the Woolworth store.

It was also Eimert rather than Stockhausen who got Ligeti a post working in the electronic studios. This was a completely new world for him, one he had heard about a few years earlier but without ever having heard any actual music until the broadcast of Stockhausen's piece, just before his flight. It took him a few months to come to terms with the equipment, which was a far cry from the computerized world of today's electronic studios. It involved working with many separate pieces of equipment: there were pitch and noise generators which produced the raw material, and filters, echo chambers and ring-modulators which were used to modify the initial result.

Ligeti's first serious experience in the electronic studio involved assisting Koenig in the realization of the latter's *Essay*. One of Koenig's aims in this piece was to get away from any suggestion of instrumental sounds, and a primary means of achieving this (in parts of the piece) was to create a web of sliding sounds, or glissandos, such that one could never quite tell where individual sounds began and ended. So it is no surprise that Ligeti's own first essay in the electronic medium used similar resources; in fact it is called *Glissandi*. If one compares *Glissandi* with most of the other work being produced in the Cologne studios at the time, two aspects immediately stand out: its liveliness, and its good humour. The opening moments may sound characteristically studious, but that impression soon disappears. Stockhausen apparently liked *Glissandi* – at least in comparison with the other non-

Stockhausen pieces of the period – but Ligeti was not satisfied, and did not let the work out into the public arena until decades later.

In fact, he was by no means committed to the electronic medium. Alongside the desire to reconstruct *Visiók*, Ligeti also had in mind a vocal work which would be based on an imaginary language. In Budapest, he had already thought of writing a piece based on 'the formal characteristics of speech'. Eventually, this would lead to *Aventures*, but when Ligeti described his ideas to Stockhausen in the course of a walk, Stockhausen persuaded him to realize his concepts via electronic music. The result was his second electronic work, *Artikulation*, sketched in January and February 1958, and realized in time to be given its first performance on 25 March – an astonishingly brief period, when one considers the primitive equipment available, and the sophistication of the result. Ligeti's main assistant in the studio was Koenig, but the young English composer Cornelius Cardew, another recent arrival in Cologne who later became Stockhausen's first personal assistant, also lent a hand.

Artikulation, at less than four minutes, is about half the length of its predecessor, and moves at a markedly faster pace. However, it is notable on far more accounts than this. Compared to other works produced in the studios at the time, and especially those by relative newcomers to electronic music, it is surprisingly colourful, lively and, above all, witty. Previous electro-acoustic works had a great propensity to be inadvertently funny, either because of incongruous juxtapositions thrown up more or less fortuitously by the serial organization scheme, or because certain 'noises' were disconcertingly reminiscent of assorted bodily functions. In *Artikulation*, on the other hand, the humorous, often slightly scatological connotations of many sounds are willingly accepted and exploited, while 'incongruities' are integral to the basic idea of the piece. It is no surprise to learn that in addition to all its 'speech-like' intentions, another inspiration for the work was the paintings of the Catalan artist Joan Miró, which Ligeti often had in his mind while composing the piece – not so much specific paintings as the whole quirky world of Miró, with its upside-down figures, its bright, almost cartoon-like splashes of colour, and its mixture of humorous and ominous elements.

The composition process, carefully documented by Rainer Wehinger about a dozen years later, was a considered mixture of order

and chaos, and offers a fascinating insight into the conflicting factors driving Ligeti's first significant 'avant-garde' work. Whereas *Glissandi* consisted mainly of sustained sounds, notated in advance in a 'score' on graph paper, the basic material of *Artikulation* was a vast number of tiny sounds, patched together from various sources (in effect, all the kinds of sounds produced in Koenig's and Stockhausen's latest pieces), and then assigned to various boxes according to a carefully worked out system of 'common properties'. The composer described these sounds as, for example, 'grainy, brittle, fibrous, slimy, sticky and compact' – exactly the kind of subjective, tactile categorization that had so disgusted the young Boulez and Stockhausen when Pierre Schaeffer had communicated the same to them a few years earlier in the Parisian studios dedicated to *musique concrète* (a form of tape composition in which the source materials were not electronic, but all kinds of 'real' sounds recorded via the microphone). Above all, though, Ligeti was constantly on the look-out for those sounds which, though produced electronically, sounded like speech: not just as vowels or consonants, but also in terms of speech-like inflections.

Using the properties of speech as a model for musical structure was no novelty in the Cologne studios; on the contrary, it was almost an in-house ideology. One of the founding fathers of electronic music in Cologne was Werner Meyer-Eppler. By training, Meyer-Eppler was a physicist, but his post-war rehabilitation had involved a shift of discipline, and he was named professor at the newly founded Institute of Phonetics in Bonn (along with Düsseldorf, the neighbouring town to Cologne). His approach to phonetics and linguistics was radical and experimental, heavily involved with the newly developing field of communications theory. He was clearly a charismatic figure; Stockhausen had attended his classes from 1954 to 1956, and even began a doctorate (he later described Meyer-Eppler as 'the best teacher I ever had'). The meticulous classification of speech sounds that underlay the preparatory work on Stockhausen's *Gesang der Jünglinge* was inspired by Meyer-Eppler, as was the permutation of syllables and phonemes in the actual piece. And even though by the time Ligeti was working in the electronic studio, Stockhausen had rejected the idea that the methods of (soft) scientific research in linguistics and communications could be directly applied to music, he was still fascinated by them, and inclined to prefer them to the vast majority of 'theories of music'. Nor was it just a matter of Stockhausen: Koenig, whom Ligeti regarded as his greatest mentor in matters concerning electronic music, had established contact with Meyer-Eppler as far back as 1951.

There was no real score for *Artikulation*, just a copious array of preliminary charts and tables to ensure that virtually every combination of pitch, length and timbre occurred. Subsequently, fragments from different boxes would be picked out at random and set next to one another – basically just 'to see what happened', from a dramatic-narrative point of view as much as a musical one: whether the different materials could flow into one another (Ligeti called this 'permeability'), or whether they remained obstinately irreconcilable. And on this basis the dramaturgy of the actual piece was evolved, not as an abstract structure, but as a sequence of mini-scenes without words.

What really stands out, in the end, is the sheer memorability of the piece. Apart from *Gesang der Jünglinge*, the early electronic works of the 1950s tend not to be, frankly, very memorable. Odd details stick in one's mind (not always for the best of reasons), but even with pieces one has heard several times, one is more likely to have a general impression of a piece than a precise, continuous, moment-by-moment one. But with *Artikulation*, everything from the watery gurgling at the outset to the furtive, acrimonious whisperings at the end strikes home immediately.

Despite its obvious secession from the High Seriousness typical of the Cologne studios, Stockhausen liked *Artikulation* too, and when he went on a lecture tour to America later that year it was one of the pieces he referred to in his lectures on electronic music. He was still advocating the piece some years later; when he gave a concert of electronic music at one of the early Cologne New Music Courses in 1965, *Artikulation* was again on the programme, and he included it in a subsequent series of radio programmes on electronic music.

In parallel with *Artikulation*, Ligeti began a third electronic piece which, had it succeeded, would probably have been hailed as a precursor of the 'spectralist' movement that flourished in Paris from the late 1960s onwards. Although the general tendency of the Cologne pieces had been to move as far away as possible from any suggestion of 'natural' sounds (Koenig being, in this respect, even more extreme than Stockhausen), there had been a couple of pieces – by Karel Goeyvaerts and Bengt Hambraeus – that had flirted with synthetically produced overtone series, that is, with the technological simulation of instrumental timbres. This involved linking each 'fundamental' (i.e. the actual note heard by the listener) with chords of pure electronic tones representing the 'overtones' which play a crucial role in making an oboe note sound different to, say, the same note on a cello. Ligeti planned to go a great deal further: 'My idea was that a sufficient number of overtones without the fundamental would, as a result of their combined acoustic effect, sound the fundamental … I imagined that slowly, different composite sounds would emerge and slowly fade away again like shadows, I intended to produce forty-eight layers of sound.' However, the results sounded dreadful, in Ligeti's view, and he decided that such dense textures could be better explored with an orchestra. Significantly, this *Pièce électronique No. 3* (an early instance of his fondness for French titles) was originally to be called *Atmosphères*, which later became the title of the first piece fully to realize his dreams of a purely textural music.

The *Pièce électronique No. 3* was finally reconstructed in 1995, at the Royal Conservatory in The Hague, but remains a curiosity, rather than part of the canon. For Ligeti, its failure signalled that it was time to abandon the electronic studios; his dream of a completely controllable music, with unlimited sonic resources, had turned out to be an illusion. He does not regret the two years spent there – he feels that he learned a vast amount, and would have been a quite different composer were it not for this experience, just as Messiaen, whose direct experience of electro-acoustic music was much briefer and a great deal less satisfying, insisted to the end of his life that electronic music had influenced him enormously. In Ligeti's case, it was a matter of trying to go beyond the limits, and finding nothing but limitations. He has never been tempted to return to the studios: he simply prefers the sound of conventional instruments, and says that if electronic sounds were some day to acquire the 'nobility' of a Stradivarius or a Steinway grand he might have a different attitude.

Besides, electronic music in the 1950s was a rather anonymous medium (more so than the contemporary *musique concrète* in Paris). Relistening to the 1950s repertoire at a distance of forty years or so, one finds some attractive pieces, especially from 1958 onwards, and most of these pieces turn out to be by significant composers: Ligeti, Berio and Maderna, for example. But whereas one can pick these composers immediately from their instrumental works of the same period, with the electronic pieces it is often easier to pick the studio of origin (the WDR studio in Cologne, or the Studio di Fonologia in Milan) than the composer. Only Stockhausen seemed able to put a personal signature on his electronic works without resorting to stereotypes.

One of the major events in Cologne early in 1958 was the première of Stockhausen's *Gruppen*, on 24 March, with a trio of composers: Stockhausen, Boulez and Maderna, conducting the three orchestras. It made an enormous impression on many composers, including Ligeti's friend György Kurtág, who missed the performance but was able to listen to a tape in the Cologne studios a few months later, on his way back to Budapest after studies in Paris. He had graduated from the Liszt Academy in 1955, much later than Ligeti, and his initial experiences with professional musicians had been utterly dispiriting. After the 1956 uprising he too had tried to flee the country, by the same route as Ligeti. But he left it too late – only a week after his friends had made their escape, he learnt from Vera's mother that the rail option had now been completely blocked. However, he had been allowed to go to Paris, where he had studied with Messiaen, Milhaud and Max Deutsch (a former Schoenberg pupil), but above all with the psychologist Marianne Stein. It had not been a happy time for him, and he suffered a nervous breakdown which left him utterly bereft of self-confidence and incapable of composing.

It is no exaggeration to say that Kurtág was overwhelmed by *Gruppen*, the bold, utopian conception of which radiates a confidence utterly at odds with his own self-doubts. As he later said, 'If Dostoyevsky once said that Russian literature came from Gogol's *The Overcoat*, then the whole of twentieth-century music after 1950 comes from *Gruppen*.' However, it was to be another year before he could bring himself to complete a work, a string quartet which he designated as his Opus 1 and dedicated to Marianne Stein, the style of which would be closer to the angular sparseness of the matchstick structures he had often constructed in moments of depression than to the sonic opulence of *Gruppen*.

Ligeti's response to *Gruppen* was less euphoric, though still enthusiastic. He had watched Stockhausen at work on the piece and had discussed its technical methods on countless occasions – it was as if the work had been the focus of an advanced composition seminar.

A rehearsal of Stockhausen's *Gruppen* for three orchestras (only two are visible here); this post-war masterpiece preoccupied Stockhausen during the months following Ligeti's arrival in Cologne.

He regarded Gruppen as an 'exemplary work' of its kind, comparable to *Gesang de Jünglinge* or Boulez's *Le Marteau sans maître*; yet while fascinated by the revolutionary new world of sound that the piece opened up, he was less convinced about the methods Stockhausen had used to produce it.

Around the time of Kurtág's Opus I string quartet, Ligeti was approached to write an article for the periodical *die reihe* ('the series'). *die reihe* had been founded a couple of years earlier by Eimert and Stockhausen as a forum and showcase for the newly emerging European avant garde; it was published in Vienna by Universal Edition, who already published Boulez and Stockhausen, and were soon to become Ligeti's first publisher. There had already been three issues – one on electronic music, one on Webern and one on current 'Musical Craftsmanship' – and now Stockhausen and Eimert were planning a big issue on 'Young Composers'. Initially Metzger had been approached to write the article on Boulez, but one can imagine that formal analysis was not to his taste, and he finished up contributing a couple of abrasively witty critiques of Adorno's cautious response to the new avant garde.

So initially, Ligeti was asked to make an analysis of Boulez's *Le Marteau sans maître*, a recent work that had already made a big impression on him, as on many others. But it used a compositional method – 'chord multiplication' – which no one in Cologne was familiar with, and Boulez was not disposed to help (his own book, *Penser la musique aujourd'hui*, published in the early 1960s, is notorious for its wilful obscurantism on technical matters: Ligeti says he still cannot understand it). So the assignment proved too intractable, and instead he made an analysis of the first piece from Boulez's earlier *Structures I* (1951–2) for two pianos, an example of 'total serialization', in which the pitch, length, dynamic and touch for each note is determined by the same serial grids.

Articles of this kind served a double purpose. On the one hand, they aimed not only to publicize the new avant garde, but also to give it some kind of intellectual-theoretical legitimacy, locally as well as internationally. According to Ligeti, the group was 'generously tolerated' in Cologne, but scarcely given the status and power it was beginning to acquire at the Darmstadt courses. But there was also a more practical side. None of the group was making a living from their works. Stockhausen and Koenig had full-time posts at WDR, but the rest led a financially precarious existence. In commissioning young composers such as Ligeti to write analytical articles, radio introductions to their own works, or series of talks on modernist father-figures like Debussy or Webern, Eimert was able to give them some welcome additional means of support, though it was some while before Ligeti's German was fluent enough for him to write his radio texts unaided – his assignments were often shared with Helms or Koenig. In other cities, other radio producers – Ulrich Dibelius in Munich, Karl-Amadeus Hartmann in Hamburg and Josef Häusler in Baden-Baden – did the same.

There is no doubt that the articles had an additional function for Ligeti at that time. Quite apart from making him known as part of the group of young radicals, writing about other composers such as Boulez enabled him to clarify his own ideas, and where appropriate to articulate a certain distance. His analysis of Boulez's *Structures Ia* is a case in point. On the one hand, Ligeti provided an immaculately detailed account of what Boulez had actually done (still quoted today as a 'classic' exposition of early serialism); on the other, he provided a sharp critique which probably delighted the highly competitive Stockhausen, just as much as it annoyed Boulez.

This is typical of Ligeti's response to the Western avant garde, which almost from the start was a mixture of fascination and scepticism. In this particular case, the Boulez analysis was a means of clarifying his own dissatisfaction with the 'equality of parameters' adopted by the serialists – the idea that such things as dynamic levels and articulation (legato, staccato etc.) were structurally just as important as pitch and rhythm. Even though he admired works such as *Le Marteau sans maître* and *Gruppen* which were a product of this thinking, he did not accept the concept itself.

In 1959 Ligeti was invited to lecture at Darmstadt for the first time, but on the subject of Webern rather than on his own work. This is not as surprising as it might seem in retrospect. As a composer he was known, even in Cologne, merely as the composer of a single, rather

Ligeti in 1958, on the verge of composing works that would establish his place in music history

striking four-minute electronic work. On the other hand, he had produced several interesting radio texts on other composers, including Webern, who was still a central figure for many composers fourteen years after his death. Stockhausen still thought of Ligeti primarily as a theorist.

In some respects, Ligeti's attachment to Webern seems curious. After all, even though Webern had acted as patron saint to the European avant garde in the early 1950s (and even to Cage and Feldman, around 1950), it is hard to imagine what relevance his sparse, ultra-motivic late works could have for a young man dreaming of a music without themes and harmonies. Perhaps it was, indeed, partly the theorist in Ligeti that was drawn to Webern – the fact that one really could account for what was going on, and that there were clearly definable rules and procedures, even though the more obviously traditional aspects of Webern's late work (the sonata forms, for instance) tended to be scrupulously ignored by the Cologne-Darmstadt avant garde.

There is certainly precious little connection between Webern and *Apparitions*, the orchestral work Ligeti worked on during 1959. This began as an attempt to reconstruct *Visiók*, but soon turned into something quite different: an entirely new kind of orchestral music greatly influenced by the 'global' way that sound and texture were handled in the electronic studios.

In describing *Apparitions*, Ligeti recalls a particularly vivid dream he had as a small child, clearly related to his fear of spiders. Though its impact was visual rather than aural, it is not hard to see how it relates to Ligeti's music at this period, as well as later:

As a small child I once had a dream that I could not get to my cot, to my safe haven, because the whole room was filled with a dense confused tangle of fine filaments. It looked like the web I had seen silkworms fill their box with as they change into pupas. I was caught up in this immense web with both living things and objects of various kinds – huge moths, a variety of beetles – which tried to get to the flickering flame of the candle in the room; enormous dirty pillows were suspended in this substance, their rotten stuffing hanging out through the slits in the torn covers. There were blobs of fresh mucus, balls of dry mucus, remnants of food all gone cold and other such revolting rubbish. Every time a beetle or a moth moved, the entire web started shaking so that the big, heavy pillows were swinging about, which, in turn, made the web rock harder. Sometimes the different kinds of movement reinforced one another and the shaking became so hard that the web tore in places and a few insects suddenly found themselves free. But their freedom was short-lived, they were soon caught up again in the rocking tangle of filaments, and their buzzing, loud at first, grew weaker and weaker. The succession of these sudden, unexpected events gradually brought about a change in the internal structure, in the texture of the web. In places knots formed, thickening into an almost solid mass, caverns opened up where shreds of the original web were floating about like gossamer. All these changes seemed like an irreversible process, never returning to earlier states again. An indescribable sadness hung over these shifting forms and structures, the hopelessness of passing time and the melancholy of unalterable past events.

The realization of *Apparitions* required a huge score, with up to sixty-three staves for those passages where each instrument has its own individual part. Ligeti subsequently learnt from the *New York Times* that this had 'set a record' (which he went on to break with the score of *Atmosphères*). However, his memory of writing the score is typically 'de-mystifying': because it was so large, it could not be put on any table he had, so he had to work on the floor, wearing whatever garments were already beyond repair.

Right from its opening moments, *Apparitions* introduces many elements of what was to become the 'Ligeti sound': very low chromatic clusters on cellos and double basses, celesta clusters, and a mini-anthology of string timbres – tremolos, rapid alternations between bridge and fingerboard, vibrating and muffled plucked sounds (including the ones discovered by Cerha), and bowed and struck sounds with the wood of the bow. Above all, the dynamics inhabit extremes; for much of the time the music is barely audible, which makes the occasional loud outbursts all the more startling (the first of them, a bass drum stroke, is marked 'like a detonation'). Gradually the strings move up through the middle register; there is a sudden wild outburst, and they settle in the stratosphere, right at the top of their range, with an 'echo ensemble' of three violins and trumpet providing a sudden surprise resonance from the back of the hall.

Uniquely in Ligeti's output, the formal proportions of this movement are based on the 'Fibonacci series', an arithmetic series discovered
in the late Middle Ages which has a close relation to the 'golden
section' familiar to painters and architects. Each number in the
Fibonacci series is the sum of the two preceding numbers (1 1 2 3 5 8 13
21 34 55 89 etc.). The further one goes up this series, the closer the
ratio of neighbouring numbers becomes to that of the 'golden section'
(1:0.618). In this century, musicologists have been fascinated by the
possibility that composers from many different eras might have
applied it to the time proportions of their works; the evidence is often
compelling, but rarely conclusive. In the post-war era, on the other
hand, many composers have employed it quite explicitly: both
Xenakis and Stockhausen did so under the direct influence of Le
Corbusier's architectural use of it.

In Ligeti's case, typically, the situation is a little more complex.
One of his colleagues at the Liszt Academy had been Ernö Lendvai,
a composer and theorist. Lendvai had been developing the thesis that
Bartók's later work (and to some extent Kodály's too) made conscious
and extensive use of the Fibonacci series. Ideas of this kind were
regarded by the communist authorities as indefensible 'formalism',
and Lendvai had promptly been put on a list of 'unreliable' teachers,
as indeed had Ligeti. Though Ligeti had his doubts about Lendvai's
propositions (which do indeed seem to have some shaky aspects), he
felt obliged to show solidarity with him, and had even written a couple
of brief articles in his defence. During the Cologne years, he was still
intrigued by Lendvai's ideas, and though an attempt to apply them to
harmonic structure in the unfinished *Pièce électronique No. 3* had
proved an utter failure, he still found the Fibonacci numbers a useful
basis for shaping duration in his new orchestral piece. However, as the
musicologist Gianmario Borio later pointed out to him, he made so
many small adjustments in the process of composition that hardly a
single Fibonacci number was left. Be that as it may, ever since
Apparitions, analysts have hastened to find golden sections and
Fibonacci proportions in Ligeti's work. They may even be there, says
Ligeti, but not by design: he used this particular kind of conscious
numerical structuring once, and only once.

The second movement of *Apparitions* brings one even closer to
Ligeti's style of the 1960s. At first sight it might seem simpler than the

With an older generation at Darmstadt, 1960: (right to left) Ligeti, composer and former Webern-pupil Stefan Wolpe, and Eduard Steuermann, pianist from the Schoenberg circle, along with course director Wolfgang Steinecke and cellist Ludwig Hoelscher

first, for there are none of the complex changes of metre and time signature, but this is because the bar-lines have stopped having any metrical significance. Ligeti has realized that the way to create a 'continuous' music is to get rid of any sense of metre: the bars of 2/2 (or 6/4) are now just a means of synchronizing the musicians via the conductor. The result is a fluid approach to musical time – indeed, one could describe the difference between the two movements of *Apparitions* in terms of the difference between solids and fluids. Whereas the first movement consists mainly of static blocks of sound, here everything is in motion: tremolos, tremolandos, and upward and downward sweeps which ricochet from one part of the orchestra to another, first between different groups of strings, then later in the woodwind as well. Then comes another 'wild' outburst, longer than the one in the first movement, and much more significant in terms of Ligeti's subsequent works. Here each of the forty-six strings has its own part, mostly leaping extravagantly from low to high. This is the first example in Ligeti's music of what he calls 'micropolyphony': a dense counterpoint in which one can no longer hear the individual voices, but is simply aware of changing degrees of activity, and perhaps of broad movements in register from low to high, or vice versa (though here almost the full range is in constant use). The score instructs the players to perform 'with extreme force. Every string player plays as intensely as if he were a soloist. Energy is more important than perfect intonation'; the latter concession is logical enough, since individual parts can only rarely be heard. This episode is followed by a scarcely less radical one in which the bassoonists play without the reed, and the brass players strike the mouthpiece with the palm of their hand: this kind of 'extended technique' was just beginning to be developed by young Polish composers like Penderecki. After this, the music seems to be returning to the gentle flutterings of the opening, but there is another shock in store: a sequence of loud eruptions initiated by the percussionists, one of whom smashes a sackful of empty bottles with a large hammer. (As a more effective but riskier alternative, Ligeti has suggested placing metal bars inside a wooden crate; at the specified moment, the percussionist – wearing protective goggles – hurls a half-gallon bottle into the crate!)

In large part, it was thanks to Mauricio Kagel that *Apparitions* got a first hearing. A couple of years earlier, Kagel had written *Anagrama*, a remarkable piece for vocal soloists, speaking choir and ensemble, and he was now seeking to arrange its first performance at a festival to be mounted in Cologne by the ISCM (International Society for Contemporary Music) – an organization committed to the promotion of new music originating from a wide variety of member nations. At first he ran up against bureaucratic obstacles: works could only be submitted by national sections, and as a 'stateless person' he was left out in the cold. He managed to get the regulations changed to permit independent composer submissions, but was then informed that there would need to be another submission by another 'stateless' composer. So he went to see Ligeti, who put forward *Apparitions*. Both works were accepted.

Not surprisingly, the première of *Apparitions* created a sensation. More unexpectedly, the response was essentially positive – it was not just another standard new music 'scandal', but was regarded as an indication of quite new musical possibilities, which indeed soon assumed major importance for the avant garde, even if *Apparitions* itself was rather overwhelmed by its successors. It was a sign of Ligeti's growing status within the Cologne group that he was now invited to write something which touched on his own work. The result, 'Wandlungen der musikalischen Form' ('Transformations of Musical Form'), was to be the first of three theoretical articles on his own work. In retrospect, Ligeti rather regrets them, precisely because the articles suggest a theoretical, somewhat dogmatic approach to composing which reflects the spirit of the times, but is far removed from his actual intentions.

Although Ligeti clearly attaches great importance to *Apparitions*, the piece has never really caught on with the public, not even with a new music public. Perhaps it is not so hard to see why. Compared to earlier works, it is obviously a 'breakthrough', and leaves the world of Bartók firmly behind, engaging with the new world of the avant garde in a distinctive way. It contains all sorts of elements that point the way forward to *Atmosphères* and subsequent works: clusters and other kinds of dense textures, extremes of registers and dynamics, and wildly flailing 'super-espressivo' passages. But what it lacks, especially in the first movement, is that sense of continuity, of gradual unfolding, that is essential to so many of the later works. Perhaps because of its commitment to golden section proportions, the music keeps stopping and starting, reflecting the 1950s avant garde's obsession with fragmentation, rather than Ligeti's dream of a continuous music. To some extent, Ligeti is the prisoner of his chosen system.

The same festival that brought Ligeti his first major success also created a major rift in the Cologne group. Metzger, now a firm Cage adherent, had set up a counter-festival in the studio of the painter Mary Bauermeister, featuring Cage and the Fluxus artist Nam June Paik; in the course of this anti-ISCM festival he read out a 'Cologne Manifesto' which claimed that 'art has missed its opportunity', and that 'its present stance is one of abolishing itself' – apparently its post-Hegelian duty …! Stockhausen came in for direct criticism as the author of an article, 'Music and Function', 'in the course of which music is partly assigned to fulfil spiritual tasks; as if, having nothing better to do than be preoccupied with itself, it could depend on the Holy Ghost to give it something more committed to do.' A few months later, Stockhausen hit back, recording his response to

Metzger's tirade: 'During the Manifesto I was thinking: Mary, bring me a glass of whisky and make Metzger a steak – his brain and mine are so dried out.'

The real breaking-point, however, had come earlier on in the festival: on 11 June there was a concert featuring Nono's attractive but conventionally post-Webernian *Coro di Didone*, and the premières of Kagel's *Anagrama* and Stockhausen's *Kontakte* for piano, percussion and four-track tape. *Kontakte* is now regarded as one of the major works of the period and a milestone in electro-acoustic music, whereas *Anagrama* is (quite unjustly) forgotten; but on that occasion it was *Anagrama* that won the day. To Stockhausen's dismay, when Ernst Brücher held a reception afterwards at his home, everyone was talking about Kagel's work, not his own. This was the first time in years that he had found himself on the back foot; subsequently he said that he had 'never felt so alone'. Though Kagel took part in the première of Stockhausen's *Carré* in October, the following months saw an increasing antagonism between the composers. This peaked a couple of years later in Palermo when Kagel demonstrated publically against Stockhausen's *Klavierstück X*.

Ligeti was caught in the personal cross-fire. He was friendly with both composers, and had reason to be grateful to them both. How could he take the side of one against the other? Yet increasingly, this is what he was being expected to do. Having initially been offered the orchestration classes at the Cologne New Music Courses with which Stockhausen was planning to supplement and perhaps replace Darmstadt, he found his name suddenly missing from the prospectus. But by this stage, he had long since sized up the situation, voted with his feet, and left Cologne for Vienna.

4

*My attitude overall is that I'm never inclined
to shock.*

Ligeti in conversation with
Lutz van Salfield

Celebrity and Scandal 1960-66

Though the 1960s, mercifully, brought no substantial addition to the traumas Ligeti had endured under fascism and communism, they were still far from comfortable. He had begun to establish a name within the avant garde, but this in itself was no guarantee of success or security. The early 1960s in particular were nomadic years for him, spent wandering from one momentary opportunity to another. These were years in which other leading members of the Darmstadt group were furiously establishing their own territory. In France, Boulez was establishing a virtual 'school' whose influence was such that if a young composer in Paris did not subscribe to a Boulezian aesthetic (a certain kind of harmony, an aura of elegant abstraction, lots of xylorimbas and vibraphones etc.) his chances of official acceptance were greatly reduced. Initially, the results were impressive: newcomers such as Gilbert Amy, Jean-Claude Eloy and Paul Méfano made brilliant débuts which, in the long run, they did not really build upon (though one could not foresee this at the time). Stockhausen, too, began to acquire the status of a guru, not through establishing a dogmatic style, but, on the contrary, as the prophet of perpetual change.

With only *Artikulation* and *Apparitions* behind him, Ligeti was in no position to stake out comparable territory. But, in any case, it was not in his nature to do so. Back in the 1920s, Erik Satie had declared: 'There is no School of Satie: I should be opposed to it,' and though Ligeti never shared Satie's obsessive dedication to frivolity, one could imagine him saying much the same sort of thing about any putative 'Ligeti School'. In fact, it may have been a horror at being cast in the role of prophet that partly accounts for the way that his output in the early 1960s see-saws between obviously 'major' works, and others that seem to cast doubt on the whole idea of Great Works, at least in relation to the 1960s avant garde.

Ligeti's first product in the 1960s was certainly 'major'. In the wake of *Apparitions*, he wrote a new orchestral work, *Atmosphères*, and following his success at the ISCM Festival, the Südwestfunk

(South West German Radio) retrospectively commissioned it for the Donaueschingen Festival, one of the primary showcases for the European avant garde. This was the festival that had given the first performances of Stockhausen's first orchestral work, *Spiel,* and Boulez's *Polyphonie X* in the early 1950s, and had recently commissioned Penderecki's first major orchestral work, *Anaklasis.* Ligeti's *Atmosphères* was to substantially eclipse *Apparitions,* and is the first work in which his new style emerges fully fledged; it remains one of his best-known works.

Atmosphères is written for 'large orchestra without percussion'. Even in this subtitle, there is an air of secession from avant-garde orthodoxies, since percussion sections of epic dimensions were a primary feature of the 1950s modernist orchestra. Stockhausen's *Gruppen* had called for no fewer than twelve percussionists, Boulez's *Don* (the opening part of *Pli selon pli*) for seven, while Nono's *Diario polacco* calls for a small army of drummers and cymbal players. But the absence of percussion is more than a polemic feature: percussion writing is, above all, about sounds that burst forth, growl or glitter for a moment, and then die away. *Atmosphères,* on the contrary, explores a new form of musical continuity – not thematic or harmonic, but steered by timbre and texture.

Atmosphères was not entirely alone in this. As the 1950s came to an end, a new spirit began to emerge in European music, and especially among those Eastern European composers able to operate outside the confines of communist cultural politics. Ironically, at much the same time as Ligeti fled from Hungary, the cultural situation in Poland had started to ease up, and the Stalinist shackles restricting musical style rapidly disappeared. A first Warsaw Autumn Festival of new music was held in 1956, another in 1958, and thereafter it became an annual event. By the 1958 festival, middle-generation composers like Lutosławski, Schaeffer, Serocki and Szabelski were already drifting towards the Western avant garde, and two young radicals had begun to make an impression: Penderecki and Górecki.

Instead of just trying to emulate the rather abstract structures of composers like Boulez and Stockhausen, the Poles soon adopted a more colourful, intuitive approach, comparable to that of the 'tachist' (action) painters. Typical examples include Lutosławski's *Venetian Games,* with its 'controlled chance' elements, and Penderecki's

Threnody for the Victims of Hiroshima, with its screaming clusters and whole array of unorthodox performance techniques.

Polish works from this period usually consisted of a number of short, often clearly contrasted sections; Ligeti's concern, however, was with a 'music without beginning or end'. For a couple of years, Stockhausen too had been talking in similar terms, particularly in connection with his idea of 'moment form', in which each moment of a piece stands by itself, but is nevertheless related to all other moments. The first important expositions of this were the electronic work *Kontakte*, and *Carré* for four choirs and orchestra. Ligeti does not rule out the possibility that *Carré* and even Penderecki's *Anaklasis* may have had a background influence on his work, but his intentions in *Atmosphères* were very different. Far from being concerned with a Stockhausen-like 'autonomy of the moment', his work sets out to erase any idea of the isolated moment – everything is always in a state of transformation, part of a more or less turbulent flux. Moreover, whereas Penderecki's piece contains many passages involving an element of chance, a highly simplified, 'free' notation, and a virtual encyclopaedia of novel string effects (striking the body of the instrument, playing behind the bridge, and so forth), *Atmosphères* is notated with meticulous exactness, and only uses unorthodox playing techniques (albeit to great effect) at the very end of the work, where the wind players blow through their instruments without sounding any pitch.

Ligeti describes the overall form of the work as something 'to be realized as a single, broad-spanned arch, with the individual sections being fused together, subordinate to the broad arch', even though the last ninety seconds, which start with a clear reminiscence of the start of the second movement of *Apparitions*, do have the effect of a coda, of an 'echo' of the main body of the work. In theory, there are twenty-two sections, each carefully timed by the composer in the score to reach a total of eight minutes, thirty-four seconds (which did not prevent Leonard Bernstein, during his brief flirtation with the avant garde in the early 1960s, from making a typically adrenaline-laden recording which lasted well under seven minutes). However, as the composer suggests, a good performance is one in which one does not hear these subdivisions as 'new sections', but rather as shifts of emphasis or direction.

Even more than *Apparitions*, *Atmosphères* looks and sounds quite unlike other avant-garde works of that period, or of any earlier period.

One could find some distant precedent in the 'Farben' movement from Schoenberg's Five Pieces for Orchestra (1909) and the third of Alban Berg's *Altenberglieder* (1912), as both of them are pieces which begin with a static chord constantly changing in orchestration; Ligeti, however, goes a great deal further. At the beginning of *Atmosphères* the whole string section and a few wind instruments enter with a cluster spread over several octaves; but the result is by no means as abrasive as one might expect, since the players enter very quietly (*pp* and *dolcissimo*), producing an almost dematerialized effect. In his programme note for the première, Ligeti talks of seeking to create an 'uninhabited, imaginary musical space'; one aspect of this 'zero population' is that, on the surface, nothing happens – for the first minute, the instruments just hold their notes, and gradually fade out until only violas and cellos are left. But the result is riveting: it is as if one was looking at a huge Rothko canvas in a room where the lighting was gradually reduced until only a lower corner was still visible. Then these remaining instruments, initially playing almost inaudibly, without vibrato, 'senza colore', start to throb a little – to rise and fall in level – even though their notes stay the same. Now other instruments re-enter, the strings with a tremolo that slowly speeds up, and the woodwinds with the reverse process. Suddenly the pages are black with notes, but the result is still essentially static. Ligeti compares this passage with a wood whose trees are clearly covered by leaves stirring in the wind, even though the individual leaves cannot be seen.

At a more theoretical level, *Atmosphères* applies certain categories from electronic music in a more material way than *Apparitions*. The Cologne studio composers made a distinction between 'stationary' sounds (those which were essentially static, like conventional single chords) and 'non-stationary' sounds (those which involved a degree of internal activity, which might or might not actually change the width of the sound, and could also lead to a shift of register). Ligeti transfers these criteria to his chromatic clusters, which can be either stationary, as at the beginning, or non-stationary, as later on.

It is in *Atmosphères* that one also sees the first clear evidence of Ligeti's intermittent attraction to scientific models (though he insists that his music itself is never 'scientific'). There are passages where a basically static surface is 'disturbed' by events which pass through the whole ensemble, like the ripples that spread when a stone is thrown

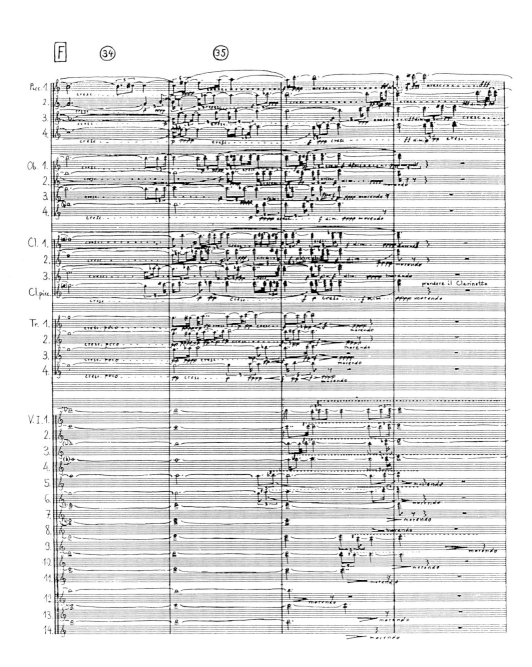

*Opposite, the start of an
'unrecordable' passage from
Atmosphères: four piccolos
ascend into the stratosphere
(reproduction of the
composer's manuscript).*

into a pool. Elsewhere there are sudden unexpected eddies and whirlpools, local 'turbulences'. *Atmosphères* also provides the first protracted use of 'micropolyphony', in a manner much more varied and subtle than the outburst in the second movement of *Apparitions*. About halfway through the piece, there is a passage which starts with a middle-register cluster in the strings, and gradually drifts higher and higher, culminating in a shrill, notoriously unrecordable chord for four piccolos. Suddenly the music plunges from top to bottom (with a cluster for eight double basses), and over this the remaining strings enter with a labyrinth of twisting melodic figures. Heard individually, these figures would sound a little like Bartók, but the point is that one cannot hear them as such – they just create a sense of inner motion within a dense band of sound. Here too, Ligeti makes an analogy with physical processes, namely with crystals 'growing' in a supersaturated solution. The crystals are always latently there, but there is a certain point at which distinct formations become visible. Ligeti's idea in using micropolyphony is 'to arrest the process, to fix the supersaturated solution just at the moment before crystallization' (*Ligeti in Conversation*), that is, just before the moment where individual melodic lines become perceptible.

The preparation for the Donaueschingen première of *Atmosphères* had its worrying aspects. Although conductor Hans Rosbaud had a proven track record conducting new works from the serialist school, this piece was something new, and Ligeti, who for some reason had not been invited to the rehearsals leading up to a radio recording (since released on CD), was alarmed to find at the dress rehearsal that Rosbaud was underplaying the continuous aspect of the work, and making the form far more sectional, far more 'chopped up' than the composer had intended. However, a conversation with Rosbaud was enough to rectify this. The actual performance at the première remains, for Ligeti, one of the best he has ever heard, and it was so enthusiastically received that the nine-minute work had to be repeated immediately – not a common occurrence in the history of new music. Alas, this performance was not recorded.

It is customary now for writers to describe the performance as a breakthrough for Ligeti, his first great public success. Ligeti, typically, has a more sceptical view: he thinks it had a novelty value for the critics, but questions whether they really understood what the work was really about. Nevertheless, the difference between the acclamation accorded to *Atmosphères* at Donaueschingen and the absolutely negative, even outraged, response to Xenakis's *Metastasis* six years earlier, was perhaps an indication that the era of orthodox post-Webernism was over, and that 'texturalism' was an idea whose time had come. Be that as it may, there is no doubt that *Atmosphères*, along with the subsequent organ piece *Volumina*, made Ligeti a name to conjure with in avant-garde circles. Indeed, nearly forty years later, *Atmosphères* remains the major classic of the brief texturalist period – only Penderecki's *Threnody* has retained comparable status.

Following *Atmosphères*, Ligeti was now well placed to assume a prominent place in the avant garde. Yet far from hastening to follow up on the success of this work, he seems to have gone out of his way to undermine any idea of himself as 'the next great composer'. Whether from irony, self-doubt or just a sense of fun, virtually every work for the next two years had aspects that could only be regarded as provocative; and while he now claims that it was never his intention to shock, that is not how it looked in the early 1960s.

The works after *Atmosphères* ranged from silence to entropy. In August 1961 Ligeti was invited to give a course on new music as part of a 'European Forum' in Alpbach. At the end of the course, each of the guest lecturers, who included artists and theatre people, were asked to talk for ten minutes about the future of their art. Ligeti was appalled at the prospect, and said straight out that he had no idea what would happen in the future, and, for that matter, nor had anyone else. But the organizers were persistent. As Ligeti recalls, 'There was the mayor of Alpbach and the mayor of Innsbruck, and they were so terribly friendly and nice, and took me very seriously. They said: "It doesn't matter what you say." Then I thought: since I can't say anything valid about the future – I'm not a prognostician or an astrologer – I won't say anything. So I said: "I won't say anything." – "That's OK, do whatever you want." Then I thought: I'll stay silent for ten minutes. So I asked, "Can I …" – "Doesn't matter what you do – anything will be acceptable." So I kept quiet for ten minutes, but there was a huge scandal.'

Though Ligeti may have stayed quiet for ten minutes, the audience did not. After a minute, Ligeti started writing some comments on the blackboard which must surely have been intended to provoke, whatever the composer claims. These included 'Please don't clap or stamp your feet' and 'Don't let yourself be manipulated!' The result was uproar, further fuelled by additional written comments of 'Crescendo' and 'Più forte'. Before the ten minutes were up, attempts had been made to drag Ligeti off the rostrum.

The resultant 'non-event', formally described in the list of Ligeti's works as *The Future of Music – A Collective Composition*, not only pursues the trends of the 'silent piece' and the 'happening' notoriously inaugurated in 1952 by John Cage's *4'33"* (at the première of which the pianist David Tudor sat at his instrument for the specified time without making any intentional sound) but also ties in with the activities of the emerging neo-Dada, 'anti/post-art' Fluxus group, one of whose members, Nam June Paik, Ligeti had already got to know in Cologne. Some time in 1958 Paik had given a 'private' happening in his flat, just for Ligeti and Koenig. The basement flat was a model of austerity, the only furniture being a mattress, and a pianino in a state of terminal disrepair. First Paik placed tiny Japanese toys on the pianino keys, then he gave each of the composers an apple, telling him to eat it and wait until he came back. Next he left through the front door, and went up the basement staircase. Ligeti and Koenig ate the apples and waited. After half an hour, there was still no sign of Paik. Then suddenly he burst in, screaming,

The face of extremism: Fluxus artist Nam June Paik was notorious for 'actions' which shocked and scandalized audiences.

A Décollage Happening in Düsseldorf, June 1962. Paik is second from the right onstage; two places to his left is Wolf Vostell, the main German figure in the Fluxus movement.

through a hitherto unnoticed door from the garden. Both composers were suitably astonished.

A couple of years later, Ligeti recalls, Wolf Vostell (a German member of Fluxus) had arranged to have an affluent audience in their evening finery driven out into the countryside and simply left there in the rain. The irreverence and novelty of many happenings appealed to Ligeti, and at one stage he found himself co-opted into the official Fluxus ranks, mainly because there was a brief period when George Maciunas, the principal theorist and impresario of Fluxus in America, decided that the musical avant garde in Europe shared his own anarchic ethos. This illusion did not last long – as soon as Maciunas found out that figures like Ligeti, Stockhausen and Berio were signed up with leading European publishers, he abandoned them. A few years later he was demonstrating outside a Stockhausen performance in New York, brandishing a placard inscribed 'Stockhausen – Patrician "Theorist" of white supremacy – go to hell!'. It is precisely this hasty transformation of fresh, new ideas into ideology that has always sent Ligeti running for cover.

However, in 1961 Ligeti did supply one archetypal Fluxus work, the *Trois Bagatelles* for piano dedicated to David Tudor, who had given the first performance of Cage's *4'33"*. Ligeti pays the work due homage by having three movements, as Tudor's Cage première had, but Ligeti establishes a distance by having only two silent movements – the first movement comprises a single soft note.

His next piece was *Fragment*, written for the sixtieth birthday of his newly-acquired publisher, Alfred Schlee of Universal Edition, and largely based on a chord extrapolated from the name S–C–H–L–E–E (in German notation, equivalent to E flat–C–B–E; 'L' has to be ignored). Even the ensemble looks eccentric, an ultra-low group of contra-bassoon, bass trombone, contrabass tuba, bass drum, tam-tam, harp, harpsichord, piano and three double basses. This seems decidedly sepulchral for a birthday piece. In fact, the ensemble is taken from the instrument- ation of the first movement of *Apparitions* (though the latter uses normal trombone and tuba), and the whole piece turns out to be self-parody – a satire of the work that Universal Edition had just accepted for publication. And just as the choice of instruments focuses on just one aspect of the *Apparitions* orchestra, so the musical events, such as they are, apply a magnifying glass to certain moments in the first movement of *Apparitions*.

The piece starts with a low, barely audible rumbling, after which the three double basses sustain a soft 'Schlee' chord (two notes of which are exactly the ones that opened *Apparitions*). So one sits and waits for the next thing to happen. One has to wait for quite a while, because for the next three or four minutes, the basses just hold their notes, with the bow position drifting very slowly from the bridge to the fingerboard. Then comes a thunderous stroke on the bass drum and a drastic crescendo from nothing on the contrabassoon, followed by a minute or more of stasis, a brief, furious outburst in which the harpsichord seems to come in too late, another long pause, and a very loud final chord, with the piano holding its notes till they die away completely. And that's it. Ligeti once described *Fragment* as 'making *Apparitions* completely ridiculous'; that is surely an exaggeration, but this piece of self-mockery does show that Ligeti was aware very early on of the danger of lapsing into mannerism.

The *coup de grâce* of this phase was the *Poème symphonique* for 100 metronomes, conductor and ten performers. It was scheduled as the final event at the 1962 Gaudeamus Music Week, to take place at an official reception at the Hilversum City Hall (though Ligeti did not know in advance that it would have this status). As with Ligeti's 'talk' *The Future of Music*, the organizers were obviously quite unaware of what they were in for – word about John Cage and happenings (including *The Future of Music*) had not reached Hilversum. The director Walter Maas, whose tireless activities on behalf of new music in Holland extended from the late 1940s to his death in the mid 1990s, blithely ordered the metronomes from a German company, little suspecting what would happen. After all, there were ten performers and a conductor, and Ligeti was emerging as a highly regarded, serious composer, so what reason was there for suspicion?

It was a classic disaster scenario, and Ligeti has given a graphic account of it. Even the hours preceding the performance were fraught with problems. The 100 metronomes were stored in ten wooden crates in a corner of the city hall where the performance was to take place. Once Ligeti had managed to open up the crates with hammer and pincers, he found that the brand-new metronomes were all carefully packed for shipping, with the winding key secured to the bottom of each instrument. To ensure customer satisfaction, they were all fully wound; but the score specified that the metronomes had to be completely run down at the start of the performance, and even at the fastest tempo setting, this took a good half hour! By this stage, Ligeti relates, 'I was covered with sweat, alone, and panic-stricken. How on earth was I going to get all these preparations done before the beginning of the reception – how was I going to get the 100 metro-nomes set up on pedestals in the banquet room of the city hall before the guests arrived, and cover them with black cloths so that the public would have no idea what sort of music was going to be performed?'

Somehow, with just a few minutes to spare, he got the instruments ready. Then came another problem. The score also prescribed that the conductor (Ligeti) and performers were to wear formal dress, so that afternoon some of the performers had gone off to a local dress hire shop to get tuxedos for themselves, and for him too. But because of the panic over unpacking the metronomes, he had no time to try his suit until the reception was only minutes away. He was still bathed in sweat; some composer friends hastily rubbed the worst off with a towel, and helped a very sticky Ligeti into his coat and tails. It now turned out that the stiff shirt was far too large, and no-one could work out how to fasten the ornate buttons and clasps, or tie a proper

Thirty-three years after the initial scandal: Ligeti with some of the 100 metronomes for a performance of the *Poème symphonique* at the Royal Academy in 1995

bow tie (the other performers, who had presumably solved these problems, had already gone off to the banquet hall with their instruments). At least, as Ligeti wryly comments, his appearance was perfectly in keeping with the Fluxus aesthetic.

The cameras of Dutch Television were already setting up to record the event. The Mayor of Hilversum, in full ceremonial regalia, gave a long address concerning the lofty aims of art, and then the crowning performance began. The conductor entered with the ten players (all composers participating in the Music Week), each of whom had ten clockwork metronomes, with the mechanism run down. At a sign from the conductor, the players wound up their metronomes, and set the speeds for each one (different for each). Then, after a pause of a few minutes (!), the conductor gave another sign, the players set the metronomes in motion and quietly left the stage, following the conductor. The piece was over when the last metronome ran down.

The result, says Ligeti, was a 'maxi-maxi-scandal'. The listeners, an invited 'society' audience with practically no knowledge of new music, were perplexed. After the final tick there was an 'oppressive silence', followed by howls of protest, and the organizing officials too were furious. Ligeti was confronted by a very elderly man who turned out to be Willem Marinus Dudek, the building's architect; Dudek insisted that his noble edifice had been insulted and desecrated by Ligeti's work.

In the following days, Ligeti found out that arts censorship was by no means confined to communist countries, even if it operated more covertly in the West. The *Poème symphonique* had been scheduled to be televised the next day, but when Ligeti's host Walter Maas turned to the appropriate channel, he found that instead of the Gaudeamus event, there was a soccer match. Maas immediately phoned the station, and was told that the broadcast had been cancelled 'at the urgent request of the Hilversum Senate'. A day or so later, Ligeti asked to see the film, but was denied permission. Six years later, when he was in Stockholm, Swedish Radio hired a copy, and he got to see the sticker on the canister: 'For internal use only – not authorized for broadcast.'

For all its provocative aspects, the *Poème symphonique* was clearly intended as more than a prank. Certainly, like many of its predecessors it was partly meant to be a critique of the current musical situation. Its misfortune was to be performed for an audience that, even at a festival of new music, had not the faintest idea what the critique was about. On the other hand, the composer's claim that it is a 'very, very serious piece' might seem a little implausible, even though the basic paradox of an erratic clockwork, of innately predictable processes whose interaction and duration is quite unpredictable, subsequently turned out to be ur-Ligeti.

However, hearing the piece today – even if only on a CD recording – gives a very different perspective. One can still doubt the profundity of Ligeti's intentions, but the result is extraordinary, and must surely have astounded the composer. Trying to estimate the effect of the piece, one would probably imagine an initial entropy – a sort of white noise – in which there is simply too much simultaneous information for one to make judgements about innate order or chaos. This would finish up, via various intermediate stages, as the desolate ticking of isolated survivors. Such an account, even if it is accurate as far as it goes, does little justice to the actual result. Within a few moments, swirls and eddies become audible within the mass of pulses – almost exactly the kind of 'turbulence' deployed in *Atmosphères*! The random scattering of so many events produces all kinds of crescendos and sudden accents, and after a few minutes there are even some tiny breaks in the texture. At times, the whole 'ensemble' seems to gather into a common metre, and by the halfway-point even individual pulses become audible for a moment. As the piece proceeds, its remorseless repetitions sometimes sound like an anticipation of the American Minimalist movement that came into being a few years later. One cannot help being reminded of pieces like Steve Reich's *Clapping Music* or *Drumming*, in which ceaselessly repeated figures gradually drift out of phase with one another. One even seems to glimpse various ethnic drumming traditions ... So what starts as a remorselessly 'textural' piece finishes up as an audibly 'polyrhythmic' one.

In Vienna too, textural music was rapidly becoming a preoccupation of the city's avant garde. Next to Ligeti, the most significant exponent was Friedrich Cerha, who had already impressed him a few years earlier with his unusual violin techniques. Meeting Cerha again after completing *Apparitions*, Ligeti was astonished and excited to find him working on an orchestral piece called *Fasce* ('Fields'), which involved exactly the same kind of textural explorations as his own piece. Cerha then embarked on a cycle of orchestral pieces called *Spiegel* ('Mirror'), some of them also involving electronic music, which not only rivalled and even outdid Ligeti's scores in terms of physical size (*Spiegel I* uses 106 staves at one point), but also proved to be among Cerha's most significant works; in particular, *Spiegel II* for 56 strings remains a classic of early texturalism.

The other wing of the Vienna radicals was dedicated to 'musical graphics'. Taking their cue from certain works by Cage and his group (and also perhaps from Bussotti's *Five Pieces for David Tudor*), Anestis Logothetis and Roman Haubenstock-Ramati had begun writing works which frequently contain little or no conventional notation, and often depend on exquisitely drawn 'pictures' to convey musical shapes and gestures. Haubenstock-Ramati (who like Ligeti had lost almost all of his family in the Nazi concentration camps) had previously established a reputation with short, exactly notated orchestral pieces in the 'post-Webern' tradition such as *Les Symphonies de timbre* and *Séquences* for violin and orchestra; he then made a gradual transition to graphics via 'mobile forms' – pieces in which relatively conventionally notated music can be realized in many different ways. Logothetis, on the other hand, had written one ultra-complex orchestral score, obviously in imitation of Stockhausen's *Gruppen*, which had remained without prospect of performance (one wonders how many other composers of this era have similar skeletons in their cupboards). Seeing himself caught in a musical cul-de-sac, he had leaped almost directly from precision to its very opposite, writing 'graphic' orchestral pieces like *Labyrinthos* and *Mäandros* on a single sheet of paper.

However, Ligeti was not tied to this environment, musically or socially. Whereas Cologne had been a provisional substitute home, Vienna was to prove a launching pad. Ligeti soon found himself being invited to lecture in many parts of Europe, from Spain to Scandinavia. The most significant and lasting of these contacts came from Stockholm. It had a long upbeat: back in 1956, just before the Hungarian uprising, the composer Mátyás Seiber, Hungarian by birth but living in England, had paid a visit to Budapest, and had met the young Ligeti. Seiber, who had studied with Kodály in the 1920s, was a highly regarded composition teacher in London, where his students had included one of the most notable Swedish composers, Ingvar Lidholm. When a position teaching solfège became available at the Stockholm Conservatorium in 1959, Seiber recommended Ligeti, who was invited for interview. He did not get the job, but his presentations on Bartók and Kodály made a strong impression. A few months later, some young Swedish composers at the Darmstadt Summer Courses were even more impressed by his Webern lectures, so early in 1960 a private invitation came to lecture on Webern and related topics. In addition, Karl-Birger Blomdahl, Sweden's leading senior composer with modernist sympathies, was keen to attract Ligeti to the Swedish Royal Academy of Music, especially in the wake of the *Apparitions* première, where a Swedish contingent had once again been present.

By the time Ligeti returned to Stockholm he was no longer regarded as just a theorist, but as a significant new actor on the avant-garde stage. This reputation was enhanced when Sixten Ehrling conducted a performance of *Apparitions* in April 1961, and followed it up a year later with *Atmosphères*. Sadly, Seiber had been killed in a car crash during a lecture tour in South Africa in September 1960; the dedication of *Atmosphères* – 'in memoriam Mátyás Seiber' – was presumably a retrospective token of gratitude, just as that of *Apparitions* had been a way of thanking Eimert. In Stockholm Ligeti was now asked to work with young composers. This was a very different situation to his lecturing activities back in the Budapest days – clearly there was no question of giving lessons in traditional harmony and counterpoint. But what, in the era of Cage and Stockhausen, was one to teach? There was real doubt about the validity of conventional craft. Or rather, there were sharply diverging views. Stockhausen, in his Darmstadt courses, completely disregarded the past, and set tasks and objectives couched entirely in terms of current developments; Berio, on the other hand, sometimes asked prospective students to write a fugal exposition in late Baroque style. In Stockholm, Ligeti opted for the 'radical' solution, encouraging students to work immediately with the most contemporary means available, including unconventional notations (later on, he was to change his mind, and encourage a more traditional grounding).

While in Stockholm, he worked on a composition for solo organ, *Volumina*, which transferred the cluster style of the orchestral works to a single instrument. He was not working in isolation, for though Sweden may have been something of a musical backwater in the mid 1950s, compared to France or Germany, by the start of the 1960s it was enjoying a renaissance, and alongside progressively inclined 'middle-of-the-road' figures like Karl-Birger Blomdahl and Ingvar Lidholm there was a flourishing avant garde: its two main figures were Bo Nilsson and Bengt Hambraeus. Nilsson, still in his early twenties, was prodigiously talented and had been promoted since his late teens by Stockhausen and Tudor (his name features prominently in Cage's *Lecture on Something*); he was, however, about to self-destruct artistically, just after completing a spectacular, flamboyant cycle of works on poems by Gösta Oswald (who had committed suicide at a similar age). More relevant from Ligeti's point of view was Bengt Hambraeus, who had been at the electronic studios in Cologne a couple of years before Ligeti (Nilsson came a little later), and being an organist, had realized a piece (*Doppelrohr II*) inspired by the innovative organ stops designed by Rössler. Then, at the very end of the 1950s, he had written a series of pieces called *Konstellationer* ('Constellations') for organ and organ sounds transformed on tape. These were the first pieces to move on from the fragmentary, serialized textures of Messiaen's *Livre d'orgue* – which had seemed enormously radical back in 1952 – and establish the organ as a potentially up-to-date avant-garde instrument.

This, then, was the environment surrounding the composition of *Volumina*. Furthermore, in Stockholm Ligeti was able to collaborate with the young organist and composer Karl-Erik Welin, who shares the work's dedication with Hans Otte, the composer and head of the music department at Radio Bremen, who had commissioned the piece (this was Ligeti's first 'real' commission). Welin had a congenially irreverent view of the 'king of instruments', and a limitless interest in its more unorthodox possibilities.

In *Volumina*, Ligeti indulged his own slightly sceptical fascination with the Cage-inspired graphic notation that Haubenstock-Ramati and Logothetis had been exploring in Vienna, and the piece contains virtually no trace of conventional notation. The rationale for this is firstly that – in contrast to *Atmosphères* – there is only one player making all the major creative decisions; moreover, when an instrument like the organ plays clusters in a reverberant acoustic, the exact pitches are largely inaudible anyway – one just has an impression of the average range and kind of activity. So there would be something rather perverse about writing a terribly complex, exact score if the same results could be achieved just as satisfactorily through carefully guided and circumscribed improvisation. But here too, there is a paradox at work: the actual graphic layout of the score may suggest a high level of freedom, but it is accompanied by a deluge of verbal instructions that makes it clear that the players are by no means free to do what they like. Players in the plural? Yes indeed: apart from the organist proper, there are two registration assistants whose role is scarcely less vital, since the organist's hands are so constantly occupied in realizing a musical continuum that other hands are needed to effect all the changes of timbre (registration) that are at least as essential to the piece as the actual notes. Neither the performer nor the listener reads the score of *Volumina* in a conventional way. For the performer, it presents a series of objectives to be realized; for the listener, it gives a guide to these objectives, but the comparison of the score to what one hears can rarely be a direct one – the point at issue is fidelity to

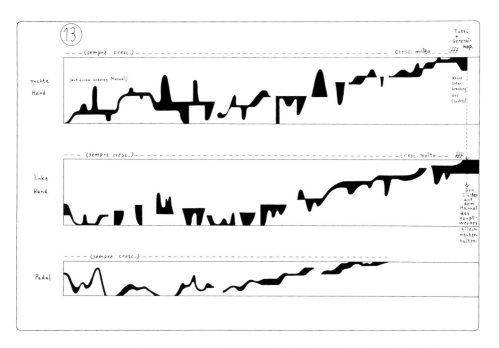

New paths in music notation: part of the 'graphic' score of *Volumina*. The three levels of the score (top to bottom) are for right hand, left hand and pedals.

the composer's idea, not to the literal reproduction of every dot and squiggle on the page.

In many respects, *Volumina* is like a photographic negative of *Atmosphères*. Though both are continuous cluster pieces, one is for large orchestra, the other for a soloist (albeit a soloist dependent on two assistants). Both start with broad clusters, but the piece for many players does so softly, while the one for a single player begins thunderously. One piece is meticulously notated, the other only very loosely, but they both pursue many of the same strategies, such as the extrapolation of pentatonic and diatonic (black- and white-note) clusters from a chromatic cluster at the beginning of both pieces.

There is another provocative aspect. The organ is, after all, not only the 'king of instruments', but is also associated primarily with churches and cathedrals, with sacred sites. Though the organ repertoire is not uniformly dignified, the conduct of organists is. From a listener's point of view, the organist is a remote figure, often placed out of sight in an organ loft. Even when visible, the organist is likely to move in a restrained, ritual manner, not least because the lack of the piano's sustaining pedal rules out the extravagant gestures of the virtuoso pianist – the hands must remain glued to the keyboard. In *Volumina*, however, the organist must often sway to and fro in a most 'unseemly' manner to execute the prescribed clusters and glissandos. Certainly, the treatment of the organ is utterly unconventional. And yet, Ligeti insists, somewhere in the background of the piece, there is a sort of latent passacaglia (a 'monumental' Baroque form, based on a constantly repeated bass line) and he says that it feels as though the ghosts of Bach and Reger are lurking there too.

As with *Artikulation*, there was an association with painting. Ligeti describes *Volumina* as 'an empty form where, as in de Chirico's pictures, there are faceless forms, overwhelming spans and distances, an architecture consisting only of framework, without a tangible building actually being there'. One could also regard the work as a first venture into the part-terrifying, part-burlesque world of Bosch and Breughel that is further explored in the Requiem and his opera *Le Grand Macabre*.

Though it may be the least overtly 'scandalous' component of Ligeti's output in the wake of *Atmosphères*, *Volumina* too casts doubt on his later denial of shock tactics. After all, extremes tend to shock, and in terms of the early 1960s, there could be nothing more extreme than the opening of *Volumina*, where the organist plays a massive, extremely loud cluster, involving every note on the instrument. This had some unforeseen consequences that were to make the work notorious before it had even been played.

Ligeti had tried out *Volumina* on a mechanical-action chamber organ in the Vienna Conservatory, and all seemed to be well. But when Welin tried out the opening in a rehearsal on the Göteberg Cathedral organ, the electrical circuits were immediately overloaded, smoke poured out of the pipes, and there was a stench of burning rubber; in addition, it turned out that various lead and tin components had melted. When the insurers were brought in, they discovered a bizarre cause of the melt-down: on some previous occasion, someone had made a running repair to one of the fuses, using a sewing needle instead of fuse wire! Needless to say, the insurance company declined to pay up. News of this got back to the church council in Bremen, and they promptly withdrew permission for the concert – they were already concerned enough that another scheduled première, Hans Otte's *Alpha Omega*, involved dancers. So the scheduled 'broadcast première' had to consist of a tape which Welin had already made at the Johanniskyrkan in Stockholm (the organ had been carefully checked first). But there were still problems; a few minutes before the broadcast, Ligeti realized that the tape used to record Welin was too short to accommodate the whole piece, and that the last few minutes must be missing, as indeed they were. The first 'real' performance took place a few days later in Amsterdam.

It was not just composers and performers who formed Ligeti's circle of friends in Sweden. Perhaps the closest relationship of all was with the musicologist Ove Nordwall, with whom Ligeti maintained a constant correspondence throughout the 1960s. Composers tend to be suspicious of musicologists: they are not sure whether they have come to praise them, or to bury them. Yet musical scholars seem to have been prominent among Ligeti's friends, more than is the case with any other major composer. He probably did not even see them as potential chroniclers (though almost inevitably, they became that too), but as intellectuals with knowledge and ideas that fascinated him. Apart from Ove Nordwall, they have included Harald

Ligeti with his friend and first biographer, the Swedish musicologist Ove Nordwall

Kaufmann, Erkki Salmenhaara, Ulrich Dibelius, Josef Häusler and many others. Yet Nordwall's position was a special one; apart from writing the first Ligeti monograph, he became a virtual 'confidant', and one cannot imagine a full account of Ligeti's earlier years which did not draw on his inside knowledge.

But though Sweden was to be a regular port of call for Ligeti for many years to come (before long, he was speaking Swedish fluently), his home base was not Stockholm but Vienna. One can imagine various reasons for this. It had been his immediate refuge after fleeing from Budapest, and of all the major Western European cities, it was the one with the closest links to Hungary, both geographically and historically. It became his family base, and his son Lukas was born there in 1965. It was also a city imbued with musical tradition – something that was more important to Ligeti than to his iconoclastic Darmstadt and Cologne colleagues. And the new-music ensemble Die Reihe that Cerha and Kurt Schwertsik had founded in 1958 offered him the highest performance standards, virtually on his doorstep.

However, Darmstadt too became an important forum for Ligeti. In 1962, he was invited to give ten seminars on 'timbre composition'; in other words, he was now welcome as a composer talking about his own work. Thereafter, he would be invited in that capacity almost every year, and though the Darmstadt courses never played a major role in commissioning his works, they were the source of some notable performances.

A case in point was Ligeti's next work, *Aventures*, for three voices (soprano, contralto and baritone) and seven instrumentalists, and its sequel *Nouvelles Aventures*. The premières were both given in Hamburg, in performances conducted by Cerha and Andrzej Markowski. But the performances which really established the works' reputations, and led to the first gramophone recordings, were given in Darmstadt, with Bruno Maderna as conductor.

As it turned out, *Volumina* was to be Ligeti's first and last flirtation with indeterminate notation. In *Aventures* and *Nouvelles Aventures*, the vocal parts are sometimes fairly loosely notated, and in terms of the early 1960s, they look pretty provocative, but they are still a great deal more specific than the score of the organ piece. As with *Volumina*, however, the most loosely notated passages are supplemented by a deluge of verbal annotations, so much so that the publishers had to issue translations in a separate booklet. As noted earlier, the basic ideas for *Aventures* date back to the period of *Artikulation*, and involve the creation of an imaginary language (shades of Kylwiria), according to what Ligeti now calls 'a secret recipe' (one aspect of which involved associating particular vowel sounds with each note of the chromatic scale). Here the Cologne group's 'Joyce evenings' had proved useful; even though Ligeti did not care much for the general ambience of Joyce's work, he found the writer's way of 'treating language as raw material' instructive. Another contributing factor was a post-Cageian 'emancipation of the voice', in which grunts, whispers and groans were just as welcome as conventionally sung notes. Once again, such ideas were in the air. In addition to Kagel's *Anagrama* (1955–8), Cage's *Aria* (1958) had made a big impact in Europe, especially when interpreted by Berio's wife Cathy Berberian. Berio himself had been

Preparing a performance of *Aventures*: Ligeti with one of his greatest advocates, the composer and conductor Bruno Maderna (plus obligatory cigarette)

inspired to write *Visage* (1961), a spectacular twenty-minute showpiece for female voice and tape in which the only 'real' word used is 'parole' (Italian for 'word').

In picking up from *Artikulation*, Ligeti was once again addressing the issue of humour in music, but from a different perspective. Whereas *Artikulation* was an essentially lively, cheerful work with some dark shadows, here the approach is more complex and ambivalent – however much laughter certain passages (intentionally) cause, the *Aventures* pieces are anything but jokes. There is a parallel here to Kagel's *Match* for two cellos and percussion, written at much the same time. In the concert hall, one sees that piece as a wonderfully bizarre contest between two cellists, with the percussionist acting as an increasingly perplexed referee; on a recording, on the other hand, the piece comes across as (for the most part) intensely serious. The same ambivalence is present in *Aventures* and its sequel, even when they are only heard, not seen. Partly, this is because the musical invention is too striking for the piece not to be taken seriously; but it is also because the two works constantly tread the tightrope between the sublime and the ridiculous.

As a starting point, Ligeti put together 'a kind of "scenario" by joining five areas of emotions; humorous, ghostly-horrific, sentimental, mystical-funereal and erotic. All five areas or processes are present all through the music, and they switch from one to the other so abruptly and quickly that there is a virtual simultaneity. Each of the three singers plays five roles at the same time' (*Ligeti in Conversation*). So in addition to there being no actual words – to this extent, *Aventures* makes the experience of the opera-goer who does not understand the words universal – there are also no fixed characters; even though one assumes a classic sexual triangle as the basis for the various solos, duos and trios, at another level each character is all of the characters. This inevitably leads away from the continuous style of the preceding orchestral works and *Volumina*; here, on the contrary, one finds a kaleidoscopic form, with quick successions and superimpositions of different moods.

It is in *Aventures* that one first encounters some of the principal hallmarks of Ligeti's work in the 1960s (other than the stationary and non-stationary clusters of *Atmosphères*), the foundations of what the composer half-ironically came to refer to as the 'Ligeti Style'. Perhaps the most striking of these is what he calls 'super-cooled expressionism'. For many listeners, one of the most 'difficult' aspects of the Second Viennese School is the tendency (more pronounced in Schoenberg and Webern than in Berg) to write vocal lines which constantly leap across the entire range of the voice. There are antecedents enough for this in Wagner – especially in *Tristan* and *Parsifal* – but they are reserved for 'extreme' moments. In Webern, Wagner's exception becomes the norm, and perhaps it is only because of the brevity of Webern's songs and the solo movements in the cantatas that this hyper-expressive lyricism still 'works' – and even here, one tends to regard the extravagant leaps with a certain detachment, rather than 'living' them as one might in Wagner and Strauss. In Ligeti, this goes one step further: in the Allegro appassionato of *Aventures*, for example, the leaps are so extreme as to confront the listener with a fairly polarized choice: either to be involved and shocked, or else withdraw to a safe, Brechtian distance, where the extravagance of the gestures may even be a source of amusement. Hence the balancing act between the sublime and the ridiculous that often gives his music of the mid 1960s an unsettling edge.

Originally, Ligeti intended to write just one work – *Aventures* (yet another French title beginning with 'A'), in a single movement. This reflected the prevailing avant-garde ideology, particularly espoused by Stockhausen, that one should not write works in 'movements' but be able to integrate the most diverse ideas within a single, unique formal process. Yet precisely because of the intensity of the music he was writing, Ligeti came to the conclusion that twelve minutes was about the longest time that an audience could sustain the necessary concentration, and so cut the piece off, more or less arbitrarily, after a contralto solo. A few years later he 'completed' the original concept with a second piece entitled *Nouvelles Aventures* – an ironic reference to the eighteenth-century French penchant for 'sequels' (the most notorious being Sade's *La Nouvelle Justine*).

Another Ligeti 'hallmark', hinted at near the beginning of *Nouvelles Aventures* and expounded at slightly greater length in a section called 'Les Horloges démoniaques' ('The Demonic Clocks'), is what the composer calls his 'meccanico' style: a web of overlapping, regular pulsations, each at different speeds. The obvious source for this is the *Poème symphonique* for 100 metronomes. But there the relationship

between individual layers was arbitrary; in the 'meccanico' style it is planned with meticulous care.

Compared to its predecessor, the form of *Nouvelles Aventures* is relatively stylized (as witness its division into two main sections): there are far more set pieces, suggesting the self-contained arias and other forms of Baroque and Classical 'number opera' rather than the more continuous 'music drama' of *Aventures*, and the listener has much less incentive to construct an imaginary plot. More significantly, though the new work is by no means short of provocations, many of them seem directed against the Darmstadt avant garde as much as against a general public: this is the first piece in which Ligeti makes unmistakable and unashamed reference to the musical past. So alongside sections with picturesque neo-Baroque titles such as 'Commérages' ('Gossips') and indeed 'Les Horloges démoniaques', there is a hocket – a medieval technique of overlapping two or more parts so that sound in one coincides with silence in the other – and a chorale. With the possible exception of the hocket (medieval and Renaissance polyphony did enjoy a certain cult status among the avant garde), these features must have seemed deplorably regressive in tone. Apart from the blatant historical references, the most striking single aspect of the second section is a Grosse Hysterische Szene ('Grand Hysterical Scene') for the soprano. On the one hand, this formally complements the baritone and contralto solos of *Aventures*. But at another level, it conjures up the classic *bel canto* mad scenes of Donizetti, among others, with the striking difference that in this case no exact notes are prescribed.

As for instrumental innovations, the sack of bottles which provocatively augmented the percussion section in *Apparitions* has many successors in the *Aventures* pieces. In *Aventures* these include twanging elastic bands, a large book, wooden furniture (attacked with a cudgel), a paper bag (inflated and popped) and a suitcase. But these sites of domestic devastation are mild in comparison with the arsenal called for in *Nouvelles Aventures*, which also demands the ripping of a silk cloth and all kinds of paper, and the destruction of a tin can, a large bottle, a wooden lath and a pile of dishes on a metal plate, as well as featuring a beaten carpet and – *pièce de résistance*! – a large tin toy frog.

Finally, the *Aventures* pieces mark Ligeti's first real engagement with the idea of virtuosity. Not that he had been writing 'easy' music up to this point; the orchestral scores, especially *Atmosphères*, push many instruments up into extremely high registers, and *Volumina* has a virtuoso manner, even if none of the notes are exactly prescribed. But in *Aventures* and its sequel, the idea of pushing voices and instruments to extremes – of testing the limits of possibility – comes to the fore.

In parallel with *Aventures*, Ligeti began work on a Requiem. The stimulus for this had come two years earlier, while he was in Stockholm: he had been approached to write a work to celebrate the tenth anniversary of the Nutida Musik ('New Music') concert series, and proposed a requiem. This may have seemed somewhat incongruous, given the circumstances of the commission, but his proposal was accepted anyway.

The Requiem is a key work in Ligeti's output. At first sight, it seems to be part of a wave of Eastern-European religious works, such as Penderecki's *St Luke Passion*, that emerged in the mid 1960s as the communist grip on artistic expression started to wane. But that is really not the case. The Requiem has many motivations, but none of them are religious or theological. It focuses on the obsession with the terror and magic of 'last things' in much the same way as Ingmar Bergman's film *The Seventh Seal*, but also, at times, explores the same intersection of fear and farce as the *Aventures* pieces (and later, the opera *Le Grand Macabre*). Back in his student days, Ligeti had already twice projected a requiem setting, partly as a clandestine act of solidarity with Catholic friends, but primarily, one imagines, in an attempt to exorcise personal fears. One of these settings, for chorus and small ensemble, was going to feature a cuckoo call – not as a joke, but rather as a symbol of futility.

Whereas *Nouvelles Aventures*, with its 'hoquetus' and 'chorale', makes amused and fleeting reference to models from various eras of early music, the Requiem's engagement with Renaissance music in particular is deadly earnest. The principal model is not the transparent imitative counterpoint of Palestrina which Ligeti had been required to master as a student, but the dense, often non-thematic polyphony of Ockeghem, composed almost a century earlier (towards the end of the fifteenth century). Whereas Palestrina's music tends to be clearly and elegantly articulated by cadence points, in a piece like Ockeghem's Marian motet *Intemerata Dei mater*, one can go for as long as two minutes without finding any obvious resting-point. Just as one pair of voices seem ready to call a temporary halt, another pair has slid into

Giovanni Pierluigi da Palestrina, the Renaissance master who was a focus of Ligeti's early counterpoint teaching in Budapest, later providing models for the composition of his Requiem

action, resulting in what is often called a 'seamless' texture. One can see the appeal of such music to a composer fascinated by continuity, whose preferred method of ending is not the carefully prepared close, but an abrupt and unexpected halt, 'as though torn off'.

However, there is one way in which Palestrina does have a significant impact. In *Palestrina and the Treatment of the Dissonance*, the text Ligeti had studied back in the Budapest years, Knud Jeppesen had used his careful analysis of the Renaissance composer's works to extrapolate a whole series of rules for composing in 'Palestrina style'. It is precisely this aspect that Ligeti latches onto in composing his Requiem, and retains in later works. But whereas Jeppesen's rules have universal application to all Palestrina's works, and any attempt to emulate them, Ligeti is free to modify or reinvent the rules from one work to the next, always building on the experience gained so far. So such things as the maximum number of consecutive notes that can ascend or descend, and the chains of intervals that are permissible, are not so much laws as algorithms: even more than in serialism, it is the composer who makes the rules.

Technically, the Requiem drives the idea of micropolyphony to an extreme. Writing the enormously complex Kyrie took up six months

well. As if to say, we do not have to live in fear; or you could put it like this, we are certainly going to die but so long as we are alive we believe that we shall live for ever ... one dimension of my music bears the imprint of a long time spent in the shadow of death both as an individual and as a member of a group.' He goes on to say that someone who has genuinely lived in fear does not set out to write 'terrifying' pieces, but to present that fear in alienated form. The actual text of the Dies Irae sequence has long fascinated precisely because it seems to have the same aim – Ligeti views it as 'an extraordinarily colourful, almost comic-strip, representation of the Last Judgement' in which the colourful, lurid imagery is, precisely, designed to overcome fear.

A significant feature of this 'comic-strip' aspect is that the imagery changes every few lines, and since Ligeti had decided to set the text almost pictorially, this involves many changes of mood and texture, in complete contrast to the monolithic character of the Kyrie. The music swings between opposites: from frantic, near-chaotic moments (slightly reminiscent of certain passages in Stockhausen's *Carré*) to others of almost complete stasis. In part, the Dies Irae is also Ligeti's homage and farewell to Webern. The leaping lines typical of Webern's vocal writing are pushed here to an extreme – even more in the solo mezzo-soprano's part than in the chorus – and deliberately taken (almost) to the point of absurdity.

Earlier, in composing *Atmosphères*, Ligeti had faced a decision between redefining harmony or obliterating it, and had chosen the latter course. In the Lacrimosa that ends his Requiem (no place here for the affirmations of a Sanctus!) he returned to the same question, and chose the other option. As he puts it: 'I asked myself: how can I work with intervals or with particular fixed pitches, without going back to tonal music? That means: no chord progressions, in either a tonal or atonal sense. Can one find a way of working with intervals and even harmonies, which are innately obsolete materials, in a way different from before?' Though the harmony of the Lacrimosa still inhabits the world of chromatic clusters, there are many points where the two solo voices, and indeed the orchestra too, converge onto a clearly focused interval – a tritone, perhaps, or a major second – in a way that creates a point of rest, and even suggests a cadence. This was to become a recurrent feature of Ligeti's music over the next few years.

However equivocal the intentions underlying the Requiem, it comes across quite unequivocally as a 'great work', shattering in its impact, and utterly unforgettable. The early 1960s saw a sudden outburst of avant-garde works that made 'big statements': Boulez's *Pli selon pli* and Stockhausen's *Momente* were the most striking examples, with Berio's *Epifanie* and Penderecki's melodramatic *St Luke Passion* not far behind. Yet these grandiose utterances seem quite at odds with Ligeti's more sceptical outlook. So what is one to make of the Requiem? Is it really an intended comic strip that inadvertently turns into a masterpiece? That seems too extreme an interpretation. But at any rate, it was a long time before Ligeti was to make such apocalyptic gestures again.

In any case, by the mid 1960s the outlook of the avant garde was beginning to change. If previously, to some degree, it had been locked up in a heroic, utopian 'ivory tower', it now started to become very aware of the social spirit of the times. The emerging mood of disrespect for authority of any kind would explode a few years later, in the uprisings of 1968. But already, a sense of scepticism, embodied in a 'negative engagement' with tradition, was beginning to emerge.

In this context, Ligeti's next work, the Cello Concerto composed in 1966 to a commission from the radio station Sender Freies Berlin, was almost predestined to be an 'anti-concerto'. During the 1950s, though there was no shortage of virtuoso solo pieces from the avant garde, the very idea of a concerto reeked of the past, and anything suggesting it was scrupulously avoided by the leading figures of the Cologne-Darmstadt group. Only the Italians had broken ranks: Nono had included a piece for concertante flute (*Y su sangre ya viena cantando*) in his early García Lorca triptych, Berio had written a *Serenata*, also with a virtuoso solo flute part, as well as *Tempi concertati*, which has a neo-Baroque 'concertino' of flute, violin and two pianos, while Maderna, impervious to all orthodoxies, had recently written an oboe concerto (and went on to write two more). But Boulez, Stockhausen, Kagel and Ligeti too had given the concerto genre a wide berth.

Now, in the 1960s, there was a shift of ground. What started to work against the former purist renunciations of the concerto was not only a growing 'pluralism' – an acceptance that the 'prohibitionism' of the 1950s was no longer necessary or useful, and that inconsistencies and 'impurities' could also play a valuable role in art – but also the irresistible rise of a new generation of virtuosos committed to new music. In the late 1950s, there had been just two figures: the flautist Severino Gazzelloni (for whom Berio had written his *Serenata*) and the pianist David Tudor. Tudor's performance of Cage's anarchic *Concert*, where there is no score, just individual parts, had already made an enormously influential case for the anti-concerto – for a work which makes enormous demands on a particular player, but overtly deprives him/her of 'star' status. But now there were new figures, especially in Germany, and even more especially in Cologne: the Kontarsky piano duo, the percussionist Christoph Caskel, and above all the cellist Siegfried Palm, to whom Ligeti's concerto is dedicated. Temperamentally, all these virtuosos lay somewhere between the flamboyant Gazzelloni (a sort of avant-garde James Galway) and the brilliant but utterly self-negating Tudor. One could demand the near-impossible of them, without necessarily having to place them in a musical spotlight.

Accordingly, the solo part of Ligeti's Cello Concerto is enormously demanding, but these demands are almost sadistically concealed – for much of the time, the cello hardly emerges from the rest of the ensemble. In the opening minutes, this is partly because the entire ensemble is semi-inaudible. The cellist enters *pppppppp* (!), with the instruction 'Entry inaudible, as if coming from nothing'; only after twenty seconds is the player instructed to 'very gradually become apparent, with a scarcely perceptible crescendo'. When the other strings enter, at a relatively crass *ppppp*, they too are to 'enter imperceptibly'. These days, Ligeti claims that the extraordinarily soft markings at the outset were simply a response to the tendency of most orchestral musicians to play much too loud, and thus do not necessarily have to be taken literally, and that the music should always be clearly audible. But perhaps this statement too should be taken with a pinch of salt: the idea of an ultra-virtuoso performing prodigious feats that cannot quite be heard – they may even be easier to see than to hear – does seem very typical of 1960s dialectics. Kagel's *Sonant* includes a movement in which the players simply mime their very elaborate parts.

Ligeti's concerto is in two movements. As with *Aventures* and *Nouvelles Aventures*, it was originally planned as a single movement, with twenty-seven more or less contrasting sections. But during the process of composition, which lasted barely a month, the first section grew so long that it became a movement in its own right. Once again, this movement is preoccupied with notions of near and far – of creating the impression of huge spaces. Ligeti graphically described the ending as seeking 'to create the impression of a vast soap bubble that may burst at any moment'.

The first movement of the Cello Concerto is probably the first piece of Ligeti's 'Western' period that strikes one as 'beautiful' in terms of conventional aesthetics. Not that Ligeti was concerned with the pursuit of 'beauty' *per se*, then or later (he once said, 'I find it quite easy to make up beautiful tunes and then elaborate on them, but I think that this compositional device is very stale.'). The real quest was for a luminosity of sound, achieved through exquisitely calculated instrumentation, and for illusions of closeness and distance (illusions in the sense that the players always sit in exactly the same place), and it is the successful realization of these musical conceptions that results in beauty. At the same time, what is beautiful for the listener can be quite terrifying for the performer. The obsessive succession of entries 'on the verge of inaudibility', especially those for the wind instruments, seem to court disaster, and the extraordinarily high passage with which the cello ends the movement, six octaves above the double basses, involves notes which barely exist on the instrument: it is a near-silent *salto mortale*.

The second movement comprises the remaining twenty-six sections of the original idea. However, the boundaries between the sections are somewhat blurred, at least at the beginning of the movement, and even the increasingly sharp demarcations towards the end of the second movement do not necessarily make the overall form any easier to grasp. On the contrary, the many contrasting fragments create a sort of anti-form, in which the distinctions between foreground and background, between principal and secondary, are continually being twisted out of shape. As Ligeti puts it: 'one notices a constantly changing motion, as though the same landscape, like in a dream, were to keep turning out differently. Formally that could be regarded as a set of variations, yet they are not variations, but a constant spinning-out (like a big "development"), where one doesn't know which musical ideas are actually being "developed". In this spinning-out, using the "window technique", seemingly foreign inserts are added, but

Ligeti with cellist Siegfried
Palm, one of the great
interpreters of the 1960s
avant garde, at a rehearsal
of his Cello Concerto

subsequently, as the form evolves, the windows turn out not to be
foreign material, but "windows on the same landscape". By the end
one no longer knows what was a window and what wasn't; and
besides, there are windows within the windows.'

This sounds like the description of an engraving by Maurits Escher
(or a painting by the surrealist René Magritte). In fact, Ligeti did not
encounter Escher's work until a little later, but one can readily see why
he was fascinated by it when he did. Whether the resulting form is
successful, however, is another matter. Listened to in retrospect, the
Cello Concerto (and especially the second movement) sounds like
a drawing board for the next five years; an astonishing number of new
factors are introduced, such as the mellifluous circling around three
or four notes at the opening, the wisps of melody, the rapid string
figurations alternating between two or more strings, explosive 'fast
as possible' cadenzas, and cloudy, disembodied textures, as well as
'blow-ups' and extensions of ideas from earlier works, such as the
hectic string declamations from *Apparitions* and the 'meccanico'
tickings and octave doublings (both hocket-like and in slithering
demisemiquavers) from *Nouvelles Aventures*. Nevertheless, many

of these features will be more richly and satisfyingly explored in subsequent works.

The relatively anarchic form of the concerto may partly reflect the influence of the philosopher Theodor Wiesengrund-Adorno, whose relationship with the Darmstadt Summer Courses went back to the immediate post-war years. Adorno, like Nietzsche, was a composer as well as philosopher, and had studied composition with Alban Berg. In the immediate post-war years he had been a key figure in the reconstruction of German musical culture, and when he saw a struggle emerging between the advocates of the Second Viennese School and those of Stravinsky's neo-classicism, he pitched into the debate with a highly influential book, *Philosophie der neuen Musik* ('The Philosophy of New Music'), which came down emphatically on behalf of Schoenberg (Stravinsky, in effect, was dismissed as a highly talented barbarian). Adorno's relationships with the radical composers had not always been smooth. Schoenberg took a substantial dislike to him in later years, especially after Adorno advised Thomas Mann on the novel *Doktor Faustus*, which Schoenberg regarded as an attack on himself, since its central figure is a 'twelve-note' composer (perhaps he also had difficulty understanding Adorno's rather convoluted post-Hegelian writings). When the young Stockhausen first went to Darmstadt in 1951, he too found himself in direct conflict with Adorno, whom he ended up accusing of 'looking for a chicken in an abstract painting'; a few years later, Adorno responded with an essay entitled 'New Music is Growing Old'.

By the early 1960s, however, the differences between Adorno and the Darmstadt avant garde had been largely reconciled; he was an active supporter of Boulez and Stockhausen and, probably as a result of conversations with his former pupil Metzger, was even displaying a cautious interest in John Cage (much to the dismay of former colleagues from the Schoenberg circle, such as the pianist Eduard Steuermann). However, it had often been noted that his actual writings on music still seemed rooted in the 'old days' of the Second Viennese School; his theories did not seem able to embrace the new composers he claimed to endorse. Adorno responded in 1961 with a Darmstadt lecture entitled 'Vers une musique informelle' ('Towards an Informal Music'), which pays due homage to Boulez and

especially Stockhausen, but then goes on to advocate 'a music which has cast off all external, abstract, rigidly demarcated forms, and which, completely free of heteronomous impositions and their extraneous elements, gains its constitution not from external legitimations, but from the objective, compelling force of the phenomenon itself.'

Ligeti had already got to know *The Philosophy of New Music* in Budapest in the early 1950s, and had met Adorno when he first went to Darmstadt in 1957. Like most of the Darmstadt group, he had mixed feelings about Adorno: he admired him and found him a fascinating conversationalist, but also could not help laughing a little at this Ultimate German Professor who seemed to be dancing in attendance around the Young Turks of the avant garde. He also felt that Adorno's 'insights' into new music could be startlingly naïve when compared to what he wrote about older music, and that he often seemed to be out of his depth.

Ligeti had even more mixed feelings about 'Vers une musique informelle'. Not so long after completing *Atmosphères*, he was sitting at table with Boulez and Adorno, and the latter was outlining to Boulez the ideas which would be central to his lecture on 'informal music'. It sounded like a description of *Atmosphères*, and Ligeti was barely able to restrain himself from saying, 'Professor, I've already composed something like that!' But when the lecture was finally presented (and then published in revised form), Ligeti was frankly disappointed: he described it to Ove Nordwall as 'an essay that shouldn't have been written, or if so, not in that form'. When he next met Adorno, he was unsparing in his criticisms, though the discussion ended cordially. However, when it came to formulating his essay for a Darmstadt symposium on musical form, Ligeti found himself making constant reference to Adorno's writings (though not to 'Vers une musique informelle'). Though Adorno too gave a lecture at the symposium, he did not attend Ligeti's; but when he read the essay the next year, he wrote Ligeti a 'terrifically friendly' letter insisting that they had come up with the same ideas independently. And when he finally heard *Atmosphères* (about six years after the original conversation at table), he told Ligeti that this was exactly the kind of 'informal music' that he had imagined!

In his own essay, Ligeti claims that 'there are no established formal schemes any more; every individual work is forced, not least by the historical constellation, to exhibit a unique overall form, appropriate only to itself.' He goes on to say that nowadays (that is, in the 1960s) the idea of formal components signalling that the music will go in a particular direction is out of the question, but this does not mean that formal 'functions' are a thing of the past: 'Various kinds of structures and motion, different possible ways of deploying planes of sound, interweavings, contrasting and merging formations, dislocations and fusions, assemblages and decompositions and so forth all serve as functional elements in the form: it's only the unambiguous marker, pointing in one direction, that is no longer there ... the causal relationship of transformations is reversible, following the chicken-egg principle: every moment of the transformation is both cause and effect within the process being described.' Ligeti uses an architectural analogy to suggest the many different kinds of form that are now available: 'The possibilities range from single-room, enormous, empty buildings to winding subterranean labyrinths, and isolated homes spread over a wide area.'

The metaphor of the labyrinth seems to describe perfectly the second movement of the Cello Concerto, whose form constantly twists and turns, coming back to similar points from different directions; and indeed, it is not hard to think of the concerto's first movement, where an almost motionless continuity is intermittently interrupted by small 'events', as exemplifying the third architectural type. But this flirtation with anarchic dialectics was temporary. It too was about to become ideology, and at that moment Ligeti would flee from it.

5

Among the music he did
in 61 with God Goldman
[left] and Rudolph Staphou
[right], during a celebration
in the Nineteenth Century
Brooklyn Bequested in
1961. A Brooklyn Jazz
fantasia was given its
premiere.

*I always have periods where I turn to to
quite different kinds of music and measure
myself against that.*

Ligeti in conversation with Ulrich Dibelius

Away from the Volcano 1966–70

Perhaps it has always been in Ligeti's nature to swim against the current, without making any great song and dance about doing so. During the early 1960s, while the avant garde was seeking to become an alternative 'establishment', Ligeti's was one of the few sceptical voices. While Boulez and Stockhausen were demanding consistency and stylistic purity, Ligeti took a delight in the bizarre and incongruous.

Yet in the years immediately preceding the civil uprisings of 1968, when the avant garde turned towards pluralism and even anarchy, Ligeti's own work became ever more focused and consistent, homing in on a limited number of 'fingerprints' which were constantly refined. The major trends of the late 1960s, such as the collage movement, in which composers quoted and superimposed everything from Mahler symphonies (Berio's *Sinfonia*) to national anthems (Stockhausen's *Hymnen*), or live electronics, where instrumental sounds were transformed in concert by electronic equipment, or the passion for 'extended techniques' which saw trombones being played with clarinet mouthpieces, and violins bowed against one another (Globokar's *Laboratorium*) – all this passed him by. Only the American minimalist school, in which complex rhythmic patterns emerge beneath a surface of seemingly endless repetitions, seemed to find parallels in his work; and even this, as we shall see, was largely fortuitous.

This does not mean that Ligeti had entered a reclusive phase, and much less that he had lost interest in the world around him. During these years he led much the same nomadic life as before, continuing to teach in Stockholm, Darmstadt and elsewhere, with Vienna as his home base (largely replaced in 1969 by Berlin). These were the years when the first official honours started to come his way: membership of the Swedish Academy of Music in 1964, a Koussevitsky Foundation Prize in 1965, the Beethoven Prize of the City of Bonn in 1967 (for his Requiem), membership of the Berlin Academy of the Arts in 1968, and so forth. But though such recognition is always welcome (and marginally useful), one cannot imagine Ligeti being overwhelmed by it.

What is clear is that Ligeti now resolved to devote as much time as possible to composition. In December 1964 he had written to Nordwall: 'I want to work a lot more, and faster. Hence the necessary conversion of all aspects of daily life to "telegraphic style", so that more time is left for composition.' Accordingly, though one could never describe Ligeti as a prolific composer, his output in the mid and late 1960s rose from about one substantial work a year to two or three.

Parallel to the Cello Concerto, and seemingly as a pendant to the Requiem, Ligeti wrote *Lux aeterna*, a short piece for sixteen-part choir, which is as monistic in style as the concerto is diverse. Like the Introitus and the Lacrimosa of the Requiem, it is a music without figures – or at least, so it seems on the surface. Yet here, picking up from aspects of the Lacrimosa, Ligeti makes his first serious break with the chromatic cluster style of the previous works. The external techniques are much as in preceding works; on paper, the music does not look so different from the Introitus, but it sounds very different – now the materials are virtually diatonic, albeit with no trace of conventional tonal harmony.

Once again, the historical model is Ockeghem; but this time it is not a matter of the 'varietas' approach used in the Introitus, but of the multi-speed unison canons (passages in which the notes sung by the first singer are imitated exactly by the others) that the Flemish composer had deployed in his *Missa prolationum*. Needless to say, there are differences: in Ockeghem the voices enter at the same time, and gradually drift apart in exact arithmetical ratios, whereas Ligeti adopts a freer approach, though still a carefully regulated one. At the opening, for example, the four sopranos and four altos enter one after another, with each new note sending out multiple echoes, but at varying paces: sometimes the new pitch drifts gently through the ensemble, allowing many of the previous notes still to hang in the air; at other times it pans across quickly, like an acoustic eraser. There are no chord progressions in the conventional sense, but constantly changing harmonic fields in which (unlike cluster composition) each individual note is clearly audible.

Though it without doubt belongs to the 'continuous' genre (like *Atmosphères*), *Lux aeterna* audibly falls into three parts; that is, there are three separate canons – the first for the eight female voices, the second for all sixteen voices (though beginning with the eight male voices) and the third for the four altos. The way in which these canons are linked and, to some degree, subdivided internally involves a new feature which assumes prominence in Ligeti's works for the next few years, and which he calls an 'interval signal'. This consists of an interval (such as an octave or a tritone) or a chord (he is particularly fond of the combination of major second and minor third) which appears suddenly, out of the blue, either to mark the end of an evolutionary process, or to punctuate one that is under way. In *Lux aeterna* the 'chords' are used to divide the canons, while the 'intervals' (always octaves) appear once within each canon: as the culmination of the first one, in the middle of the second, at the point where the female voices join in (here, the entry on the syllables 'Re-quiem' recalls the 'Re-spi-ce' chords in Tallis's *Spem in alium*), and again, halfway through the third canon, splitting up into a chordal 'interval signal', and inaugurating a sustained coda.

Lux aeterna is far more than a spin-off from the Requiem: it could stake strong claims to be regarded as the most exquisitely 'perfect' *a cappella* work of the post-war era. Its 'virtuosity' lies not in external display, but in the absolutely perfect intonation – hideously difficult to achieve and maintain – that is required to project its extraordinary harmonic luminosity: in a good performance it reveals the same sort of cold yet burning harmonic radiance as the motets of Victoria. In addition, there are a couple of instances of typical Ligeti-sadism: of extreme demands which the performers must not only meet, but meet in such a way that their 'extremism' is concealed. One is the first 'interval signal', where the basses enter for the first time (i.e. with no chance to warm up) on a high falsetto chord; the other, towards the end of the work, is the entry of three sopranos and all four tenors, as softly as possible, on a high B (Beethoven makes comparably monstrous demands in his *Missa solemnis*).

Ligeti's next work, *Lontano*, marked a return to the orchestra. But although, superficially, it again belongs to the 'continuous' genre, and once again calls for extremely large score paper (albeit with more restraint than its predecessors – here sixty staves suffice), the result is very different, and was perceived by many commentators as showing, for the first time, a deliberate swing away from the avant garde. This impression must have been strengthened by the composer's comment that while composing the work, he constantly had in mind some lines from Keats's 'Ode to a Nightingale' (scarcely a poet one would associate with the Darmstadt avant garde):

The same that oft-times hath
Charm'd magic casements, opening on the foam
Of perilous seas, in faery lands forlorn.

This time the orchestra is a conventional late-Romantic one, with no percussion or keyboards; the only unusual instrument is an (optional) contrabass clarinet. And though the score looks quite unlike anything from the nineteenth century, the orchestration is, deliberately, full of allusions to the Romantic era, and to Bruckner in particular. The large number of staves required for the score has more to do with the multiple divisi found in Debussy and Richard Strauss than with the mass effects of *Atmosphères*. At times the orchestra functions as a massive chamber orchestra, which is one reason why Ligeti dedicated the work to Südwestfunk Symphony Orchestra, as well as to its conductor Ernest Bour. As he puts it: 'the orchestral musicians are truly the soloists in the piece.'

If the first movement of the Cello Concerto marks the beginning of Ligeti's love affair with orchestration, *Lontano* is the first full-blown declaration. The work's distance from the 'abstract' modernist style of the avant garde is spelt out in an instruction on the first page: 'The piece must be played with great expression; apart from the indicated rallentandos and accelerandos other fluctuations in tempo are permissible' – in other words, the give and take of Romantic rubato.

Yet here lies one of the supreme 'Ligeti paradoxes'. *Lontano*, which seems to represent a rejection of the modernist aesthetic of preceding works such as the Cello Concerto and *Lux aeterna*, actually uses exactly the same musical materials as *Lux aeterna*, but here the canons are transposed, the order of the second and third canons is reversed, and the transitions are substantially recomposed. In effect, it is a re-reading of the choral piece (or in Renaissance terms, a 'parody') which aims to draw entirely opposite conclusions (though Ligeti still insists that 'to perform *Lontano* properly, one must be very fond of Ockeghem'). On the one hand, there is the contrast between coldness (*Lux aeterna*) and warmth (*Lontano*); but despite its title, *Lontano* is not consistently 'distant', but seems constantly to draw close and then back away. The sense of 'space' also has a vertical dimension: Ligeti describes how he 'imagined a vast space of sound in gradual transformation, not through dense chromaticism but through a constantly changing pattern of colour like a moiré fabric'.

Lontano is an orchestral *tour de force*, all the more remarkable because it has virtually no recourse to surface virtuosity. But far more than that, it is an astonishing exploration of the emotive power of orchestral sonority, the way in which moods can be inflected and even overturned by the subtlest changes of instrumentation. For Ligeti, these manipulations of the orchestra have not only to do with musical tone colour, and different kinds of historical associations, but with colour and light in a quite literal sense. Ligeti has a vivid synaesthetic sense, that is, he associates sounds with actual colours. In a conversation with Josef Häusler not long after the première of *Lontano*, he emphasized just how strong these associations were while composing the piece. Taking the third and final section as an example, he describes the start of the canon as 'a gradual passing into dim, deep regions' which is suddenly lit up as if from behind, whereupon a new element enters which is somehow diffuse, but gets brighter and brighter until 'the music seems to shine, to be radiant'. The diffuse light narrows to a single note, a high D sharp, after which 'suddenly there yawns an abyss, a huge distancing, a hole piercing through the music. It is a moment that has an irresistible association for me with the wonderful painting by Altdorfer, *Alexanderschlacht* in the Alte Pinakothek in Munich, in which the clouds – these blue clouds – part, and behind them there is a beam of sunlight shining through.' Presumably, few if any of these associations attach to the parallel passage in *Lux aeterna*; this is a particularly striking example of the way the composer has completely reconceived existing material.

Though Ligeti's reference to Altdorfer might easily suggest a Romantic composer at work, *Lontano* does not inaugurate a Romantic phase in Ligeti's work, though it undoubtedly served as an inspiration for the neo-Romantic movement that surfaced in Germany in the 1970s. It also gained him a new publisher. Ligeti had already left Universal Edition in favour of Peters Edition, which had published all the works from *Volumina* to *Lux aeterna*; he now moved to Schott in Mainz, probably the most powerful and influential of the German publishers. No great dramas attached to these moves (unlike those made

Opposite, 'A sudden eruption of light': the luminous sky of Altdorfer's *Alexanderschlacht* profoundly influenced a moment in Ligeti's *Lontano*.

by some of his contemporaries), and good relations with the former publishers remained; it was just a matter of getting a better offer.

If Schott were anticipating a whole succession of pieces like *Lontano*, they would have been disappointed. What they did get was a sequence of increasingly exquisitely crafted works which may have been at odds with the generally disruptive trends of the late 1960s, but are now ranked, in many cases, among the period's 'classics'. However, one wonders what they made of Ligeti's next work, *Harmonies*. This piece, a curious by-product of the composer's desire to change his harmonic focus, is the first of two studies for organ. If one compares the score of this piece with that of *Lontano*, it is hard at first to believe that they come from the same composer. Every moment in *Lontano* shows enormous sophistication; *Harmonies*, on the other hand, consists of a seemingly bland succession of 231 chords, with no clear indication of rhythm. There is no evidence of need for a virtuoso technique, so what makes this an 'étude'? Well, it is a 'composer's study': a study in composing with deliberately restricted means. In writing the enormously complex micropolyphony of the Requiem, Ligeti had been very conscious of the need to set himself rules and limitations, so as to give some focus and not to let the music run out of control. Here, the intention is absolutely the reverse: to see how meaningful musical processes can be extracted from almost absurd constraints.

Except at the very end, the piece uses only the manuals of the organ (i.e. no pedals). Each chord consists of ten notes – that is, all ten fingers are constantly in use – and each chord differs from the previous one only in that one finger has been moved up or down a semitone (usually but not always alternating between hands). Like *Volumina*, the piece needs registration assistants; since the organist's hands are constantly on the manuals, the alternative would be to have no changes of tone-colour at all! But in *Harmonies*, it is not just a matter of stop-changes. Ligeti asks for 'pallid, very alien, "decaying" colours ("artificial consumptiveness")', achieved through reduced wind pressure, and recommends various strategies, such as substitution of a vacuum cleaner (!) for the normal bellows, slowing the electric fan down, and taking out low pipes so that some air escapes (in a recent recording, Ligeti removed the high-precision Swiss weights from the wind reservoir, and substituted his own body). The result of this is that the pitches constantly waver up and down, and the harmonic structure is largely obliterated! So what looks on paper like a harmony exercise turns out to be an exercise in subverting harmony.

The incentive to write *Harmonies* came from Ligeti's long collaboration with the Hamburg organist Gerd Zacher; alongside Welin, Zacher had been the principal exponent of *Volumina*, as well as many other avant-garde works. Ligeti's motivation to write his next work for solo keyboard, *Continuum*, was more arbitrary, even though it resulted in one of his best-known works. The Swiss harpsichordist Antoinette Vischer, who had already commissioned works from composers such as Berio, Earle Brown and Isang Yun, approached Ligeti for a piece, with the offer of a generous commission fee. The very idea of writing 'new music' for a historical instrument may seem curious enough (though Kagel had recently written a wonderfully 'dialectical' *Musik für Renaissanceinstrumente* in which the instruments of Praetorius's *Syntagmum musicum* seem to arise, spluttering and furious, from a 300-year burial), but by this stage the harpsichord had already made many appearances in Ligeti's work: in the orchestra of *Apparitions* (as well as the related *Fragment*) and the Requiem, and also in the ensembles of *Aventures* and *Nouvelles Aventures*. However, the title is, as Ligeti says, deliberately 'an anti-harpsichord title, because the harpsichord is the discontinuous instrument par excellence. And I was attracted by writing a continuous kind of music for such an instrument.' That does not mean that he was aiming to write 'against' the instrument; on the contrary, he insists, it is only by writing entirely 'in the spirit of the instrument' that one can push it to extremes – in this case, speeds so extreme that separated repeated notes seem to fuse into a single line: 'a continuous sound ... that would have to consist of innumerable thin slices of salami'. (Elsewhere he compares the effect to the wheels of a railway engine, which seem to stand still once a certain speed has been reached, or even, viewed through another train window, to turn backwards.)

To produce this continuous sound, two things are required: the first is an extremely fast speed (the marking is *prestissimo*), so fast that the ear can barely distinguish individual notes. The other requirement is that the hands remain almost glued to the keyboard throughout – there is no scope for broad leaps, or any kind of figure that would necessarily slow things down (the only momentary respites for one hand come when the page has to be turned). This immediately raises questions as to how the form of the piece is to be shaped: with Bach, in addition to tonality, there would be some consistent motive or figuration, but here? As it happens, Ligeti's solutions are not so different from Bach's, however dissimilar the effect. In *Continuum*, as in many Bach preludes, the primary factors are changing registers, and the repetition and constant modification of patterns. In the first part of the piece, the hands remain in overlapping registers; in the second they gradually drift apart. The same kind of 'soap bubble' imagery that Ligeti evoked in relation to the Cello Concerto recurs here – he makes the comparison with having to blow up a balloon: 'That would be a model for the piece: always stretching, further and further, and at some point the maximum tension is achieved, and then suddenly there is a qualitative alteration.' The two hands drift apart, each one in 'close position' (like two desynchronized five-finger exercises), until suddenly there is a change of registration and both hands, snapping back into synchronization, spread out to a tritone-plus-octave 'interval signal'. But the hands go on drifting apart until the bottom one seemingly runs out of notes and comes to a halt, before joining the right hand up in the stratosphere for the conclusion of the piece.

As for patterns, when describing *Lontano* Ligeti had already made a comparison with moiré effects, where the superimposition of two innately regular patterns seems to create a third, much more complex entity. It was around this time that Ligeti first encountered the engravings of Maurits Escher, which have continued to fascinate him ever since. In a typical picture such as *Concave and Convex*, everything seems entirely logically constructed; every detail is meticulously put in place. Yet in terms of the real world, it is all wrong: you cannot tell what is up or down, what is in front and what is behind. The flat surface of the picture bristles with three-dimensional effects, but they are all ambiguous, and while every detail makes sense in itself (or several different senses), there is no way of looking at the picture that makes all the details fit together, except in a purely abstract, non-realistic way. In short, Escher's pictorial world rests on paradox, just as Ligeti's musical one does. We have already seen evidence of the role that paradox plays in the conception of *Continuum*, but nowhere is this conscious homage to Escher's play with illusion more apparent than in its handling of musical patterns.

Concave and Convex by Maurits Escher; visual and aural illusions fascinate Ligeti, and he finds many parallels between Escher's art and his own.

The problem is this: how, given absolutely continuous, ultra-rapid regular motion in both hands, can one make individual notes 'stand out' on the harpsichord, an instrument that does not accept the notion of loud and soft (except in terms of a chord being louder than a single note, and some registrations being louder than others)? Two basic 'tricks' are involved. Firstly, whatever note is highest or lowest will tend to stand out, especially if there is more than the minimum (semitone) distance between it and the next note, and if it has been newly introduced into the texture.

However, what makes these notes emerge from the texture is not just a matter of hand positions, but of regular rhythms. Even though, in his 1965 lecture on musical form, Ligeti had emphasized and endorsed new music's rejection of clear metres and regular pulsations (except in the quasi-satirical case of his 'meccanico' passages), he was about to move away from this doctrinaire position, as indeed were many other composers, including Stockhausen. *Continuum* marks a first step in this direction. The very rapid pulsation can create an impression of shimmering stasis; but if, for example, the right hand brings in a high C sharp every third note, one hears this as a regular pattern sticking out from the 'continuum', and if one then introduces, say, a low note every fourth note, then another regular pattern is created, in a 3:4 ratio to the first one. And if the hands play notes in the same register (or overlapping registers) on the two manuals, then all kinds of 'interferences' can be created between the two layers.

Using the harpsichord forced another issue into the foreground. It was already evident from the preceding works that Ligeti was getting tired of clusters, and looking for a more differentiated harmony. But on the harpsichord, virtually any dissonant chord with four notes or more tends to sound like a cluster, especially if it is within a narrow register (e.g. less than an octave). So whereas earlier pieces investigated the possibility of diatonic harmonies, in *Continuum* they become the norm.

This combination of diatonic figures with multiple repetitions naturally suggests the work of the American minimalist composers who had emerged in the USA in the mid 1960s: Terry Riley, Steve Reich and, a little later, Philip Glass. Whereas the group of New York composers around John Cage had aroused a certain reluctant fascination in Europe, this new movement was widely considered beyond the pale. There were many reasons for this. For a start, its insistent patterns were completely at odds with the European avant garde's passion for non-repetition, just as its blatantly diatonic motives were the antithesis of post-serial abstraction. Its affiliations with West Coast psychedelia and rock music were regarded as highly suspect (the highly successful LP of Terry Riley's *In C* had a euphoric 'rave review' by the editor of *Crawdaddy* magazine on the back cover, and its successor, *A Rainbow in Curved Air*, was packaged just like a psychedelic rock LP). In any case, the meditative ambience promoted by Riley was a red rag to the European left: clearly, this was yet another American 'opiate for the masses'. Above all, though, minimalism had the temerity to be boisterously cheerful, something which the European avant garde could only regard as sheer irresponsibility.

Not unnaturally, the dislike was largely mutual. Riley's enthusiasm for Stockhausen did not last much beyond his teens, Reich had been unconvinced by European serialism while studying composition with Berio at Mills College, Oakland, and when Philip Glass went to study with Nadia Boulanger in Paris (Boulanger had provided the Continental 'finishing school' for many American composers of the preceding generation), he rapidly acquired an aversion to the Boulez camp: 'these maniacs, these creeps, who were trying to make everyone write this crazy creepy music.' Conversely, Heinz-Klaus Metzger is supposed to have made a habit of going up to the desk in hotel lobbies where muzak was playing, and asking the receptionist to 'please turn off the Phil Glass'.

Looking at *Continuum* in retrospect, Ligeti too is struck by its similarities to minimalism, but at that time (perhaps surprisingly) he did not know the minimalists' work. Later, when he did hear it, it made a great impression on him.

A year later, Ligeti wrote a second étude for organ, *Coulée*, which involves an ingenious kind of cross-breeding: it revisits the instrument in terms of the motion within stasis of the harpsichord piece. Here the challenge is not only to the fingers, but also involves finding registrations such that, as Ligeti writes in his preface, 'Despite the great speed, the impression of a sort of continuous trill motion [is] retained ... the listener must be able to hear that what is happening is not a sustained chord but rather an internal motion (even if it is insanely fast).'

The comparison with *Continuum* is fascinating: the composer is clearly very conscious of the need to be 'the same, but not the same'. The openings are near identical: only the interval involved is different (a minor third in *Continuum*, a perfect fifth in *Coulée*); and the general strategies are similar: gradually changing patterns with rhythmic 'moiré' effects. But the form of *Coulée* is even more 'continuous' than that of the harpsichord piece: there are no punctuating 'interval signals', and virtually no change of register until the last part of the piece, where both hands gradually drift up to the very top of the instrument, and suddenly break off, in the classic Ligeti manner, as if they had fallen off the top of the keyboard. Comparing the work to Ligeti's first organ étude, the most significant difference, perhaps, is the use of the organ pedals, which had played no role in *Harmonies* except at the very end, as a semi-ironic way of pointing out that the piece was over. In *Coulée*, the pedals are present almost throughout (though not at the end). At first they simply provide a sustained backdrop, a sort of resonance from the keyboard *continuum*; but after about a minute, they come up to the same volume level as the keyboard, and form a very slow-moving 'chorale layer'.

The trio of keyboard solos were concerned once again with a 'continuous' form, and a single textural focus, but the various chamber pieces written in the later 1960s are each much more diverse in character, exploring and extending various 'Ligeti fingerprints'. But their diversity is still inward-looking, in sharp contrast to the pluralism that dominated most other European new music at the time. Even the ensembles seem defiantly traditionalist. Stockhausen is writing for his own live-electronic ensemble, Berio's *Sinfonia* matches the Swingle Singers with a symphony orchestra, Kagel (in *Acustica*) writes for neo-futurist noise-makers, while Hans Werner Henze (Schott's other front-runner in the late 1960s, and a recent convert to leftist radicalism) is constantly looking for provocative vocal and instrumental possibilities. Ligeti, on the other hand, writes a wind quintet, a string quartet and a piece for string orchestra.

The Ten Pieces for wind quintet written for the Stockholm Wind Quintet embody Ligeti's approach to diversity. As with the earlier Bagatelles extrapolated from *Musica ricercata*, there is no question of a structurally unified work. Ligeti describes the Ten Pieces as 'a series of colourful cartoons' – rather like the Dies Irae sequence in the Requiem, though with none of that work's apocalyptic overtones! A closer parallel, perhaps, would be with the kaleidoscopic form of the Cello Concerto's second movement, with the difference that here the short sections are explicitly separated into movements. One other obvious difference between the Ten Pieces for wind quintet and the Bagatelles written over a decade earlier is that the former are 'original compositions', rather than arrangements, as the Bagatelles were. This means that instead of adapting existing music to a certain kind of ensemble, Ligeti was able to begin with a personal conception of the wind quintet, and derive the music from this concept. Part of this conception involves a conscious to-and-fro between the idea of a unified ensemble and that of five disparate individuals. So every second movement is a mini-concerto featuring one instrument as soloist (and dedicated to the appropriate member of the Stockholm quintet). In these solo movements one sees further evidence of a drift away from the Darmstadt avant garde. Far from exploring innovative 'extended techniques', these movements concentrate on the sounds and techniques (sometimes virtuoso, but not always) most characteristic of each instrument; the models are not Cage and Kagel but, as Ligeti himself points out, Stravinsky and Richard Strauss.

Following common practice in post-war works, the flautist and oboist double on several instruments: the flautist also plays alto flute and (in the last two movements) piccolo, while the oboist doubles on cor anglais and oboe d'amore. The lower-pitched alternative instruments (alto flute and cor anglais) are used at the start of the work, which means that over the course of the whole piece the ensemble moves from being a relatively unified, low-register ensemble to a diverse one, covering the widest possible range.

The first piece is in effect *Atmosphères* for wind quintet, with the instruments entering on a soft, *dolcissimo* cluster, with the same basic marking (*molto sostenuto*) and tempo as the orchestral work; here, however, every instrumental part is clearly audible. The second piece, featuring the clarinet, has a typically 'extreme' marking: *Prestissimo minaccioso e burlesco* (*minaccioso*, 'menacing', will turn out to be a favourite marking in the opera *Le Grand Macabre*), while the third starts in 'cloud' style, but gradually becomes more focused, culminating (though not ending) in a sharply unison melody. The fourth is a breakneck flute solo which gradually fuses with the two accompanying instruments (clarinet and bassoon), while the fifth is a 'fast as possible' version of the 'meccanico' genre, as is, initially, the sixth, before an oboe solo intervenes. The seventh is a paradox piece: it is marked *Vivo, energico*, yet almost nothing happens until the end, where an outpouring of individual melodies rising to a climax is typically 'torn off'. The eighth movement is equally ambivalent: it begins as a quartet, with the horn, the latent soloist, absent. The ninth movement, for just three instruments (piccolo, oboe, clarinet) seems to pick up where the first left off: a high-register unison calculated to cause hyperventilation, which splits up into astringent, piercing howls.

A rehearsal of the Ten Pieces
for wind quintet with the
players for whom it was
written, the Stockholm
Wind Quintet

The final movement is marked *Presto bizarro e rubato*, with a wild but sporadic bassoon solo (*con violenza*) that finally peters out against a held piccolo note. At the end of the score Ligeti, ever-suspicious of the 'grand finale' mentality, places a quotation from Lewis Carroll's *Alice's Adventures in Wonderland*:

> ... but – There was a long pause. 'Is that all?' Alice timidly asked. 'That's all,' said Humpty Dumpty. 'Goodbye.'

The emergence of so many clear stereotypes in Ligeti's music from the 1960s raises all sorts of questions. Is the music not in danger of becoming an exquisitely refined patchwork of known quantities? What kinds of unity can be created using what seem to be such clearly demarcated musical territories?

These issues are addressed head on in the five-movement Second String Quartet, also written in 1968, which is Ligeti's first substantial instrumental work to involve more than two movements. Why? Among other reasons, so that the same compositional strategies – 'the generation of different types of movement resulting from bundles of polyrhythmic voices' – can be explored in terms of different contexts or, more precisely, different textural surfaces. Each of the last four movements concentrates on a different 'Ligeti fingerprint': the second is in the 'floating' style, the third is a 'meccanico' piece, the fourth is a variant on the 'wildly gesticulating' type, here compressed into a very narrow range, while the fifth sets out in 'tremolo' style. But with the exception of the fourth, each movement basically pursues the same sort of course: a drift from one register to another is punctuated by an 'interval signal', then the drift resumes from a different starting-point, and so forth.

But the quartet is also, like *Lontano*, a piece that explores a relationship to tradition, without seeking to be 'traditional'. Whereas the Cello Concerto was an 'anti-concerto', the Second String Quartet is by no means an 'anti-quartet'. Ligeti comments that 'the entire string quartet tradition from Beethoven to Webern is there somewhere ... even sonata form, although only like an immured corpse' (just as Bach and Reger lurked in the background of *Volumina*). Though the five-movement structure may suggest Bartók's 'arch forms', it is surely more significant here that the outer movements are relatively diverse in character (especially the first), whereas the inner movements are more 'specialized', concentrating on one particular type of texture.

In a conversation with Josef Häusler just before the première of the quartet, Ligeti talked about his ambivalent attitude to tradition: there was the desire always to do something new, not repeating the past (not even his own), yet there was at the same time the increasing desire to make allusions to the past, and even to pay some discreet homages – in this case, one to Bartók in the fifth movement. He suspects that 'perhaps I somewhere harbour the need, when I cut myself off from tradition so radically, to secretly maintain an umbilical cord, like an astronaut who is bound by a cord to the satellite, although he moves about freely in space.'

There was another powerful motivation. For Ligeti, as for many other musicians, the quartet is the élite genre, the one where the achievements of the past are so formidable that one hesitates to match oneself against them; but at the same time, to do so is the ultimate test, the only way of demonstrating that one is working at the highest possible standard (and the idea of 'niveau' – of quality, of standard – is one that constantly arises in Ligeti's conversations). Whereas the *Métamorphoses nocturnes* had provided a means of seeing how he measured up against Bartók's quartets, in the Second Quartet the yard-stick is the entire quartet repertoire. Here, rather than pursuing new stimuli, he pushes what he knows to the limits, and the resulting work makes enormous demands on the players: the kind of virtuosity required of the soloist in the Cello Concerto is now par for all four players.

The Second Quartet also involved a more specific technical challenge, rather similar to the one that Lutosławski had faced four years earlier in writing his string quartet. Both composers had established highly personal styles based on techniques implying large ensembles – clusters and micropolyphony for Ligeti, and sequences of twelve-note chords for Lutosławski – and for both, the challenge was to adapt these ideas to a small ensemble. In Ligeti's case, this meant a quartet without themes or motives, only textures and types of movement. And once again there was an influence, or at least point of reference, from the visual arts: Cézanne, whose paintings led Ligeti to ask himself how, in a musical context, 'can colour replace contours, how can contrasting volumes and weights create form?'

Ligeti at the 1969 Darmstadt
courses, where Continuum,
his first 'illusionist' piece, was
given its first performance

Contrasts of the most extreme kind are present from the outset: the
first movement leaps constantly from almost inaudible threads of
sound to '*fortississimos*', and from near-stasis to frantic activity. At first
the impression of micropolyphony is created by having all instruments
play flickering, irregular lines at the very top of their range, where
the individual pitches are almost indecipherable (and are further
'smudged' by little microtonal inflections). Throughout the movement, the four parts drift in and out of focus; towards the end there
is a sequence of wild outbursts, marked 'tutta la forza', 'as if crazy',
in which the sheer number of notes in each instrument creates the
impression of far more than four players; the last of these outbursts
gradually crumbles into a soft, shuddering bundle of sound,
terminated by an ethereal near-chromatic scale which leaps elegantly
between high and low registers.

The second movement is strongly reminiscent of *Lontano*, though
here the lines are not diatonic but chromatic and, again, microtonal in
part (Ligeti emphasizes that these 'swerves' in intonation are not
precise quarter-tones, but generally smaller intervals). At the opening,
the composer calls for a different kind of tone production on almost
every note: with and without vibrato, *col legno, sul ponticello, sul tasto,
flautando* etc., and the loud outbursts in the middle of the piece call
for a deliberately scratchy, rasping tone in which the pitch largely
disappears. The movement ends, like the first, with a descending scale,
but this time it is compressed into the narrowest possible range.
The third movement marks the first occasion on which Ligeti devotes
a whole movement to the 'meccanico' principle, while the fourth is
unique in Ligeti's output: a dense, ferocious music that seems to be
constantly trying to break out of its narrow confines, but only
succeeds for a moment, towards the end. Ligeti compares it to
a dwarf star, in which 'the same mass that is contained in our sun
is compressed into a millionth part of the volume', whereas the fifth
movement 'spreads itself out, just like a cloud'.

At the 1968 Darmstadt courses, Ligeti was mainly involved in
a series of lectures and discussions entitled 'Is the Nineteenth Century
Dead?', a topic that tied in well with a concert performance of
Lontano. The next year, he may have felt rather like a fish out of water.
Certainly, his series of seminars on *Continuum* and the Ten Pieces for
wind quintet must have seemed utterly at odds with the main focuses

and controversies of the courses. The centrepiece of the 1969 courses was Stockhausen's seminar series, which turned out not to be a 'composition class' at all, but a series of performances of the 'text compositions' *Aus den sieben Tagen* ('From the Seven Days'). In these pieces, the 'score' consisted only of brief texts whose contents struck most participants as both mystical and mystifying: 'Play a vibration in the rhythm of the universe' was a characteristic instruction. Anything more at odds with the leftist, post-1968 uprisings mood of the participants would be hard to imagine, and controversy raged. Stockhausen was being accused of obscurantism, élitism, imperialism, exploitation, and just about everything else imaginable. Even some of his players – not the Cologne colleagues, but a Parisian group centred on the composer-trombonist Vinko Globokar – began to dissent, questioning Stockhausen's right to authorship of their joint efforts.

There were other signs that Darmstadt had decided that the nineteenth century was indeed dead. 'Multi- media' was a buzzword on everyone's lips – not in our present-day, computer-age sense, but as a halfway house between Cage and Wagner, featuring the informal interaction of visual and acoustic arts. And the 1969 courses also saw the emergence of the 31-year-old Helmut Lachenmann as leading figure in a new movement, *Verweigerungsmusik* ('Music of Denial'), which involved a left-wing critique of conventional notions of 'beauty'. It is hard to imagine that Ligeti's natural curiosity would have extended to any of these causes. Everything seemed to be driven by ideology, and he had had more than enough experience of that.

His next ensemble work, *Ramifications*, was something of a leftover; it was a commission attaching to the Koussevitsky Prize he had received some years earlier which, not for the last time, had fallen well behind schedule. *Ramifications* returns to the idea of 'blurred' intonation from a different perspective. Here there are two string sextets (the piece can also be performed with two string orchestras), one of which is tuned a quarter-tone above the other. But even this does not signal a conversion to quarter-tone composition: the quarter-tone clusters Penderecki used in works like the *Threnody* did not tempt Ligeti, and nor did the idea of quarter-tone melodies. His interest was in inflecting the twelve notes of the chromatic scale, not in doubling their quantity. In any case, *Ramifications* operates on the assumption that the initial difference in tuning (actually slightly more than a quarter-tone) will not remain constant: the 'higher' ensemble will constantly find itself sliding down towards the normally tuned one, and then have to back off (up) again. Once again, the aim is to 'smudge' the harmony. In a note on the work, Ligeti describes the result as 'hyperchromaticism'; but, as in other works of the period, there is a constant to-and-fro from chromatic to diatonic which one can still detect beneath the blurring. A continuous Escher-like game is being played with the listener's capacity to sort out what is going on; a couple of moments where suddenly only one ensemble is playing, and harmonic 'normality' is restored, have an almost shocking effect – one realizes how much one's ear has been taking for granted.

The differences between the 'solo' and orchestral versions are by no means straightforward. In the latter, the blurring is more drastic, and there is relatively little scope for the ear to try and decipher all twelve parts. But then, the way the ear averages out the slightly discrepant intonations of several performers playing the same part also means that the harmony sometimes seems to be clearer than in the solo version.

If *Ramifications* is, ultimately, a secondary work within Ligeti's output, the Chamber Concerto for thirteen instruments that follows it is quite the opposite: even more than the Second String Quartet, it is a *locus classicus*, a showcase for the style Ligeti had developed in the course of the 1960s, every feature of which is presented in immaculately polished form (which may be why Ligeti describes it as a 'lighter sister-work' to the quartet). But for that very reason it was also a potential source of difficulty, since it 'summed up' the 1960s in a way that was almost too definitive. Perhaps this is why it also makes a tentative move towards a new approach, a micropolyphony in which individual lines become somewhat more audible. Recalling Ligeti's 'crystal culture' metaphor, one could say that from now on, the process of crystallization is arrested just a little later on, as the first formations are beginning to become apparent.

The title 'chamber concerto' implies that not only is every player a soloist – as was already the case in *Lontano* – but also that their parts are often virtuoso. The work is notable for its alternation between moments where the instruments fuse into a single block of sound, and those where their individuality is emphasized. The search for a 'fused' sound is reflected in the instrumentation, and not just in the instruments that are chosen (including a Hammond organ), but also in those that are significantly omitted – the substitution of a bass clarinet for the bassoon, and the omission of the 'penetrating' trumpet from the brass. On the other hand, this is by no means a 'colourless' ensemble, as some of the more extravagantly virtuoso passages make clear.

The interplay between fused timbres and (slightly) more audible melodic lines is immediately apparent in the first movement, which is another example of the 'blurring' strategy. Here the basic idea was 'the surface of a stretch of water where everything takes place below the surface ... suddenly a tune emerges and then sinks back again. For a moment the outlines seem quite clear, then everything gets blurred once more.' The 'tunes', tentative at first, grow more strident, and then the whole texture seems to break apart and hang in the air; extending Ligeti's metaphor, the effect is rather like a slow-motion film of a huge rock being thrown in a pool, where the spray flies in all directions (though not without perceptible patterns), and is just in the process of settling when the film grinds to a halt.

The three remaining movements follow the pattern of the Second Quartet (albeit without its fourth, 'dwarf star' movement): a slow, static movement which grows more animated, a 'meccanico' movement, and a volatile, hyperactive finale. The second movement is notable for an experiment in superimposing different tempos which foreshadows some of the polymetric investigations of the 1980s: after the static opening there comes a passage in which the tempo changes almost every bar, and at each change, one instrument carries on playing in the previous tempo, so that at times as many as five players are independent of the conductor's beat. Nevertheless, the chance element is kept under strict control. 'Freedom here,' says Ligeti, 'is a bit like driving a coach and six and slackening the rein; all six horses still run at much the same speed, as each of them conforms to the speed of the others.'

The 'meccanico' movement is much more complex than its equivalent in the quartet, though not much longer. Like the previous movement, it falls into three main parts (plus a short coda of trills and accents): the first in a narrow central range, the second more widely spread, and the third polarized between high and low. The final movement is a Presto which initially harks back to the end of the first movement; in the middle, a sudden frantic solo for the pianist, 'hammering like a madman' in the top register, gives way to a toccata-like passage in the bottom register, a shimmering, swirling sequence for strings and woodwind, and a sudden, quizzical ending.

Within a few years, the tide of musical thinking in Europe was to change considerably, swinging away from innovation at all cost to a re-evaluation of more traditional qualities. But in the cultural context of 1971, still dominated by the avant garde, the title of Ligeti's next orchestral piece, *Melodien* ('Melodies'), must have sounded like an act of wilful, even perverse repudiation – a return to the past. Second Quartet and Chamber Concerto were already quasi-traditional titles, but in a more neutral way – they did not imply any particular stylistic agenda, apart from a possible evocation of the Second Viennese School. But *Melodien*? It is not surprising to find Stockhausen commenting, somewhat disparagingly, 'The pianist Kontarsky recently told me that Ligeti spoke of being fed up with his works up to now – he wants to compose clear melodies.' What is surprising, perhaps, is that Stockhausen too had just written a piece for two pianos, *Mantra*, which was also the beginning of a 'return to melody'. Yet the two composers' motives were very different. For Stockhausen, a work like *Mantra* represented a conscious about-face after the semi-improvised, noise-dominated works of the late 1960s, such as *Kurzwellen, Spiral* and the *Aus den sieben Tagen* collection. For Ligeti, on the other hand, *Melodien* was partly a matter of taking an approach already present in the Chamber Concerto somewhat further and making it more explicit.

But perhaps the intentions are also more drastic. Resuming the aquatic metaphor that Ligeti uses in conjunction with the opening of the Chamber Concerto, one could say that *Melodien* is an exercise in muddying the waters, in breaking away from 'Ligeti characteristics' that were in danger of becoming too comfortable. There are no obvious cluster harmonies (until the very end), no interval signals, no 'meccanico' set pieces, no outbursts of 'super-cooled expressionism', and no drastic breaks in continuity ('as though torn off'). But even without so many of the familiar surface markers, the music is unmistakably Ligeti's, even if it is suddenly a different Ligeti. The musical form is shaped by gradual drifts in register, closing in on single notes and broadening out again, and the whole sound of the orchestra is distinctively his. Nor are the standard components of the

'Ligeti style' entirely absent – but they have retreated to the background, as one activity among many.

Indeed, questions of near and far, foreground and background are, as ever, very much in Ligeti's mind. As the preface to the score points out, the work has three basic 'strata': 'a "foreground" consisting of melodies and shorter melodic patterns; a middle plane consisting of subordinate, ostinato-like figurations; and a "background" consisting of long sustained notes.' What strikes one at the opening of *Melodien*, however, is not so much the melodies as the dense network of scale figures swirling upwards: a new topos in Ligeti's ensemble works, though it appears in *Continuum* and *Coulée*. Gradually, these figures are filtered up to the top range (by taking away the lower notes), gaps start to appear in the initially continuous rhythms, and the melodic and background layers assume more prominence. Thereafter the music seems to compress and dilate alternately, and the balance between the three planes constantly shifts. Towards the end of the work, a return to the upward swirls of the opening is as close as Ligeti's work had come so far to a conventional 'recapitulation'.

It was around this time that Ligeti found his music thrust into the spotlight by Hollywood, through Stanley Kubrick's film *2001: A Space Odyssey*. It seems that Kubrick had not originally intended to use Ligeti's music in his film; he had heard some of it, was impressed, and gave copies of it to another composer, from whom he had commissioned the actual film score, as an indication of the sort of music he wanted. Not surprisingly, this other composer was not able to produce Ligeti requiems to order, and on receiving his score, Kubrick decided to stick with the originals, excerpts from *Atmosphères*, *Aventures*, the Requiem and *Lux aeterna*.

All of this was news to Ligeti, who had no idea that his music was being cinematized. The first he knew of it was when an American friend told him that there was a new film that seemed to have a lot of his music in it. He went along, armed with a stopwatch, and discovered that there was over half an hour of it! Naturally, he was furious, even though he liked the film, and asked his publishers to take action. The matter never went to court, since MGM's lawyers, while conceding that they could not win the case, indicated that they were prepared to spin things out ad infinitum, and suggested a fairly modest out-of-court settlement. In the meantime Kubrick, unabashed, went

Film producer Stanley Kubrick, famous for *A Clockwork Orange*, and for *2001: A Space Odyssey* which made liberal use of Ligeti's music

The poster for *2001: A Space Odyssey*; Kubrick's unauthorized use of Ligeti's music launched the composer unexpectedly into international celebrity.

on to use more of Ligeti's music in 1980 for another film, *The Shining*. This time, however, he did seek (and gain) permission.

Leaving aside moral rights (not a concept that elicits much sympathy in the film industry, unless one can base a script on it), one has to concede that Kubrick's use of Ligeti's music was brilliantly effective – Ligeti thought so too – and the film album, which set Ligeti's music next to a hyper-glossy Karajan version of the Blue Danube Waltz, *Also Sprach Zarathustra* and an excerpt from Khachaturian's *Spartacus*, created a new level of interest in his work in the USA.

6

Fresh Beginnings 1970-80

The early 1970s, too, were a turning-point for new music, but in a very different sense to the 1950s and 1960s. If you went into the student union office in a German conservatory, the chances are that there would be a poster of Che Guevara on the wall, and for a young composer, the politically correct thing would be to set texts by poets like Pablo Neruda. Yet despite the outward show of (political) radicalism, the general mood among the young was already one of conformism. Apart from isolated instances of post-68 desperation such as the terrorist activities of the Baader-Meinhof gang, 'leftism' became a very comfortable attitude to espouse.

Around this time it was becoming overwhelmingly apparent that not only were many of the established avant-gardists getting into a rut, but the younger generation of composers was providing very little that was new or individual. In some cases, their adherence to left-wing causes was used both as an alibi for lack of innovation, and as a stick for beating their modernist elders, who were accused of forming an élitist modernist clique. In Darmstadt, this attitude had already begun to surface in 1969, when most of the aggression was directed towards Stockhausen and his *Aus den sieben Tagen* performances. Ligeti was teaching there too, but was not drawn into the emerging controversy.

Three years later, it was a different story. Following lectures by musicologists Carl Dahlhaus and Reinhold Brinkman, Ligeti found himself in a discussion in which the middle-aged avant garde was accused of conspiring to exclude the young. This was too much: Ligeti protested that he and his contemporaries would be delighted to see and hear works by young composers which were not imitations of Boulez, Stockhausen, Ligeti, Riley and Cage, but set out to replace them with something new. When the 'new wave' did come, in the mid 1970s, it proved to be a 'retro' wave, and ironically, many of the young conservatives – von Bose, Müller-Siemens, von Dadelsen and others – were Ligeti's own students.

Ligeti's inclusion of the American minimalist Terry Riley in his list of much-emulated composers was one of many significant by-products of an invitation to Ligeti to be composer-in-residence at Stanford University in 1972, his first major invitation to the USA. Stanford was in the process of establishing a reputation – which it maintains to this day – of being a pioneer in computer music, thanks mainly to the ground-breaking work of the composer John Chowning, who at the time was working on *Turenas*, probably the first real 'classic' of computer music. But Ligeti had no idea of this. As he later told Chowning, he had simply got this invitation from a university in California, thought it would probably be nice and sunny, and since he was getting behind with commissions and could do with a congenial working environment, he gladly accepted. In fact, it was two or three months before he visited the computer lab, but when he did, and Chowning played him *Sabelithe*, a piece composed the previous year, he was intrigued, even though he only heard the piece over tiny office loudspeakers. When Chowning gave the first public presentation of *Turenas* a few months later, Ligeti was in the audience. This time, hearing the glittering, splintery sounds at the beginning of the work execute 3D loops-within-loops through the hall, and doubtless struck not only by the novel sonorities but also by the extraordinarily clean, hiss-free sound, he was very impressed indeed. Though not tempted to return to electronic music himself,

Fog over San Francisco – an image underlying Ligeti's *San Francisco Polyphony* (1973–4), a work commissioned as a result of his time spent at Stanford University

he willingly advocated the new approach. Since 1969 he had been living mainly in Berlin, as a fellow of the German Academic Exchange Service (DAAD), and on returning to Berlin after his stay in the USA, he secured opportunities for Chowning to give presentations in Berlin and Darmstadt. This led to Chowning gaining a residency in Berlin as well. A little later, when Boulez started planning a new electronic research program for IRCAM in Paris (the Institut de Recherche et de Coordination Acoustique/Musique, opened in 1973), Ligeti was emphatic that the Stanford approach was the way to go.

The main piece Ligeti was working on at this time was a two-movement Double Concerto for flute and oboe. At first glance, it seems to be a return to the 1960s style: the opening pages look much more like *Lontano* than *Melodien*. But there are indeed differences. The opening movement is marked 'Calmo – con tenerezza'; the marking 'calmo' is a familiar one for Ligeti, but the direction 'con tenerezza' ('with tenderness') is not. *Lontano* had been marked 'Sostenuto espressivo', but at the risk of trying to extrapolate too much from one word, 'tenerezza' does suggest a more personal, intimate emotional involvement – something that was to emerge in some works of the 1980s.

More significant, though, is a new, more determined approach to undermining conventional tempered tuning. This was partly stimulated by another excursion while at Stanford, a visit to the composer Harry Partch. Since the 1930s Partch had been well known as a pioneer of alternative tunings based on a division of the octave into forty-three parts, and had built his own instruments to perform his works. Ligeti seems to have been relatively unimpressed by Partch's music, which he found 'rhythmically primitive' (this probably refers to a lack of rhythmic polyphony, for the rhythms themselves are certainly complex), but he was clearly stimulated by the new tuning systems. Not only the solo parts of the Double Concerto but the orchestral woodwind parts (and at the climax of the first movement, the strings too) employ microtonal inflections derived from 'just intonation' (in which tuning is based on the simple number ratios of the harmonic series) in order to break away from normal tuning and create a harmony which, as Ligeti describes it, is 'neither chromatic nor diatonic, but occupies an intermediate, fluctuating position'.

American composer Harry
Partch, who built his own
instruments to explore new
tuning systems

In the first movement the flautist plays only alto and bass flute, which Ligeti matches with a strikingly 'low-register' chamber orchestra with no violins, but including a low woodwind quartet of bass clarinet, two bassoons and contrabassoon. The aim, however, is not to produce gruff, heavy sonorities, but warm, husky ones, with the woodwinds predominating, and the two soloists acting merely as 'first among equals'. In the second movement (Allegro corrente), the challenge is to use this same low ensemble to create a music that is 'of great brightness and clarity', or at least becomes so after a low, murmuring start. This involves making some hazardous demands on the players: at one point the four double bass players are all playing rapid, intricate passages in a medium-high cello register. And if the solo parts are more obviously virtuoso in this movement, the same is true for all the other players – there are no passengers here. Only twice (near the middle and the end) do the principal flautist and oboist emerge as real soloists; elsewhere, everyone is engaged in frantic activity, leading to a conclusion where, in the composer's words, 'the music glitters as though deeply frozen and moves as stiffly as a puppet.'

It was also during his stay at Stanford that Ligeti finally got to hear music by the American minimalist school. In a way, this was a curiously belated exposure: the movement had already gained a high profile by the mid 1960s, and by the end of the decade many recordings of works by Steve Reich and Terry Riley were available on major labels (Ligeti had even met Riley in the late 1960s in Stockholm). Moreover, the work that initially impressed Ligeti – Riley's *In C* (1964) – had been performed under the direction of Lukas Foss at the Darmstadt Summer Courses in 1969. But apparently Ligeti did not hear it, and maybe that was just as well: it was a scrambled, ragged performance, booed throughout (on sectarian rather than musical grounds – Darmstadt was not ready for diatonic music), and the most memorable moment was when the lead pianist's incessantly repeated high C broke a string (greeted by cheers), upon which the pianist immediately switched to a retuned neighbouring key (to groans and renewed boos).

What most impressed Ligeti about Riley's piece was that it too proposed a kind of 'continuous' form with plenty of internal activity – there seemed to be uncanny parallels with *Continuum* and *Coulée* – but did so over a long span of time, often forty-five minutes or more.

And unlike many other early minimalist pieces, the form is not static, but dynamic: the players have fifty-three exactly notated melodic fragments, each of which they can repeat as many times as they like before proceeding to the next. At first the fragments are firmly rooted in a C major scale (hence the title), but gradually they move to the notes of E minor (it is always a matter of scales and modes rather than the 'keys' of tonal music), and seem to be heading back to C when they sidetrack towards F major. These transitions, however, are increasingly blurred as the piece proceeds, because although the individual performers all play at the same tempo, they make quite different decisions as to when to move on to the next figure. The result is a process very analogous to what Ligeti had been doing, albeit in a much more precisely controlled way, ever since *Lux aeterna.*

The first clear evidence of this exposure comes in *Clocks and Clouds* (1972–3), a thirteen-minute work for twelve-part female choir and orchestra which Ligeti has tended to downplay because, in his view, it is too simplistic: the minimalist influence, he feels, is too obvious and undigested, and the 'Ligeti element' too stereotyped, too close to unintentional self-parody. This seems an unduly harsh judgement. Compared to the works which surround it, it may not be overly concerned with exploring new territory, or with self-redefinition, but it is an enormously attractive piece, and concert programmers looking for a companion piece to Messiaen's *Trois Petites Liturgies* (also for female choir) might do well to consider it – not least because the violins which are worked so hard in Messiaen's piece are omitted in Ligeti's. Indeed, the whole constitution of Ligeti's orchestra is unusual, with its solid core of woodwind (five flutes, five clarinets, three oboes and four bassoons) and next to no brass, just two trumpets which have next to nothing to do in the first half of the work, and only a discreet role thereafter. For the rest, there is a small 'keyboard' contingent of glockenspiel, celesta, vibraphone and two harps, and fourteen low solo strings (four violas, six cellos and four double basses).

The work's title comes from an essay by the Viennese-born philosopher of science Sir Karl Popper. Not that Ligeti is a particular admirer of Popper – Popper's insistence on common sense, and the need for any theory worthy of the name to be falsifiable, may have appealed to him, but his pronouncements on the arts, and in particular his disparaging remarks about the new Viennese music of his youth, were presumably much less appealing. However, in the mid 1960s, Popper had written an essay entitled 'Of Clocks and Clouds', in which he made distinction between those physical phenomena that can be exactly measured ('clocks') and others which can only be described in general terms ('clouds'), and suggested that each contains elements of the other. This immediately struck a sympathetic chord with Ligeti, since Popper's 'Clocks and Clouds' equated so exactly with his 'meccanico' and 'non-stationary cluster' styles. Equally important, however, is the idea of transition from one to the other.

The homage to Riley is clearest at the start of the work, which does indeed start 'in C', with rapid, repeated diatonic figures in the flutes and clarinets. As in the pieces from the late 1960s, the diatonic intervals are soon filled out by chromatic ones, and turn into ascending scales of the kind familiar from *Melodien*. When the choir enters, it does so in the 'cloudy' manner of *Lux aeterna*, but this time with the microtonal inflections deployed in the Double Concerto. The 'text' is a phonetic one – another instance of an 'imaginary language' – though what if anything is being said in this language, only the composer knows. The voices gradually edge up higher, and suddenly all kinds of rapid, 'clock-like' figurations take over, and are passed across to the orchestra. When the choir re-enters, the upward movement continues, but now there is another factor. Ever since the choir's first entry, the double basses have been holding a low B, as an almost imperceptible pedal point, or drone. But now that bass line starts to move, and in terms of Ligeti's music the effect is rather startling: though one could not describe the music as tonal, each change of the bottom pitch has the effect of a key change, and even more than in *Lontano* one is suddenly aware of 'harmony'. Then the alto voices initiate a new 'clockwork', which sounds like an imaginary (but Eastern European) folk music. This in turn peters out, and after an orchestral passage in which high, slow, drifting melodic lines are set against whirling figures so fast that they too seem static, the voices return, at the bottom of their range, with a 'clockwork' that gradually dissipates into a cloud.

Though one would not guess it from the music, *Clocks and Clouds* is another 'in memoriam' piece. It is dedicated to the memory of Harald Kaufmann, an Austrian musicologist who had helped Ligeti with the formulation of his Boulez analysis and the essay

'Wandlungen der Musikalischen Form' ('Transformations of Musical Form'), and had written eloquently about his work. In his programme note Ligeti recalled that their numerous conversations often gave him new musical ideas, adding that 'his early death leaves a gap in my life that can never be filled'.

Another loss, an even more serious one, came a year later. In 1973, Bruno Maderna died of cancer. He had been seriously ill for some time, yet shortly before his death he conducted a whole concert of Ligeti's work in Amsterdam, despite the composer's pleas not to risk his health any further. That was typical of Maderna, who to the very last put himself at the service of others. And in Ligeti's view, his death was the final death knell of the Cologne-Darmstadt avant garde. Certainly it affected many composers, for even more than Boulez, it was Maderna who had acted as advocate as well as colleague. Boulez, after years of indecision in which he had hardly completed a piece, wrote a major orchestral work, *Rituel in memoriam Maderna*, and Franco Donatoni, also going through something of a crisis, wrote an enormously impressive orchestral tribute, *Duo per Bruno*. For Ligeti, Maderna's death was even more distressing a blow. Through all the squabbles and rivalries, it was Maderna who had been calm and incorruptible. He had become a father-figure, and when he was gone, Ligeti felt he had somehow been left alone. It was now, after sixteen years, that he finally severed his umbilical cord to the radical modernists, with his opera *Le Grand Macabre*.

But first he wrote another orchestral work, *San Francisco Polyphony*. The title is in English since it was written to celebrate the sixtieth anniversary of the San Francisco Symphony Orchestra, a commission which came about partly as a result of Ligeti's six-month residency at Stanford University. It is a curious work in many ways: although a dialectic of order and disorder had always played a role in Ligeti's compositional thinking, it is hard to think of another work in which the balance is tipped so decisively in favour of disorder. Consciously so, too: the composer describes how 'an exchange takes place between order and chaos. The individual melodic lines and figures are innately closed and ordered, but their combination, both simultaneous and successive, is chaotic. In the overlying structure, in the governing form of the musical events, order finally reasserts itself. One can imagine various objects in a state of total disarray in a drawer, but the drawer itself has a clearly defined form: chaos prevails inside, but in itself it is well-formed.'

Unlike the previous orchestral works (though *Melodien* gives a hint of it), *San Francisco Polyphony* starts *in medias res*: it is as if the piece had already been going on for a while, and we suddenly come in, in the midst of a process that is already well under way. To that extent it resembles the 'informal' pieces that the Italian avant-gardist Aldo Clementi (another regular visitor to Darmstadt) had been writing since the early 1960s. But whereas Clementi's pieces present a dense, abstract labyrinth which is essentially 'uneventful', in *San Francisco Polyphony* we seem to be groping our way through the spider's web of Ligeti's childhood dream. It is a precarious passage: sudden, traumatic events occur without warning, and catastrophe seems imminent at every moment. One thinks of the famous Yeats line: 'Things fall apart; the centre cannot hold.'

San Francisco Polyphony is Ligeti's farewell to the textural style of the 1960s. Though the later concertos for piano and for violin have their hyperactive moments, this is the last score in which there are often literally several hundred notes in each bar. While writing the piece, Ligeti imagined that not only the notorious fog but also the general cultural climate of San Francisco was making an impact on the piece, just as it had already done on *Clocks and Clouds*. But, as he concedes, once individual melodies start to emerge more clearly, the polyphony seems to have more and more to do with expressionist Vienna – here a 'city of bad dreams' – rather than with San Francisco. The violin lines recall Mahler, and the soaring trumpet lines recall Berg: no other work by Ligeti up to this point is so charged with 'tradition' (though the Horn Trio of a decade later will equal it, in a much less disquieting sort of way). Apart from the final Prestissimo, which does indeed evoke a modern city, the work seems to have a turbulently valedictory quality, in which the farewell to modernism is also extended back to the Viennese generations that preceded the Darmstadt school.

In 1973, Ligeti's nomadic life of the preceding decade came to a relative halt. He gained a professorship at the Hamburg Conservatory, and accordingly resettled in that city, which has remained his home base ever since. One might wonder how it is that a leading composer whose teaching career had begun over twenty years earlier, and who had been invited to teach composition all over the

One of many honours: Ligeti receives the Bach Prize of the city of Hamburg in 1975.

world, should have waited so long before taking up a professorial position. The fact is, no institution had made a decent offer; there had been various negotiations, but either conditions were inadequate, or the institution had preferred another composer. And perhaps that was not so exceptional: even Stockhausen, far more didactically inclined than Ligeti, had only gained a professorship a year or so earlier, when the suicide of Bernd Alois Zimmermann left a vacant position at the Musikhochschule in Cologne.

Admittedly, as with so many other things, Ligeti's view of composition teaching is equivocal. Like many composers, he believes that composition cannot really be taught, in the sense that a would-be creative artist either has, or does not have, the necessary talent: it cannot be synthetically produced. What can be taught (and here he is in complete agreement with Kagel) is craftsmanship, which initially involves precisely the disciplined, rigorous study of such things as Palestrina's counterpoint that Ligeti had learned in Budapest. But this, ideally, should precede the serious study of composition: by the time one comes into a high-level composition class, this is one of the many things one should already be able to do.

As indicated earlier, Ligeti's first years as professor of composition in Hamburg coincided with the rise of a new generation of German composers, mainly committed to an explicitly anti-modernist, neo-Romantic aesthetic, and many of whom were his own students. In addition, it was his own current publisher, Schott, that had signed up most of them, and was promoting them as the future of German music. One has the impression that Ligeti found this situation acutely uncomfortable. On the one hand, he did not want to sabotage their prospects; on the other, he certainly did not wish to see his reasons for rejecting the Darmstadt legacy equated with theirs. For them, the modernist path was a culpable error; for him, it was a legitimate, even thrilling venture that seemed to have run out of steam. He may even have felt that they were trying to interpret his own recent music to their own ends, rather than to his. When Hans von Dadelsen (son of the eminent Bach scholar Georg von Dadelsen) made an analysis of *Lontano*, he set out to find as many links as possible to the Romantic era, just as his discussion of *San Francisco Polyphony* sought to portray it – with some justification – as modernity's final self-destructive eruption.

Perhaps the most depressing aspect of this new generation, from Ligeti's point of view, was that there was nothing new to learn from them. In rejecting the recent past, all they had to put in its place was the more distant past, plus a populist advocacy of non-radical rock music. Ligeti's own reaction to pop and rock was (and remains) mixed. Back in the 1960s, he had found the early Beatles singles pleasantly fresh and lively, but just as entertainment music – he certainly did not subscribe to the opinion of the music critic of *The Times*, who hailed them as successors to Schubert. On the other hand, he did find the *Sergeant Pepper* album genuinely impressive, and a decade later, he also found himself liking Supertramp's *Breakfast in America*, whose mixture of catchy tunes and unpredictable phrase lengths (as in the *Logical Song*) made it a firm favourite with his students. Jazz, with which he only really became familiar in the 1970s, is another matter: here he can recognize the same kind of sophistication ('elegance, simplicity and complexity, all at the same time') as in the best concert-hall music. On the whole, his tastes are for the more disciplined 'progressive' movements: the bebop of Charlie Parker, Miles Davis and John Coltrane (he particularly admires *Kind of Blue*) and Eric Dolphy (though he is less keen on Ornette Coleman's more iconoclastic 'free jazz'), as well as the bands of Louis Armstrong and King Oliver in the 1920s, and Duke Ellington in the 1930s.

None of this, however, had any significant impact on his main work of the mid 1970s, the opera *Le Grand Macabre*. Its origins go back to the late 1960s. After the success of the Requiem, Ligeti was approached by Göran Gentele, the head of the Swedish Royal Opera in Stockholm, to write, if not an opera, then at least a piece for an opera house. Even though only a few years elapsed between the first ideas and the start of composition, that period witnessed crucial changes in artistic outlook, and not just for Ligeti. In the late 1960s, the opera house was viewed by the avant garde as an emblem of backward thinking: Boulez had said that the best thing you could do with most opera houses was to blow them up, and Stockhausen steadfastly refused all requests to write an opera (ironically, since he went on to spend the last quarter of the twentieth century working on nothing but *Licht*, a cycle of seven operas!). In 1971, Ligeti's friend Kagel created a sensation with his 'anti-opera' *Staatstheater*, which Friedlinde Wagner (admittedly the renegade black sheep of the Bayreuth clan) described as the only interesting thing that had happened in opera in years.

So it is not surprising that, when first questioned about his forthcoming operatic project in 1970, Ligeti declared: 'It won't be an opera in the normal sense. I can't write a "traditional" opera, I don't want to: for me the genre of opera is irrelevant today, it belongs to a historical phase which is basically different to the situation with composition today.' Like Kagel, he was going to think of the opera house as a theatre with a particular set of technical resources, rather than as a place that performs operas. As for the text, he would not be setting a conventional libretto, but producing a 'synthetic' text in conjunction with the music (as in *Nouvelles Aventures*, which he was completing at the time the commission was first offered), and since the provisional title was *Kylwiria*, one assumes the work might well have resuscitated not only the imaginary world of his childhood, but its language too.

But all this changed. By the time he got round to work on the piece, he probably felt that *Staatstheater* had taken anti-opera as far

as it could usefully go, and in writing what he once facetiously called
an 'anti-anti-opera' he finished up with, to all intents and purposes,
'opera'. The magic world of his childhood was also set aside, and
instead he took up the Oedipus myth, completing his own libretto in
1971. Then calamity struck: Gentele was killed in a motor accident
in Sicily, and the project was temporarily shelved.

By the end of the year, though, a whole team in Stockholm was
casting around for a new topic: Ligeti himself, his close friend
Nordwall, the stage designer Aliute Meczies, and Michael Meschke,
the director and producer of the Stockholm Puppet Theatre. Ligeti
was looking for an extension of the comic-book catastrophe ambience
of the Dies Irae from the Requiem. Even his Oedipus paraphrase had
been inspired by Saul Steinberg's cartoons, and was going to be
completely devoid of antiquarian features, with only a minimum of
narrative. Now he wanted 'some kind of tragi-comic, exaggeratedly
frightening but not really dangerous "Last Judgement"'. It was
Meczies who came up with the idea of adapting *La Balade du Grand
Macabre*, a 'farce for rhetoricians' written by the Belgian playwright
Michel de Ghelderode in the early 1930s, but not performed until
twenty years later. As it happens, Ghelderode had already been
proposed as a possible source a few years earlier. During an evening
drinking session in the Darmstadt Schlosskeller, with the strains of
Sergeant Pepper pounding through the air, the Belgian composer
Jacques Calonne had mentioned the name Ghelderode in passing as
a writer whom Ligeti might find interesting. But then, presumably,
beer and the Beatles overtook the conversation.

Ligeti describes Ghelderode's play as 'exactly what I was looking
for. At last I had found a play about the end of the world, a bizarre,
demoniacal, cruel and also very comic piece.' It is set in 'Breughelland'
(Ligeti was particularly reminded of two Breughel paintings, *The
Land of Cockaigne* and *The Triumph of Death*), and describes the End
of the World, as presided over by the grotesque figure of The Great
Macabre (who in Ligeti's libretto becomes Nekrotzar – the tsar of the
dead). In the play, this Grim Reaper turns out to be a fraud, and the
'end of the world' a drunken farce – though in the opera, we are not
quite so sure …

Ghelderode is a major figure in the mid-century theatrical avant
garde, with a flamboyant approach to words, but Ligeti was emphatic

from the start that *Le Grand Macabre* was not to be a literary opera –
as in Verdi or Monteverdi, the characters are 'real' characters, not
mouthpieces for the author's ideas. For him, the scenario of
Ghelderode's play was right, but the language was wrong: too 'rich
and flowery'. Ligeti's literary inclinations have always been towards
writers who used simple language to convey extraordinary and
complex situations, writers as diverse as Kleist, Kafka, Lewis Carroll
and Boris Vian. As noted earlier, the obscure language of Joyce's
Ulysses and *Finnegan's Wake* had intrigued him from a technical point
of view, but was not really to his taste. In terms of theatre, the writer
who particularly appealed to him was Alfred Jarry, the French author
of the 'scandalous', absurdist *Père Ubu* plays.

So Ligeti asked Meschke to 'Jarrify' Ghelderode's text, making it
sharper and 'super-realistic'. But then, after Meschke had provided
a prose version, Ligeti decided that he wanted something a little more
formal, and turned parts of it into rhyming (German) verse – a
difficult task which forced him to resort to dictionaries of rhymes and
synonyms. Ligeti reports that when he sent the result to Schott, his
publishers, they corrected a few things, but then said, 'It isn't very
good German, in fact it's rather peculiar German, but we're leaving it.'
Rightly or not, he is inclined to believe that all the subsequent
translations of the libretto into other languages are probably superior
to his 'original'.

The plot is 'over the top' from start to finish – wildly burlesque in
content and gesture, and at least as reminiscent of Rabelais's *Gargantua*
and *Pantagruel* as of anything in Jarry. In the first scene, a drunken Piet
the Pot is ogling two beautiful young lovers (the 'male' is a trousers
part, in the manner of Mozart's Cherubino and Strauss's Octavian),
who are in a state of considerable sexual arousal ('I'm dripping!' – 'I'm
ready to burst!') and looking desperately for somewhere to copulate
undisturbed. In the first score, their names are Clitoria and Spermando
– subsequently, rather sadly, this was toned down to Amanda and
Amando. Suddenly Nekrotzar emerges from a grave and announces
that the world will end at midnight. He commandeers Piet as his horse
(humiliation and subjugation are the opera's stock-in-trade), and the
lovers promptly commandeer the grave.

The second scene takes place in the home of the Court
Astronomer Astradamors (the name combines references to stars, love

A Swedish Grim Reaper: A poster for the Stockholm première of *Le Grand Macabre*

and Nostradamus) and his wife Mescalina; Ligeti describes the home as a 'chaotic, shabby combination of laboratory and kitchen'. It is an S&M extravaganza: Mescalina (a conflation of Messalina and mescalin) is an oversize virago in full bondage kit – black leather and assorted implements – and Astradamors is the passive, protesting victim (optionally dressed in women's underwear). First he gets a whipping, then he is supposedly impaled from behind with a spit, but turns out to have a protective saucepan lid in his pants. Incensed at this deceit, Mescalina fells him with a karate blow, and he plays dead until she confronts him with her ultimate weapon (and the embodiment of Ligeti's childhood fears): a huge, hairy spider, which she invites him to eat – he screams with horror. After a grotesque dance, he kisses her backside, and she is in the process of stripping him of his (female) clothing when an alarm bell rings. The session is over: Astradamors is dispatched to his telescope, looking for a disaster-portending red comet, and Mescalina falls asleep. At this point Nekrotzar enters, still riding on Piet's back. Mescalina is dreaming of Venus, who appears as a vision ('entirely nude, and of consummate

Ligeti discusses *Le Grand Macabre* with Elgar Howarth, the conductor of the first performance.

beauty'). The less than consummately beautiful Mescalina abuses her
roundly for her failure to supply adequately endowed sexual partners,
and demands something better. Nekrotzar decides to answer her
prayers, and 'flings himself on the sleeping Mescalina, like
Frankenstein's monster' (though the Transylvanian Count Dracula
seems a more apt model). After a bestial 'love scene', with Piet,
Astradamors and Venus looking on avidly, Mescalina awakes.
Nekrotzar bites her in the throat, and she dies, screaming. Piet and
Astradamors hastily tip her into a nearby burial chamber, while
Nekrotzar rants on about the impending end of the world.

For the long third scene, the action shifts to the court of the
overweight, juvenile Prince Go-Go, where two competing ministers
(who can be represented as puppets) are hurling an alphabet of
Rabelesian abuse at one another ('Arse-licker, Bloodsucker,
Charlatan'). Again, one thinks of Jarry – the cavern scene in *Père Ubu*
– as well as the comparable tirade in Beckett's *Waiting for Godot*;
Ligeti cites Captain Haddock in *Tin-Tin* as another influence. They
then address the prince's education, brutally: they sway his rocking-
horse till he falls off, punch him ('posture exercises'), crush him with a
massively heavy crown, and try to stop him from eating until he has
signed papers raising taxes. The latter ploy fails, and in comes
Gepopo, head of the eponymous secret police (the Nazi reference is
not hard to decipher); the part is entrusted to a coloratura soprano.
As 'his' name suggests, he constantly stammers (a characterization
trick going back to Cavalli and the early days of Venetian opera), as
does his retinue of detectives and executioners. After prognosticating
various civic disasters, he and his forces leave. There are sounds of
a crowd outside; the ministers go to the balcony, and are knocked over
by hurled projectiles. At this point, the power relations switch, and
the child prince, who has been guzzling furiously, takes over. The
offstage crowd greets him rapturously. Gepopo returns in disguise,
as another huge, ugly spider, announcing the approach of the comet
and the apocalyptic Macabre (that is, Nekrotzar), and everyone except
the prince flees. Astradamors rushes in, the populace outside becomes
increasingly agitated, sirens sound, and finally Nekrotzar enters
through the auditorium, brandishing scythe and trumpet, riding
Piet as ever, and accompanied by 'an infernal entourage, of giants,
skeletons, fabulous monsters, devils and demons'.

A set design by Aliute
Meczies for the Stockholm
première of *Le Grand
Macabre*

Nekrotzar is in a trance, oblivious to everything but his mission. The populace wails, Piet and Astradamors get blind drunk, but he notices nothing: he is obsessed with the impending End of Time. Then he gets the idea that the glass of wine offered him by Piet is a chalice of his victims' blood, and he drinks. Piet refills his glass time after time, till Nekrotzar too is utterly drunk. As midnight nears, there are storms and earthquakes. Suddenly, Nekrotzar remembers his task, calls for scythe and trumpet, and struggles onto the Prince's rocking horse. The apocalypse comes, and there is total darkness.

The fourth and final scene (Act II, but following without a break) returns to the location of the opening. It is still dark, and Piet and Astradamors float by, dreaming they are dead. Dawn breaks, Go-Go, suffering from a hangover, wanders on stage, and is accosted by three cut-throats. As they are about to throttle him, Nekrotzar emerges from their cart, also with a hangover, and Mescalina bursts out of the tomb and sets on him. The cut-throats restrain her, bring in the two ministers, and massacre everyone except Nekrotzar, but when Piet

and Astradamors enter, Go-Go springs back to life, and produces
three bottles. Nekrotzar realizes his project has failed. As he drinks, he
shrinks into a tiny ball. Suddenly Amanda and Amando emerge from
the tomb, dishevelled but still exquisite, with the sun shining through
their hair. 'Hey, kids,' yells Piet, 'didn't you know that the world has
come to an end?' Needless to say, this is of no concern to them. Ever
since they disappeared into the tomb, the rest of the world has been
non-existent anyway: its traumas have passed them by, but now they
join the other characters in a final motto (in the manner of Verdi's
Falstaff, which is even quoted in passing):

Fear not to die, good people all!
No-one knows when his hour will fall.
And when it comes, then let it be …
Farewell, till then – live merrily!

Though it is hard to imagine an opera less Wagnerian than
Le Grand Macabre, there is one important and unexpected point of
contact. Many passages in Wagner's music dramas are constructed
on a 'bar form' principle derived from the fourteenth-century
Meistersinger ('Mastersingers'): three parallel 'verses' and an epilogue
('drei Stollen und ein Abgesang'). Ligeti describes the entire opera as
an example of the 'bar form': not only are there three main scenes and
epilogue, but each of the main scenes develops in a parallel manner,
starting as an idyll, and making a crescendo to a 'catastrophic' climax.
The first scene starts with the young lovers, and ends with Nekrotzar's
subjugation of Piet. The second scene begins as a fairly devious
domestic sex scene (one hesitates to call Astradamors and Mescalina
'lovers') and again climaxes with the entry of Nekrotzar and Piet.
The notion of an idyll is stretched slightly further when applied to
the scene with Prince Go-Go and his ministers, but this again begins
relatively calmly, and culminates in the appearance of Nekrotzar, Piet
and Astradamors, and the apparent end of the world.

The music of the opera is intentionally disparate: Ligeti describes it
as a kind of 'pop art', in the sense of the American and British painters
who had come to the fore in the late 1960s. There are any number of
references to the past, but their quality is mainly ironic rather than
nostalgic. So the Toccata which opens the work, and returns at the

start of Act II, is a tongue-in-cheek homage to Monteverdi's *Orfeo* in which Monteverdi's cornetts are replaced by car horns. In the second scene, Astradamors and Mescalina cavort to a thinly disguised mutation of the cancan from Offenbach's *Orpheus in the Underworld*, with twisted variants of Schumann's *The Merry Peasant* and Liszt's *Grand Galop chromatique* thrown in.

These references intensify in the third scene. Nekrotzar's grand entry through the auditorium is accompanied by a 'Collage' (a 'homage to Charles Ives') which starts with a twelve-note transmogrification (into pairs of tritones) of the opening of the last movement of Beethoven's 'Eroica' Symphony. Among Nekrotzar's retinue of devils are four musicians, playing violin, bassoon, E flat clarinet and piccolo. The violinist plays a ragtime on a retuned violin (quasi-Scott Joplin, but surely also a reference to the Devil in Stravinsky's *Soldier's Tale*, who likewise plays a ragtime), and the bassoonist plays a distorted version of a Greek Orthodox hymn that Ligeti used to sing at school. The other two devil-musicians are clearly pioneers of World music: the clarinet's part is 'a mixture of Brazilian and Spanish, half samba and half flamenco', while the piccolo has a pentatonic Hungarian tune that is modified to sound like Scottish bagpipe music. And there are more parodies and homages to come: the drunken Nekrotzar holds forth to the accompaniment of a neo-classicizing 'galimatias', while the musical backdrop to his final shrivelling is a 'double canon' for strings which seems to shake hands with Lutosławski's *Funeral Music*.

However witty these cross-references are, one can sense a second, less comfortable motivation. In *San Francisco Polyphony* (which seems to be about the end of a world, though not The World), Ligeti had virtually blown the 'Ligeti style' of the 1960s apart, without necessarily knowing what was going to take its place. Though the opera contains some extraordinarily impressive passages, such as the apocalyptic orchestral interlude which links the two acts, and is never less than effective, the composer's own voice is sometimes disturbingly hard to detect: it is clearly the work of a brilliant composer, but which brilliant composer? At one level, the music of *Le Grand Macabre* suggests that stylistic concessions are being made to the singers, such as the sweetly euphonious (and frankly enchanting) chains of consonant intervals given to the two lovers. But opera or not, it is not in Ligeti's nature to make such concessions, and one cannot help speculating that for once, at a period of stylistic indecision and even crisis, the stereotype of the unadventurous opera singer became something of an alibi.

Not that the vocal parts are easy! On the contrary, their technical demands are often monstrous: the coloratura arias sung by Gepopo in the third scene are all in Mozart's 'Queen of the Night' league of difficulty (the composer admits, 'I was told it was impossible, but on the first night in Stockholm, the soprano [Britt-Marie Aruhn] brought it off.'). But within a few years, Ligeti himself was expressing reservations about the work, conceding that the result was more conventional than he had intended, and that his passion for *Traviata* and *Carmen*, which had begun back in childhood, had perhaps got the upper hand.

Be that as it may, the première in Stockholm (12 April 1978) was a major success, and all seven performances were sold out. This was

Following page, a scene from the 1997 Salzburg Festival première of the revised Le Grand Macabre; Peter Sellars's production was visually spectacular, but not to Ligeti's taste.

Aliute Meczies's design for
the 'Gepopochef' in Act II
of *Le Grand Macabre*

followed by a flurry of other productions, especially in Germany: in
Hamburg (1978), Saarbrücken, Bologna (1979), Nuremberg (1980),
Paris (1981) and London (1982). Almost immediately, Ligeti slashed
a considerable amount of spoken dialogue from the work, but what
he learned above all from these various performances was that as
drama, the piece could withstand all kinds of producers' interpretations, but not mediocre singing: if a part was not well sung,
the theatrical element also collapsed. He particularly liked the
Bologna production, with designs and costumes by Topor: for him,
'it really caught the spirit of the work; it was a demoniacal romp,
a great extravaganza.'

But then came a dry period of eight years, before there was another
flood of productions in the early 1990s: in Ulm, Leipzig (1991), Zürich
and Berne. Now the piece was being presented as a revived 'modern
classic' rather than a new work, and some productions at least sought to
give it an overt contemporary relevance. In Leipzig, for example,
Breughelland was very explicitly equated with East Germany (something
that certainly did not please the composer). In the wake of these revivals,
Ligeti decided to revise the work – we shall return to this later.

The opera had a rather surprising dedicatee: Ligeti's son Lukas, born just eight years earlier in Vienna, in 1965. Partly, this is surprising because, rightly or wrongly, one has the impression of Ligeti slowly drifting away from his family during this period: Kurtág continues to talk about them, but Ligeti does not. And it is from Kurtág that we gain some insight into the even more surprising dedication of a major work to an eight-year-old. It seems that Lukas was becoming a 'double' of his father, perhaps to a startling degree. Back in his early years, Ligeti had drafted the plans for the imaginary land of Kylwiria, which could have been the subject of his opera. Now, says Kurtág, Lukas was evolving his own imaginary realm, in some respects even more detailed than his father's. In many respects, the parallels were to continue. Lukas too became a composer – as did Stockhausen's son Simon, and more recently Górecki's son – and although he would move towards rock- and free jazz-inspired improvisation, he shared other fascinations of his father, such as minimalism and African polyrhythms.

Another more curious satellite of the opera, *Rondeau* ('One-Man Theatre for an actor and tape'), is likewise dedicated to Lukas Ligeti. It is a predictably macabre little piece, with more than a hint of Jarry (for instance, the scene with the Three Free Men in *Ubu enchaîné*). An actor enters, in search of a plot rather than an author, with a rhyming dictionary in hand (memories of Ligeti the librettist!); no inspiration is forthcoming, and he turns on the tape. A voice says 'You will be shot', there is the sound of a shot being fired, and the actor falls to the ground. After a while he gets up, goes off, comes back on, starts again, stumbles over his imaginary corpse, gets the shooting retrospectively annulled (shades of Hindemith's *Hin und zurück*), aggravates the tape recorder into a fresh shooting, conducts a conversation with himself as corpse, and so forth. Finally he comes to the conclusion that the Last Judgement has come (a clear cross-reference to the opera), and that he has been appointed to sound the Last Trump, which he does, on an ocarina or some other inappropriately commonplace instrument.

In parallel with the later stages of the opera, Ligeti also worked on a series of Three Pieces for Two Pianos, the first piano music he had written since leaving Hungary. The opening piece, 'Monument', is a far cry from the eclecticism of *Le Grand Macabre* – it is a harsh, uncompromising piece which harks back in some ways to the *Poème symphonique*. This 'toughness' may well be a discreet homage to the work's dedicatees, Alfons and Aloys Kontarsky, who twenty years earlier had established their careers by sailing blithely through Boulez's thorny and extremely difficult *Structures*, and had rapidly become the new music piano duo that every avant-garde composer wanted to write for. They were permanent fixtures at the Darmstadt courses, and Aloys – equally notable as performer, intellectual and bon vivant – had collaborated closely with Kagel and Stockhausen (the latter's note for Kontarsky's recording of his *Klavierstücke I–XI* includes a graphic account of the pianist's startling gastronomic activities during the recording period).

The basis of 'Monument' is the superimposition of several rhythmic cycles, each associated with a single, remorselessly repeated note (albeit with a few sidesteps to neighbouring notes): Ligeti says he 'imagined a huge, statuesque imaginary architecture, with the interferences of six layers of lattices'. The cycles are introduced one by one, in such a way that after a while motives and melodic fragments start to emerge almost arbitrarily from the collision of layers; as the texture grows ever more dense, these figures are swamped in a general mass of sound – the inscriptions on the monument become indecipherable.

The second piece has the idiosyncratic title 'Self Portrait with Reich and Riley (and Chopin in the background)'; needless to say, the title is ironic, not self-aggrandizing. *Clocks and Clouds* had been the first piece in which identifiable foreign bodies (namely the minimalists) had found their way into Ligeti's work with the composer's consent, even if he had been slightly disconcerted by the extent of their takeover. By the time of the two-piano pieces, the insurgency was clearly under control, and he felt the time had come to pay a public homage by revisiting the techniques and figurations of some of his own proto-minimalist pieces (notably *Continuum*) in terms of the new American school. At first, he says, he thought of calling the piece 'Still Life with Reich and Riley', but since painted still lifes always involve dead objects (the French term 'nature morte' – 'dead nature' – always seems more apt), this seemed an unfriendly thing to do, and he settled for the present, more collegial title. The allusion to the Presto finale of Chopin's Second Piano Sonata at the end of the work has led some commentators to divide the rest of the movement into three separate portraits, of Ligeti, Reich and Riley respectively. Quite apart from the fact that the reference to Chopin's work, as an 'early precursor of quintessentially minimalist music', was a relative (but brilliant) afterthought, this interpretation is hard to sustain. One cannot imagine Ligeti composing a self-conscious self-portrait. In personal terms, it would be completely at odds with the way he thinks, and in musical terms, it is superfluous: even during the relatively problematic mid 1970s, few composers had as strong a musical personality. It is more a matter of Ligeti pretending to be Reich and Riley in the process of trying to recompose Ligeti.

The last movement ('In zart fliessender Bewegung' – 'With gently flowing motion'), which the composer describes as a 'liquefied' variant of 'Monument', is more conventionally virtuoso. Beginning with limpid descending figures à la Debussy, the music gets ever faster and louder, and the soft 'inner melodies' picked out at the opening turn into cannon shots ricocheting between the two pianos. Just when it seems impossible for the music to get faster or louder, the whirling figures are suddenly reduced to a *pianissimo*, and an eight-part canonic chorale emerges to bring the work to a close.

In the wake of *Le Grand Macabre*, Ligeti was already laying plans for a second opera, based on Shakespeare's *The Tempest*, which he had first read in his teens (in a Hungarian translation); it was to be 'very melodic, very "magical" in its atmosphere', but in other respects it was going to pick up threads from *San Francisco Polyphony* and the Three Pieces for Two Pianos, rather than *Le Grand Macabre*. One can imagine a wonderful Ligeti *Tempest* opera, but alas it was not to be. Even at an early stage, Ligeti was a little concerned at the ambitiousness of such a project, and in the end he decided in favour of his other preferred option – an opera based on Lewis Carroll's *Alice* books: meta-logical paradox won out over transcendental magic. Perhaps, too, he was deterred by the appearance of histrionic Shakespearian blockbusters such as Aribert Reimann's opera *Lear*; and in any case, perhaps the time for a Ligeti *Tempest* would have been the era of *Lontano*, rather than that of the more objective works of the 1980s.

In fact, the only works completed in the late 1970s were a couple of harpsichord pieces which, though undoubtedly attractive, the composer is reluctant to regard as 'real Ligeti': he calls them pastiches. The pieces in question are the *Passacaglia ungherese* and *Hungarian*

Opposite, looking for the
right formula: Ligeti holds a
composition seminar at the
1976 Darmstadt courses.

Rock, both composed early in 1978. They respond, somewhat wryly, to two obsessions of his Hamburg students: 'new tonality' and the repetitive rhythmic structures of rock music.

The *Passacaglia* is based on a sixteen-note theme in a regular minim pulse; though it contains all twelve notes of the chromatic scale, when placed in unison canon with itself, at a distance of two bars, it forms a mellifluous, irreproachably consonant two-part counterpoint of thirds and sixths (an offshoot of the lovers' music in *Le Grand Macabre*), with the end of each statement of the theme fusing seamlessly into a repetition at an octave lower. So in effect, one has an endless chain of descending thirds and sixths, which has to be hoicked up a few octaves every now and then, to prevent it from disappearing off the bottom of the keyboard. Set against this are melodies in Hungarian style, the figuration of which becomes gradually faster, finishing with a flurry of semiquavers. Formally, this is a process familiar from keyboard writing of the seventeenth century and even earlier; here it becomes a historicized special case of a basic 'Ligeti paradox': a piece which seems to be slow, but turns out, without any change of tempo, to be very fast.

Hungarian Rock, on the other hand, is fast and frantic from the start. It is a chaconne – that is, a piece based on a constantly repeated chord sequence. In this case, the basic material is a four-bar sequence for the left hand, which Ulrich Dibelius compares to a jazz-rock 'chorus' (though not even the Ramones had choruses lasting under five seconds!). Every bar uses the same (2+2+3+2) rhythm – a typically Eastern European rhythmic cycle, though not exclusive to that region. The right hand begins tentatively with single notes (memories of Miles Davies?), but soon develops into an exuberant solo, punctuated by ascending scale flourishes. At the end, the solo 'explodes' in the top register, and there is a slow epilogue, whose three lines of notation last almost half as long as the rest of the piece.

Even these small-scale pieces have a certain historical significance. In the late 1970s, the Great Debate among composers, critics, promoters and theorists was about whether or not the modernist tradition should be sustained, and these arguments had mainly to do with matters of complexity, abstraction, accessibility, expression and the like. What they largely ignored was the question of a composer's roots. Even in the heyday of the 1950s avant garde, when good style was equated with internal consistency, and lack of obvious reference to any external tradition, it was accepted that composers like Barraqué and Boulez continued a tradition of 'French clarity and elegance', that Stockhausen's aggressive intransigence sounded 'German', and that Berio, Nono and Maderna had 'a typically Italian lyricism', but there was no question of local references. Nono sometimes integrated Spanish rhythms into his earliest anti-fascist works, such as the *Epitaffio per Frederico Garcia Lorca*, but that was for explicitly political reasons, and his avant-garde colleagues were generally unimpressed. When the music of John Cage started to make an impression in Europe in the late 1950s (and later, that of minimalists such as Terry Riley and Steve Reich), its 'Americanism' was hailed on the surface as freedom from tradition, but also privately dismissed as non-European barbarism.

In the 1960s, the growth of 'pluralist' trends meant that the consistency rule no longer applied. Composers could change style within a work, and even appropriate music from other eras and other cultures, without necessarily losing face in progressive circles. Henze became a radical by mixing improvisation and South American references, Berio based a movement of his *Sinfonia* exclusively on quotations from other music, from Bach to the present day, and Stockhausen wrote two major electronic works (*Hymnen* and *Telemusik*) based respectively on national anthems and fragments of non-Western music from all kinds of cultures. Suddenly, everything external was permissible; only one's own musical backyard was taboo.

Like the high modernists of the late 1960s, the young neo-Romantics of the mid 1970s tended to take this cosmopolitanism for granted: what they were reacting against was their elders' passion for innovation. Certain commentators notwithstanding, most of them were not post-modern: they were simply anti-modern. But looking back at the music of the 1970s and 80s, one of the most striking traits among composers of many different aesthetic persuasions was, precisely, a re-evaluation of their own heritages. In Germany, the young Cologne composer Walter Zimmermann wrote a cycle of works called *Lokale Musik* which applied various arcane transformation processes to the folk music of his native Franconia, and Dieter Schnebel investigated the Allemanic dialect used by Hebbel in his *Jowaegerli*; in England, Michael Finnissy extracted extraordinary consequences from folk music in his hypervirtuoso piano piece *English Country-Tunes*. Nor was the 'big league' untouched by these trends. Steve Reich, after being influenced by Ghanaian music in works like *Drumming*, returned openly to his Jewish roots in *Tehillim* and many subsequent works; Cage paid explicit homage to American tradition in pieces like *The Harmony of Maine* and *Apartment House 1776* (in which old American hymn tunes are subjected to some relatively respectful chance operations), and Kagel, who as a young man in Buenos Aires used to go the cinema with his English tutor Jorge Luis Borges, emerged clearly as an expatriate Argentinian with his *Die Stücke der Windrose* ('Compass Pieces') cycle.

Much of this passed Ligeti by. For others, the late 1960s had been a period of wild diversification, but for him, it was a time in which he had meticulously refined his own style, without any obvious reference to external influences. Even though *Lontano*, in particular, had paid elliptical homage to the music of the Romantic era, there was no question of quotations, or of even a single bar that could have come from a nineteenth-century work. But in the 1970s, this changed; works like *Clocks and Clouds* paid direct homage to the minimalism of Reich and Riley, and the opera *Le Grand Macabre* embraced pluralism in many ways, including sudden switches of style, quotation and pastiche. But it is in the two pasticcios for harpsichord late in the decade that Ligeti first returns explicitly to his Hungarian roots, and however tongue-in-cheek the initial motivation, this would prove to be a constant feature of subsequent works.

One by-product of the sustained success of *Le Grand Macabre* was an invitation late in 1982, just before the London production, to appear on *Desert Island Discs*, a popular BBC radio programme in which each week's guest chooses eight pieces of music, as well as a book and a 'luxury' (Ligeti opted for Lewis Carroll's *Alice* books, and decided to rob the Prado of Hieronymus Bosch's *The Garden of Earthly Delights*). His disc choices, played in chronological order, were:

Gesualdo: *Beltà, poi che t'assenti* (Madrigals, Book 6)
Monteverdi: *Alle danze, alle gioie* (Madrigals, Book 9)
Mozart: String Quintet in C (first movement)
Schubert: String Quintet in C (second movement)
Verdi: 'Come un fantasima' (*Simon Boccanegra*, Act III, scene 3)
Brahms: Variations and Fugue on a Theme of Handel
Wolf: *Geh, Geliebter, geh jetzt* (Spanish Songbook)
Bartók: *Bánat* (No. 22 of 27 Choruses)

The painting Ligeti would take
to his Desert Island: *The
Garden of Earthly Delights* by
Hieronymus Bosch

Given the popular nature of the programme, one should not be too surprised at the lack of Ockeghem at one end of the historical spectrum, or the music of Ligeti and his contemporaries at the other. What the selection emphasizes is the degree to which Ligeti (when not composing) could be a normal, albeit highly sophisticated, 'music lover'. His basic selection criterion, as he told compère Roy Plomley, was 'quality', but there were other factors too. Gesualdo's introduction of 'madness' into music fascinates Ligeti, while the Monteverdi madrigal was chosen because 'I am an opera fanatic, and Monteverdi is not only the first, but one of the greatest opera composers'; he finds that the late madrigals 'are also operatic music' – very dramatic'. Mozart's quintets are 'absolutely the most beautiful music', while the slow movement of Schubert's quintet (which he nominated as the piece he would take if he were allowed only one disc) is 'a mystery. The beginning of the second movement, I think, is one of the deepest, most magic and mysterious things.' (Which in turn makes one think of Ligeti's *Tempest* project.)

Simon Boccanegra was there because of his general passion for opera, but also because he said that Abbado's performance with La Scala 'is really – dramatically, musically and technically – one of my favourite operas on record'. As for the inclusion of Brahms, this may seem natural, given that Ligeti had just composed a Horn Trio commissioned as a 'homage to Brahms' (of which more later). But slightly startlingly, Ligeti commented that Brahms was really not one of his favourite composers; this piece was included partly to reflect his love of the piano (he was distressed at having to leave out favourite composers such as Bach, Beethoven, Chopin and Schumann), and above all because, once again, the performance by Rudolf Serkin represented 'absolutely the highest level of playing'. The song by Wolf is another instance of 'magic', while the Bartók chorus, for him, is 'like a crystal … completely transparent'.

Many years later, in conversation with Peter Niklas Wilson, Ligeti elaborated a little more on his 'classical' tastes. As one can imagine, he does not care for music with grand, pathos-laden gestures (though he confesses to a sneaking fondness for some pieces by Tchaikovsky). He admires Wagner, but he does not love him; similarly he gives Richard Strauss full marks for orchestration, but much less for taste. Though he finds Debussy's music 'often so unbelievably mild' he finds him a 'greater poet' than Ravel, whom he does not much care for, despite their common predilection for 'clockwork' structures. When it comes to exemplary orchestration (always a preoccupation of his), he pairs Haydn and Stravinsky, but Stravinsky also intrigues him as an artful putative 'post-modernist', able to write an opera like *The Rake's Progress* which 'is pastiche, and yet is great art'. This, admittedly, was a view from the late 1990s, but it touches on issues that would also concern Ligeti in the years immediately following *Le Grand Macabre*.

7

Ligeti in Salzburg for the premiere of the revised version of *Le Grand Macabre*, July 1997

There is no fixed idea as to where all this is leading. There is no definitive vision of the future, no overall plan, from one work to the next...I grope around in various directions, like a blind man in a labyrinth, as soon as a further step has succeeded, it's already in the past, and then there are any number of conceivable ramifications for the next step.

Ligeti: 'Rhapsodische, unausgewogene Gedanken über Musik', *Neue Zeitschrift für Musik*, 1993

Local and Universal 1980-99

If the 1970s, for Ligeti, started with a flood of new discoveries and enthusiasms that somehow petered out, the 1980s were to prove enormously fertile, not so much in terms of the number of works produced, but in terms of new stimuli and fresh impetus. Once again, this put Ligeti on a quite different course to most of his contemporaries. For many composers of his generation, the 1980s were the time for crystallizing 'late styles', and writing spectacular epics to embody them: it was a decade of 'grand adagios'. Luigi Nono's music became desolately elegiac; much of his opera *Prometeo* borders on complete stasis, with exquisitely beautiful, madrigalesque fragments drifting between the multiple loudspeakers. Stockhausen engaged with opera on a more massive scale, adding two more instalments to his *Licht* cycle, one of which, *Montag*, lasts over five and a half hours – substantially longer than any part of Wagner's *Ring* cycle. When it came to sheer length, Stockhausen had competition from the American composer Morton Feldman, once the 'miniaturist' of the group around John Cage, whose chamber pieces from the 1980s, inspired by Middle-Eastern rug patterns, often lasted several hours (his String Quartet No. 2 also breaks the five-hour barrier). Cage himself scarcely shared Feldman's monomania (though an eight-CD set of him reading his *Diary: How to Improve the World (You will only make it worse)* probably sets some kind of record). Yet even Cage adopted a fairly consistent manner in the computer-generated 'time-bracket' pieces of his final years: predominantly sustained and peaceful works whose numerical titles (*Fourteen, Fifty-Eight* etc.) simply designate the number of players.

However impressive, these were all closed worlds, impervious to external musical influences. With Ligeti, it was quite different: as with Stravinsky half a century earlier, all kinds of music could serve as an inspiration, without there being any danger of his own creative personality being submerged. His fascination with ways of subverting traditional tunings flourished; but above all, the new decade was to be a period of rhythmic discoveries, from sources as diverse as medieval

Ligeti with the American composer Conlon Nancarrow (middle), whose enormously complex Studies for mechanical pianos greatly impressed him

Europe and central Africa. The biggest revelation of all, perhaps, came from the work of the American composer Conlon Nancarrow.

Nancarrow, born in 1912 (the same year as John Cage), had started out as a jazz trumpeter before going on to study composition with revered figures such as Walter Piston and Roger Sessions. Like many young artists with leftist inclinations, he went to Spain to fight against Franco and the fascist forces in the Spanish Civil War. On his return in 1939, he faced passport difficulties and latent McCarthyism, so he left the USA and settled in Mexico City, where he started composing works notable for the complex tempo ratios between the individual voices. It was an idea that Charles Ives had pioneered back in the early years of the century in pieces such as *Over the Pavements* (Ives took the view that people did not walk at the same speed unless they were in the army, and that art could profit from their example), and in the late 1940s Elliott Carter was beginning to take the same approach. But in Nancarrow's work, the rhythmic complexities soon went beyond what human performers could manage, so he turned to the mechanical 'player piano', and embarked on a huge series of increasingly intricate Studies, for which he hand-punched the rolls himself. Not only were the rhythmic ratios of these pieces enormously complex: at times they involved speeds way beyond human physical capacities.

This music remained almost completely unknown until 1960, when John Cage received some tape recordings via a New York librarian, and persuaded his choreographer friend Merce Cunningham to use some of them as a dance score. From this point on, Nancarrow's music was at least known and admired by a small circle, consisting mainly of young avant-gardists such as Gordon Mumma and James Tenney. In the late 1960s a recording of twelve of the studies was released, but it soon went out of print. So in Europe, at least, Nancarrow remained largely unknown until the mid 1970s, when the German composer Walter Zimmermann included him in a book about non-establishment American composition called *Desert Plants*.

It was purely by chance that Ligeti encountered Nancarrow's music. Sometimes it seems strange that a composer with such immense natural curiosity should have taken so long to discover works that already enjoyed a certain esoteric circulation. But this is presumably because, at any one time, Ligeti is interested in so many different things that there is just not room for any more, unless they happen to be brought to his attention. At any rate, in February 1980 he had come across an essay by the Berlin gallery owner René Block in a Berlin Academy of Arts catalogue. Block was best known as an advocate of the Fluxus movement, but in 'The Sum of all Sounds is Grey' he also wrote about a meeting with Nancarrow two years earlier in Mexico City, and reproduced a page from the score of Study for Player Piano No. 36. Ligeti was intrigued; later, he asked one of his composition students, Manfred Stahnke, who had just spent a year in the USA, whether he had come across any of Nancarrow's work. As it happened, Stahnke had already heard a recording of a couple of the player piano studies in the Musicological Institute at Hamburg University, just before leaving for the USA, but had not had time to tell Ligeti about their composer. Now he handed over various recordings, and Ligeti was hooked.

In 1982 Ligeti invited Nancarrow to Europe, and introduced concerts of his works. These 'concerts' were necessarily on tape, since there was no instrument in Europe capable of reproducing Nancarrow's rolls, and a débâcle in Mexico City back in 1964 had led the composer to refuse to hire out his own instruments. After a presentation in Cologne, Ligeti and Nancarrow got into conversation with the musicologist Jürgen Hocker, who was also intrigued by this music, and was determined to find an instrument on which the pieces could be presented 'live'. A couple of years later, Hocker found a suitable Ampico-Bösendorfer grand player piano in Belgium, but it was in such dreadful condition that it took him two more years to get it in working order. In 1987 the restored instrument got its first public exposure in Amsterdam, at a concert in the presence of the composer; the next year, the WDR in Cologne mounted 'Music and Machine: Nancarrow and Ligeti in Cologne'. Here Ligeti resumed contact with Hocker, and encouraged him to seek out a second instrument, so that Nancarrow's studies for two player pianos could also be presented in Europe. A few years later, Ligeti too would find a use for these instruments.

The fact that Ligeti had initially asked Manfred Stahnke about Nancarrow typifies the difference between Ligeti's Hamburg students in the 1970s and those in the 80s. The 1970s group were mainly Young Conservatives, preoccupied with disavowing the modernist innovations of the older generation. Though they, along with Wolfgang Rihm, initially spearheaded the 'New Romantic' movement in Germany, it is hard to imagine that Ligeti gained any great musical stimulus from them, and it is probably no accident that his only musical response to them was the two 'pastiche' pieces for harpsichord. They had nothing to tell him that he did not already know – they simply disapproved of much of what he did know. The 1980s group, on the other hand, seem more typically 'post-modern': one can imagine them endorsing George Santayana's phrase, 'We do not nowadays repudiate our predecessors – we pleasantly bid them goodbye.'

So what, in terms of music, does 'post-modernism' amount to? It is a catchword that overran academic circles in the 1980s and early 90s, and gave rise to a flood (or was it a swamp?) of doctorates, fellowships and professorial chairs. But it also had currency outside the universities, and gave focus to a change in artistic practice. It involved a whole series of assumptions, some of them contradictory. The main one was that until recently, there had been an outlook called 'modernism' – in musical terms, extending back not just to Schoenberg, but to Beethoven or even earlier – which attached particular importance to innovation and progress (embodied in Ezra Pound's injunction 'Make it new!'), and that this outlook was now exhausted or irrelevant. That did not necessarily mean that composers had a new, 'theoretical' justification for being conservative (though some took it that way: the American composer George Rochberg, for example, started writing string quartet movements in the style of late Beethoven, Mahler, Bartók and others). But it did imply that there were no more great agendas, no more gladiatorial combats such as those between serialism and indeterminacy. Any stylistic approach, past or present, could be the object of intelligent – and perhaps slightly detached, even ironic – investigation.

Accordingly, the Hamburg classes of the 1980s found him surrounded by young composers with an omnivorous curiosity almost matching his own, and 'discoveries' became the order of the day. Often these extended way back into the past. Though Ligeti, by the time that he wrote the Requiem, was familiar with Netherlands composers such as Ockeghem, who was active in the fifteenth century, it was not until the early 1980s that he became familiar with the rhythmic intricacies of late medieval music. In the early 1970s, the German record company Electrola had established a series called 'Reflexe' dedicated to early music, and each year a 'Christmas Box' of six discs appeared. One day another student, Annette Kreutziger-Herr, brought in a disc of works by Johannes Ciconia, including a three-part polymetric canon 'Le Ray au soleyl', which particularly aroused the enthusiasm of Stahnke and two other composers, Hans Peter Reutter and Hubertus Dreyer. Ligeti himself found a recording of Solage's ultra-chromatic *Fumeux fume*, which must surely rank as one of the most startlingly eccentric compositions of the fourteenth century, and Stahnke brought in works by Senleches, as well as *Angelorum psalat*, the one surviving work of Rodericus. Common to most of these works is an extraordinary rhythmic intricacy, even by twentieth-century standards. Like the avant garde of the 1950s, the composers had found themselves in a period of notational innovation which opened up new rhythmic possibilities, and like the Darmstadt school, they were determined to push them to the limit. In some pieces by Matteo da Perugia, for example, the three parts are effectively in three different but exactly aligned tempos, and have no point of mutual contact except at the very beginning and the very end.

Yet another stimulus came from the Puerto Rican composer Roberto Sierra, a member of the composition class from 1979 to 1982. He drew Ligeti's attention to the complex polyrhythms of much Caribbean and South American music, and traces of these found their way into works from the 1980s such as the Piano Concerto. More significantly, just before going back to Puerto Rico to take up a position as Director of Cultural Affairs, Sierra also introduced Ligeti to a gramophone record called *Banda Polyphonies*, containing examples of vocal and instrumental ensembles recorded in the Central African Republic by the Israeli musicologist Simha Arom. Once again, he was fascinated by the intricacy of the music. A couple of years later he met Arom in Jerusalem, and was able to look at the meticulous transcriptions he had made of this music. When Arom published his book *Polyphonies et polyrhythmies instrumentales d'Afrique Centrale* ('African Polyrhythm and Polyphony') in 1985, Ligeti contributed a preface in which he comments on 'the proximity I feel exists between [African music] and my own way of thinking with regards to composition: that is, the creation of structures which are both remarkably simple and highly complex'. In this music, as in so much of his own, there was an element of paradox: 'the patterns performed by the individual musicians are quite different from those which result from their combination. In fact, the ensemble's super-pattern is in itself not played and exists only as an illusory outline ... What we can witness in this music is a wonderful combination of order and disorder which in turn merges together producing a sense of order at a higher level.'

Not all of the group's discoveries had to do with rhythm. Another senior American 'outsider' to attract Manfred Stahnke's attention was Harry Partch. As we have seen, Ligeti was already familiar with the music; he had even visited Partch during his Stanford sojourn in 1972, but had not been overly impressed by what he heard. Stahnke, on the other hand, was immediately inspired to write some pieces of his own which use tunings similar to Partch's, and one of these, *Partch Harp*, attracted Ligeti's attention and rekindled his own interest (never far below the surface) in new tunings.

A rehearsal of the Horn Trio
with violinist Saschko
Gawriloff, for whom Ligeti
would later write his Violin
Concerto

However, the first major work from the 1980s, the Horn Trio, pointed in a very different direction. Some years previously Ligeti had been approached by the pianist Eckart Besch to write a companion piece to Brahms's Horn Trio. 'As soon as he pronounced the word horn,' said Ligeti (long before he had actually written the piece), 'somewhere inside my head I heard the sound of a horn as if coming from a distant forest in a fairy tale, just as in a poem by Eichendorff.'

Had he written it immediately, it might have been a very different piece. The three principal instruments of horn, violin and piano are favourites of the composer (along with the cello), and had been allocated flamboyant roles in works from the 1960s, beginning with the horn cadenza near the beginning of *Nouvelles Aventures*, and ending with the wild piano cadenza in the final movement of the Chamber Concerto. Even if Maderna's death had severed the umbilical cord to those earlier pieces, there are passages enough in *Le Grand Macabre* that show that a taste for extremes was still present (as it also was in the pieces for two pianos). But by the early 1980s, the situation was very different. On the surface, Ligeti seemed to have dried up; he had not written anything for three or four years – nothing since the two pastiche pieces for harpsichord.

The Trio was the piece with which Ligeti determinedly found his feet again. An essential element of this recovery was to redefine his relationship to musical 'tradition', though only as a composer – as a listener his position had always been quite clear. Of all the major figures of the post-war avant garde, Ligeti had the least adversarial relationship towards the 'classical' tradition: Xenakis ignored its existence, Cage said it was irrelevant, Stockhausen regarded it as something to be superseded, and Boulez started out admitting only a hard-line trinity of late Beethoven, Bach and Debussy which was gradually softened (somewhat) through his work as a conductor. Ligeti, in comparison, was a straightforward 'music lover' (as one can see from his 'Desert Island Discs'), albeit at a very sophisticated level. A photograph exists of him playing the piano in his Hamburg apartment in the early 1970s; what is on the music stand is not Ligeti, nor even Webern, but Schubert's late B flat sonata.

On the other hand, when it came to composing, he was no fan of 'retro' movements. If, in some respects, he was to return to traditional elements, there had to be a contemporary sensibility as well: even when composing a 'homage to Brahms', it was important to emphasize that one was living in 1982, not 1882. The first movement of the trio opens with an emblematic 'warping' of tradition: a classic descending 'horn figure' (Ligeti was thinking of the opening of Beethoven's 'Les Adieux' sonata, among other things), but with the conventional intervals somewhat compressed, and allotted to the violin, not the horn. And there are some radical factors at work here, beneath the idyllic, nostalgic surface. The violin melodies are based on units of five semiquavers, and the horn's on triplets, creating a virtual 15:8 ratio between the two!

What this emphasizes is that the rhythmic complexities that currently fascinated Ligeti, whether in Nancarrow's studies or in African polyphony, were stylistically neutral. Whereas the first encounter with American minimalism had led to music with clear echoes of Reich and Riley, these later fascinations are not necessarily tied to a particular style (the nostalgic world of the trio is worlds away from Nancarrow): presumably this is one reason why they have been a more lasting presence in Ligeti's work. Nor, even here, has Ligeti's obsession with alternatives to tempered tuning disappeared. When the second subject appears (yes, this is indeed a conventional sonata form), the horn part exploits the 'natural' tunings of the 7th, 11th and 13th harmonics.

In the second movement – marked 'Vivacissimo molto ritmico', but also 'fresh, sparkling, light, gliding, dancing' (isn't there a hint of overkill here?) – the neo-Bartókian aspect is even clearer: a quasi-Bulgarian ostinato (3+3+2) runs all the way through the piano part. Nevertheless, the relationship of the other parts (often including the pianist's other hand) to this ostinato – that is, their independence of it – is very much of the late twentieth century. As for the third movement, a scherzo and trio, any Hungarian composer who writes an 'Alla marcia' inevitably invites comparison with Bartók. But here, thinking back to the two-piano pieces, an appropriate subtitle might be 'Self-Portrait with Béla Bartók and Steve Reich', since the violin part, which doubles the piano exactly at the outset, gradually gets out of step, creating considerable rhythmic intricacies. When the opening returns, after a smoothly flowing middle section, the horn adds all kinds of anarchically untempered contributions.

The fourth, most striking movement is a Lamento which continues the lament tradition of Monteverdi and Purcell, yet also has links to all kinds of European folk traditions, from Spain to Greece. For Ligeti, understandably, the direct inspiration lay nearer to home, in the Hungarian laments he knew from Transylvanian folk music, and to some extent in Romanian music. The basic falling figure (extrapolated from the work's opening) involves a striking inversion of the scale figures in Ligeti's previous works, which were predominantly ascending, disappearing up into the ether (the opening of *Melodien* is a classic example), rather than plumbing the depths. However, it is not the technical aspect that is important here. This was arguably the most directly emotional music Ligeti had ever written: no more 'super-cooled expressionism', but the same sort of desperate but controlled fatalism that one finds in the slow movement of the Brahms Horn Trio. In the course of the 1980s and 90s, the descending 'lamento' figure would become an increasingly prominent feature of Ligeti's work, and in almost every case, the emotional expression would be equally direct.

Attempts have been made to portray the trio in terms of reverse shock tactics, of 'épater l'avant-garde'. This really does not seem very convincing. For a start, ten years after Maderna's death, there was not much of an avant garde left to shock; secondly, conservative works rarely shock, though they may disappoint (in any case, any shock value inherent in 'returns to tonality' had been milked for all it was worth back in the late 1960s, in collage pieces like Castiglioni's enormous *Sinfonie guerriere ed amorose*). It seems more realistic to say that the trio reflects a period in which the self-doubts of the mid 1970s had, if anything, increased. On the face of it, it was a barren period, in which almost four years went by without a new work. But not for want of trying: as Ligeti said in 1992, 'stylistic problems were responsible for the big jump from the pieces for two pianos to the Horn Trio ... What we used to call the avant-garde situation has changed: there is a new generation, which I am not part of – that is, the "new expressionists". Somehow I had to find my own place and know what I was doing. My music was meant to become much more melodic, with a sort of non-diatonic diatonicism. I had to try and stay the same as I was, but without regurgitating the same old thing. I actually wrote a lot during these years: a whole series of starts on a piano concerto ... And the Horn Trio was a sort of detour.'

The years preceding the trio had indeed been far from inactive. Ligeti had made as many as twenty separate attempts to start the piano concerto, and found himself having to start afresh each time. And to the extent that the trio suggests a retreat from the modern world, it gives a quite misleading impression of Ligeti in the early 1980s. We have seen the enthusiasm with which he and his Hamburg students explored the musics of many eras and cultures. Ligeti's personal agenda as a composer was by no means to indulge his ties to tradition; to a degree, he had done that in the trio, and that was enough. His project now was to find a different kind of modernism, quite disjunct from the structural and aesthetic ideologies of the Cologne/Darmstadt years; for him, 'post-modernism' – an aesthetic buzzword of the 1980s – meant renewing the spirit of modernism by leaving one particular manifestation of it behind, and crystallizing new ones. It is in this spirit that one needs to see the endless cast-off beginnings of the Piano Concerto: it was not just a matter of starting a new work, but of launching a new personal aesthetic.

However conservative in some respects, the Horn Trio decisively broke the drought that had followed *Le Grand Macabre*. Within a year, Ligeti had completed two superb new choral works which primarily look forwards, not backwards: the *Drei Phantasien* based on poems by Friedrich Hölderlin, and the *Magyar etüdök* ('Hungarian Etudes'), in which Ligeti returns after almost thirty years to the poems of Sándor Weöres. If the trio seems, in creative rather than stylistic terms, like a 'convalescent's hymn of praise' (as Beethoven called the slow movement of his String Quartet Op. 132), then the choral pieces suggest the subtitle of the second part of Beethoven's Adagio – 'feeling new strength'.

In the course of the late 1960s and 70s, the poetry of Hölderlin, the German romantic poet who had written many of his finest poems during his final years of madness, had become something of a *cause célèbre* among the European avant garde. Maderna had led the way with a series of works which were finally brought together as the quasi-opera *Hyperion*, and the first really significant work of Nono's 'late period' was the string quartet *Fragmente-Stille: an Diotima*, also inspired by Hölderlin. Nor was his rediscovery the exclusive province of the avant garde: composers as disparate as the young Wolfgang Rihm (who tended to specialize in texts by mentally disturbed authors) and the ageing Benjamin Britten wrote striking song cycles based on his poems. Heinz Holliger also wrote a major *Scardanelli-Cycle* based on Hölderlin texts.

In Ligeti's case, what is remarkable is not so much the particular choice of poet – Hölderlin had long been a favourite of his – as the decision to set a poetic text at all. This is something he had not done since his Budapest years, some three decades earlier. The many choral works written in the meantime had either used his own phonetic concoctions, or familiar sacred texts, which had mainly been approached with a broad brush, establishing a general atmosphere rather than responding to particular words or phrases (the one striking exception being the Dies irae from the Requiem). Now, in the wake of *Le Grand Macabre*, his attitude had evidently changed: it is clear that the three poems chosen – *Hälfte des Lebens* ('Midway through Life'), *Wenn aus der Ferne* ('When from Afar') and *Abendphantasie* ('Evening Fantasies') – appealed not only on account of their 'atmosphere', but also because of the constant changes of imagery, which encourage an almost madrigalesque response (and by now, Ligeti was also a Gesualdo fan).

The music itself is part new, part familiar. The old micropolyphony is present, but it tends to set out from unison canons with clearly audible opening motives; moreover, given the often graphic responses to Hölderlin's text, it tends not to last for long. The microtonal inflections of the Double Concerto now find their way into Ligeti's choral music, but here the effect is often to suggest Eastern European folk music, rather than innovations in concert hall music. Particularly notable is the use of rhythm for dramatic effect – *Le Grand Macabre* apart, this is some of Ligeti's most passionately rhetorical music to date.

The *Magyar etüdök* are very different in character – shorter, more explicit in their references to Hungarian music, but also much more complex and continuous in their construction, as the title suggests (though it actually derives from a collection of 'virtuoso' short poems by Sándor Weöres); they are accordingly more detached in tone, as well as more light-hearted. Whereas the sixteen singers in the Hölderlin settings were essentially treated as a single choir (however soloistic their roles might be at times), in the *Magyar etüdök* the singers are divided into two or more choirs. This is particularly striking in the final piece, *Vásár* ('Village Fair'), in which the choir is divided into five groups, each advertising its wares over and over again: apples, dog-sleds, frocks and booties, mead, and a travelling circus. The groups enter one after another, each in a different tempo, and with startlingly complex ratios – 9:11:14:16:19! Impossible as this seems, Ligeti finds a way of writing it down such that one group serves as a practical point of orientation for the others.

It is typical of Ligeti – or at least, the Ligeti of the 1980s and onwards – that these kinds of technical intricacies, which were to become increasingly important in subsequent works, are not announced portentously, but with as light a hand as possible. Here one sees a basic distinction between Ligeti and most of the other major post-war figures, who have sought to associate the technical innovations of their later years with 'great works', as if one necessarily implied the other. The clearest example is Stockhausen's *Licht*, in which every part of a 24-hour work is to be derived from a single 'super-formula'; but Boulez's introduction of live electronics in *Répons*, a work that seemed to get longer every few years, Feldman's two-hour expositions of his 'Turkish rug' technique, and even Cage's family of 'number pieces' created from the same computer program, all tended in this direction.

With Ligeti, on the other hand, age has brought an increasing distrust of all grand systems: 'I'm not a guru,' he insists, 'I don't want to preach, I don't want to improve the world. All these utopias are alien to me.' The engagement with all kinds of compositional intricacies, going hand in hand with a fascination with instrumental virtuosity, is a personal passion – it does not seek to determine what anyone else does, or to make the aesthetic value of a work dependent on the espousal of particular techniques. The same sort of distrust applies to the emotional element of his work. Though it is clear that personal expression has come to play a more obvious role in recent works, it may be significant that the strongest emotional statements have tended to come in small pieces, such as the Etudes for piano (1984–).

The 1980s was also a decade in which Ligeti's interest in new mathematical and scientific discoveries was rekindled. In 1983 he saw the first computer representations of fractals, and the idea of 'self-similar' structures immediately seemed applicable to music. Not that Ligeti has ever seen himself as a 'scientific' composer (though he had once thought of becoming a scientist rather than a composer), but he is fascinated by much scientific research, and sees real parallels between the artist and the scientist. For him, both are people whose natural curiosity leads them into 'exploring connections which others have not yet recognised, and sketching structures that have not yet existed'. Similarly, though mathematics plays no great role in his music – there are all kinds of 'temporary algorithms' but few grand arithmetical designs – he is intrigued by the fact that much

Mandelbrot sets, realized as computer graphics. This kind of fractal (self-similar) structure inspired the fourth movement of Ligeti's Piano Concerto (1985–8).

mathematical research, like composition, sets out from more or less arbitrarily designed 'rules of play'.

He even became temporarily excited about the prospects for computer music. The synthesized voice of the computer Hal in Kubrick's film *2001* had actually been something of a landmark in computer sound synthesis, and Ligeti's visit to another, rather less distinguished, science fiction epic, *Tron* (released in 1982), fascinated him. Even though he thought the film itself was fairly awful kitsch, he was utterly intrigued by the high-speed computer graphics, which suggested an imminent new world; for once, he abandoned his scepticism about prophesies, and said, 'I believe (this is my feeling) that in the immediate future, in the second half of the 1980s, a "genuine" computer music will come about, which goes way beyond the principles known at present.' By general consent, this did not happen.

The early 1980s were also a period of increasing official recognition – paradoxically, at a time when Ligeti himself was least certain of his path. Not that he had ever been short of prizes and awards: *Apparitions* and the Requiem had won first prizes at the ISCM competitions in 1964 and 1966, and *Lontano* won the UNESCO Competition in 1969. He had been awarded the honorary medal of Helsinki University in 1967, been made a member of the Berlin Academy of Arts in 1968, an honorary member of the Steiermark Musikverein in Graz in 1969, a member of the Free Academy of the Arts in Hamburg in 1971 and so forth. But now the regular trickle became a flood. In 1984 alone he was awarded the Parisian Prix Ravel, the Budapest Béla Bartók-Ditta Pásztory Prize (the pianist Pásztory was also Bartók's second wife), was made a member of the American Academy and Institute of Arts and Letters and also an honorary member of the ISCM. Some of these awards were more than just honorary. In 1986 he gained the richly endowed Grawemeyer Award (for his first book of Etudes) and some years later, in 1993, the Ernst-von-Siemens Music Prize, the most spectacular of the European prizes. The ultimate prize, perhaps, was Sony Corporation's decision, of which more later, to undertake a Complete Edition of the composer's works on CD.

The Piano Concerto which had been causing him so much trouble achieved a provisional three-movement form by mid 1986, and was given its première at the Styrian Autumn Festival in Graz, Austria.

In this form, it is surely a concertino rather than a concerto, however complex and demanding the first movement may be. Hearing it in concert, Ligeti says that his 'feeling for form called for a continuation', so in the course of the next eighteen months he added two more movements; the final version had its première on 29 February 1988 in Vienna. The additions were not just a matter of making the work longer: they change the overall balance. The key movement here is the fourth, which Ligeti regards as the 'central movement' of the work. Rather than adding another slow movement and finale to create an arch-shaped fast-slow-fast-slow-fast pattern, he wrote a highly complex movement which acts as a counterweight to the first.

The first movement, which represents Ligeti's first major engagement with the African and Caribbean polyrhythms that had so intrigued him in recent years, operates on two metric levels: at the outset, the ensemble is split into two parts, one playing in 4/4, the other in 12/8. The second movement is the only one that can really be regarded as a 'slow movement', but the chaste, austere sobriety of the opening bars is soon undermined by the constant use of low instruments in uncomfortably high registers, and high instruments in their lowest range (Morton Feldman used to exhort his students to consider the possibility of a piccolo sounding below the double bass), not to mention the introduction of instruments such as ocarina and slide-whistle which virtually rule out the possibility of 'pure' intonation. The scherzo-like third movement is the one most obviously concerned with rhythmic and melodic 'illusionism' of the kind introduced in *Continuum*, and in works by Steve Reich such as *Drumming*: the individual parts are composed in such a way that when heard together they lead the listener to perceive 'virtual' melodies and rhythms which are not actually present.

Turning to the movements added after the initial première, the fourth is one of Ligeti's few pieces to adopt a 'scientific' model not just at a metaphorical level, but also at a literal one. The inspiration here is the computer simulations of fractal structures – of Julia and Mandelbrot sets – that he first saw in 1983. The basis of these structures is complete 'self-similarity': at every level, from the tiniest detail to the total form, the same basic shapes are involved. As so often, there is also a 'Ligeti paradox' at work: although the tempo is fast, the texture is so fragmentary that there is no real impression of speed.

A performance of the Piano
Concerto, with Ueli Wiget
and Ensemble Modern,
Frankfurt

As the texture builds up, we come to realize that initially we had been at the periphery of what the composer calls a 'maelstrom' – a dense kaleidoscope of interlocking segments whose hectic motion is apparent from a 'medium' perspective, but which, once one is at its centre, again becomes 'static', albeit in a much more convulsive, overwhelming way. The brief fifth movement, whose whirling piano entry curiously recalls a similar gesture which opens the second movement of Busoni's piano concerto, summarizes and extends the preoccupations of the previous movements, albeit in a way that systematically negates the traditional grand finale mentality: the more complex the processes, the more glittering and effortless their presentation.

'With the Piano Concerto,' wrote Ligeti, 'I offer my aesthetic credo: my independence both from the criteria of the traditional avant garde and from those of fashionable post-modernism.' Clearly there has to be more to a 'credo' – even an aesthetic one – than mere independence, especially when it comes from a composer who is so responsive to the artistic and scientific world around him. In this case, the implicit message seems to be: keep looking for the new and astonishing, but be prepared to find it anywhere, and not just in the places where you had got used to searching for it. Not, for example, in the extension of a familiar 'Darmstadt tradition', but in unfamiliar musics that have found their own independent paths to complexity, or in extra-musical ideas that offer rich and surprising perspectives. In many of his comments, Ligeti leaves no doubt that, in principle, he prefers complexity to simplicity, so long as the former is not just associated with having lots of notes (the almost motionless opening of the slow movement of Schubert's Quintet is also, in its own way, extremely complex). Even for the unsuperstitious and unmystical Ligeti, an essential component of great art is sustained magic, and the trance-like state he experienced as a child going to the opera is something he still seeks and finds.

The works in which all the diverse influences on Ligeti's later music are most evidently explored are the stupendous series of piano Etudes begun in the mid 1980s. Curiously, Ligeti's fascination with the étude format had been preceded by, of all people, John Cage, who wrote a set of 32 *Etudes australes* for piano in the mid 1970s, and followed them up with some *Etudes boréales* for cello and for piano, and a further 32 *Freeman Etudes* for violin – staggeringly difficult pieces which were not completed until 1990. Initially, following Debussy rather than Chopin (let alone Cage), Ligeti planned two books with six études apiece. But the second book blew out to eight pieces, and a third book is now under way (at the time of writing, there are seventeen études in all). This is not a matter of readjusting the schedule from twelve to twenty-four: the composer now regards the Etudes as an open, infinite sequence. He hopes to complete at least a fourth book, but that, he says, with tongue firmly lodged in his cheek, 'depends on God'.

Unlike Chopin or Liszt, Ligeti has written his études in the full knowledge that he will not be able to play them himself. On the contrary, he says, 'the initial impulse was, above all, my own inadequate technique ... I would love to be a fabulous pianist! I know a lot about nuances of attack, phrasing, rubato and formal structure. And I absolutely love to play the piano, but only for myself.' So these are by no means the études of a non-pianist; on the contrary, they arise not only from Ligeti's love of the piano music of Scarlatti, Chopin, Schumann and Liszt, but from his own direct physical contact with the keyboard. Stravinsky once said that 'the fingers are great inspirers', and so it is for Ligeti too. He writes: 'I lay my ten fingers on the keyboard and imagine music. My fingers copy this mental image as I press the keys, but this copy is very inexact: a feedback emerges between idea and tactile/motor execution. This feedback loop repeats itself many times, enriched by provisional sketches: a mill wheel turns between my inner ear, my fingers, and the marks on the paper. The result sounds completely different from my initial conceptions: the anatomical reality of my hands and the configuration of the piano keyboard have transformed my imaginary constructs.'

Though nearly all the études in Book 1 have evocative titles (as ever, in Ligeti's beloved French), they are usually afterthoughts, as with Debussy's *Préludes*. As Constantin Floros has shown by reference to the sketches, all sorts of different titles and references come to the composer's mind in the course of composition, but individual pieces are almost never written to a pre-existing programme. There is a generating musical idea, or perhaps a basic mood, but the 'final' title comes later. For example, the titles considered for the exuberant first étude included *Pulsations* and *En blanc et noir*. The latter would have been a homage to Debussy, but also a reference to the way in which the two hands are polarized between the white keys (right hand) and the

black ones (left). 'Pulsations', on the other hand, could have been applied to almost any of the études: it is the theme for the whole set, arising in equal part from the strongly rhythmic character of Nancarrow's études, and the regular fast pulsation that underlies many folk musics, but especially the African music that had been such an exciting discovery for Ligeti in the preceding years.

The eventual title, *Désordre* ('Disorder'), is more subtle in its references. At one level, it is ironic: nothing could be more remorselessly organized than this étude, which is one of Ligeti's two avowedly 'scientific' pieces, being based on the self-similar structures of the Koch snowflake (the exactness of the analogy is of secondary interest: what the scientific model offers here is inspiration, not legitimation). *Cordes vides* ('Open Strings') is, inevitably, a study in fifths, while *Touches bloquées* returns to the 'blocked keys' technique already explored in the second of the two-piano pieces. *Fanfares* also revisits (recent) familiar territory, namely the 'Bulgarian' ostinatos of the Horn Trio's second movement. If some of the melodies in open fifths in *Cordes vides* already had a hint of Thelonious Monk about them, in *Arc-en-ciel* ('Rainbow') Ligeti's fondness for jazz comes nearer to the surface: the piece is marked (bilingually) 'con eleganza, with swing', and the discreetly hothouse harmony seems at times to allude equally to Messiaen (another synaesthetic composer, with a fondness for 'rainbow harmonies') and to Bill Evans, providing a gentle reminder that both had a fondness for added sixths, and that Messiaen's *Turangalîla-symphonie* is exactly contemporary with the first stirrings of 'modern jazz'.

Dedications are usually a secondary consideration for Ligeti: the natural recipients are performers, commissioners and patrons, as well as friends and colleagues, especially if they have significant anniversaries coming up. So the first three études are dedicated to Pierre Boulez, on the occasion of his sixtieth birthday, while the fourth and fifth are dedicated respectively to pianists Volker Banfield and Louise Sibourd (Sibourd had given the première of the first étude of the first book, Banfield all the rest). But in the sixth and final étude, *Automne à Varsovie* ('Autumn in Warsaw'), which combines Ligeti's typical technical preoccupations with an overt emotionalism that picks up the threads from the last movement of the Horn Trio, it is a different story. The tumultuous piece is dedicated 'to my Polish friends', and clearly refers to troubled times in Poland in the early 1980s, at the time the Solidarity movement was emerging. Of two alternative titles, 'Warsaw Etude' (shades of Chopin's 'Revolutionary Etude') and 'Warsaw Autumn', the latter is particularly significant: it refers to the annual new music festival founded in 1956, which is where the whole Polish avant garde had its first springboard: older composers like Lutosławski and Serocki, as well as the young Górecki and Penderecki. But it was not just a festival for Polish composers: Ligeti had first been represented there in 1959 with *Artikulation*, and after a performance of the Requiem in 1968, a work of his had been included almost every year. In the early 1980s, the Composers' Union which played a large role in organizing the festival became very much involved in the political situation; almost all of its members supported Solidarity, and opposed the government of Jarazelski; this had actually led to the cancellation of the 1982 festival. So one can assume that at least in part, *Automne à Varsovie* is Ligeti's act of solidarity with Polish composer friends, who mounted a mini Ligeti Festival at the 1985 Warsaw Autumn: in addition to Banfield's premières of *Touches bloquées* and *Automne à Varsovie*, there were performances of *Lux aeterna*, *Ramifications*, the *Drei Phantasien*, both string quartets and the Horn Trio.

Polish demonstrators in Warsaw defiantly holding up a 'Solidarity' banner in August 1981; the political turmoil in Poland was an inspiration for Ligeti's Etude No. 6.

Ligeti at the Théâtre de l'Odéon in Paris, 1992. This picture became the basic emblem for Sony's Complete Works CD series.

There was a break of a few years between the two books of études, during which time Ligeti was mainly occupied with completion of the Piano Concerto; work on the second book began in 1988. Shortly afterwards, in 1989, he retired from the Musikhochschule in Hamburg, though he continued to enjoy contact with favourite students. He denied that this represented any great change in his life, but it did raise the question of whether or not he wanted to go on living in Hamburg. Initially he more or less divided his time between Hamburg and Vienna. The latter city, of course, took him back almost to the borders of his Hungary. It is clear that Ligeti has never lost a sense of Hungarian identity, and that if anything, it has strengthened in recent years. He has said that in principle, at least, he would like to return to a free, post-Cold War Hungary, but that, as in much of Eastern Europe – most notably in the former Yugoslavia – the fall of communism has simply unveiled a rabid nationalism which he finds just as unacceptable. For a while, this inveterate lover of French titles toyed with the idea of moving to Paris, but in the end he decided to stay on in Hamburg, not least because that environment has 'worked' for him: he knew that he could get on with creative work there, and one could always go to Vienna or elsewhere to recuperate.

The music of the Balinese gamelan was one of many kinds of rhythmically intricate non-Western music that fascinated and inspired Ligeti in the 1980s.

If the pieces in the first book of the Etudes – especially Nos. 1 and 6 – seemed formidable at the time they were published, some of the eight studies that make up the second book eclipse them considerably, at least in terms of the strength and dexterity required, and the 'presto' markings of the first book now become 'prestissimo'. The polyrhythmic explorations of the earlier études are still there, but are now allied in many cases to sheer torrents of notes which suggest that Liszt's *Transcendental Studies* have become as much of a model as the études of Chopin and Debussy.

Just as the first étude, *Désordre*, split the white and black notes between the two hands, so *Galamb Borong*, which opens the second book, divides the chromatic scale into two whole-tone scales, and allocates one to each hand. The title is 'fake Indonesian': it does not actually mean anything, but the piece is intended to evoke the shimmering of a gamelan orchestra, through a ripple of regular notes from which various melodic lines emerge at different speeds. *Fém* (Hungarian for 'metal') is a glittering, spiky piece which Ligeti says should be played 'with swing' – one of many occasions in later works which invoke the performance style of jazz. The ninth étude, *Vertige*, is the first of the ultra-virtuoso pieces in the second book: a constant and indeed dizzying swirl of descending scales which is clearly intended as a keyboard counterpart to the Shepard scales (scales which, due to a psychoacoustic 'trick', seem to continue infinitely up or down) that are found in many of Jean-Claude Risset's electronic works.

Vertige brought Ligeti back into contact with Jürgen Hocker's player pianos. Not that this was his original intention, but he happened to show Hocker the score, and Hocker commented that this piece, with its constant multi-layered chromatic scales, seemed to be an ideal candidate for a player piano version. So with the aid of a composer colleague, Hocker made a transcription, and sent a tape of the result to Ligeti. There was no immediate response, and Hocker was unsure what, if anything, to do next. Then, out of the blue, early in 1992, Ligeti rang him. *Vertige* is dedicated to Mauricio Kagel, and a performance had been planned for a concert at the Cologne Philharmonic, celebrating Kagel's sixtieth birthday. But in the meantime, the pianist Volker Banfield had been seriously injured in a car accident, and the chances of getting another pianist to learn this remorseless finger-breaker in time were slim. Ligeti proposed that the player piano version be given instead, and was so pleased with the result that he gave Hocker free rein to make other transcriptions. To date, he has made versions of *Désordre* and *Touches bloquées* from Book 1, and the whole of Book 2. These versions are not just literal transferences of the original works to the player piano: they involve additions (such as octave doublings) which exploit the mechanical instrument's ability to literally play in all registers simultaneously, as opposed to the traditional virtuoso simulations of this effect pioneered by Chopin and Liszt. Tempos are decided in consultation with the composer; in general, these are faster than the tempos prescribed or foreseen for 'live' pianists.

The tenth étude, *Der Zauberlehrling* ('The Sorcerer's Apprentice'), breaks with the tradition of French titles so as to avoid direct association with Dukas's symphonic poem (and by extension, the cartoon antics of Mickey Mouse), though there are certainly passing references to Debussy. It is another *tour de force*, the ultra-rapid repeated notes of which are a test of the piano mechanism as well as the pianist – Ligeti asks here for 'almost the speed of *Continuum*', and the aim is that the notes should fuse into a continuous flickering. *En suspens* ('In Suspension'), an 'Andante con moto with the elegance of "swing"' dedicated to Kurtág, brings a moment of repose; while *Entrelacs* ('Interlacings') reweaves threads from *Galamb Borong*.

Explicitly programmatic or quasi-autobiographical elements are rare in Ligeti's music, but there are exceptions. One of the most striking of these is the thirteenth étude, *L'Escalier du diable* ('The Devil's Staircase'). Originally Ligeti had planned to write two books with six études apiece, and since Book 1 had ended so bleakly, with *Automne à Varsovie*, he planned to have a radiant, uplifting piece at the end of Book 2 – something along the lines of Debussy's *L'Isle joyeuse*. He had in mind a line from Shakespeare's *The Tempest*: 'The isle is full of noises, sounds and sweet airs.' In February 1993 he went to Santa Monica, a town close to the Californian coast, and started work. The environment proved to be anything but restful. The weather on the west coast that winter was appalling: Los Angeles was flooded, with mudslides destroying hundreds of homes. For three days the storms were so bad that Ligeti could not leave the house. And as he puts it, 'then the island paradise turned into this *L'Escalier du diable* étude, a completely black piece.' Nor was it just the stormy weather that changed the character of the piece and turned it from a twelfth study – the eventual Etude no. 12 was *Entrelacs* – to an 'unlucky' thirteenth. Cycling around Santa Monica (he does not drive), Ligeti was appalled by the contrast between the ultra-lavish homes of the Beverley Hills millionaires and the slums inhabited by the poor: it was 'more than my once-socialist soul could bear'.

The Etude No. 14 that closes Book 2 is once again a piece of sensational difficulty. The title, *Columna Infinita*, referring to the famous sculpture by Constanin Brancusi, was another afterthought. Ligeti only knew of the sculpture by repute – he had never actually seen it; but at a certain point, it struck him that since his étude was designed to keep going endlessly up and up, it was actually rather like Brancusi's column. Since the sculptor – whose work he greatly admired – was Romanian, and had erected this sculpture in the Romanian city of Tîrgu-Jiu, a homage was due, even though the city (and Brancusi's origins) lay on the opposite side of the Carpathian Alps to Transylvania. A few years later, Ligeti received an analysis which 'proved', quite spuriously, that he had modelled his work exactly on the sculpture he had never even seen: Brancusi's *Infinite*

Constantin Brancusi's
Columna Infinita (1938)

Column consists of 162 octahedrons, and Ligeti's étude had 162 ascending sequences ...

In terms of mechanical realization, the fourteenth étude is a special case: it was conceived from the start in two versions: one for 'human' pianist, and an 'ideal' version for player piano, which is at least half as fast again as the current recorded 'live' versions. Here the player piano version is actually the original, and a first score was marked 'for player piano (ad lib. living pianist)'. This seems to bring Ligeti directly into line with Nancarrow, whose études are not really designed for human performers, though a few of them have lain at least on the border of human possibilities, and have thus posed an irresistible challenge to certain virtuosos. Yet Ligeti hedges his bets a little: he says that he does not rule out 'real' pianists playing this piece – in fact he welcomes it – but at the present, he doubts whether even the best pianists will quite be able to achieve the speed he has in mind as an ideal. So the mechanical version is a goal towards which 'live' practice can gradually aim.

Admittedly, this approach raises some questions. Does the 'mechanical' Etude No. 14 really sound so much better than the imperfect human versions? Does the music gain any otherwise unrevealed artistic dimensions from being played this fast? Back in the early 1960s, Milton Babbitt's public lectures on his new

RCA MkII Synthesizer included an electronic version of Bach's
Two Part Invention in F major which was infinitely faster than even
a Glenn Gould could have managed. But it did not actually say
anything interesting about Bach's work, or leave one dreaming of
a time when real pianists could play it that fast. What it did show
was that listeners could still hear the music at that speed – that it did
not turn into an undifferentiated blur of notes. The same reservations,
it seems to me, could be levelled at Ligeti's 'player piano étude'. It is
precisely the humane and humanist dimensions that Ligeti's studies
add to the mechanical intricacies of his models that underpin their
aesthetic status.

Sheer velocity and accuracy is not the only motivation for their
mechanical realization: both *Désordre* and *Galamb Borong* have been
recast for two player pianos, so as to make the different scales used in
the two hands more audible. Nor have the Etudes been the only
recipients of mechanical reinterpretation: *Continuum* has been given
two new, post-harpsichord lives: in a version for two player pianos,
and another for barrel organ, an instrument that Ligeti first encountered in his childhood years; in addition Jürgen Hocker has recently
made a two player piano version of the Three Pieces for Two Pianos.

The Etudes have effectively brought not just Ligeti, but
contemporary piano music generally, back into mainstream awareness.
They represent an enormous challenge to even the most skilled virtuoso, but while it is common enough to hear them being described as
'unplayable', this particular use of the epithet 'unplayable' is different
to the normal dismissals of complex new works: it involves the kind
of slightly awesome reputation accorded to Godowsky's Chopin
transcriptions. A typical response is that of Alfred Brendel, who says,
'You need three or five hands to play Ligeti. But it's worth the trouble',
and recommends them to his best students 'if they are feeling heroic'.
Accordingly, some pieces from Book 1 are beginning to find their way
into international piano competitions, and no doubt those from Book
2 and its successors will follow.

Alongside the second book of études, Ligeti began work on another
ongoing series, of more modest dimensions, but scarcely less intricate:
a series of *Nonsense Madrigals*, written for the six voices of the King's
Singers. The texts are mainly Victorian English – Lewis Carroll above
all, but also the more prosaic William Brighty Rands; in addition,

there is an English translation from Struwelpeter, and a setting of the alphabet. There is nothing very Victorian about the music, apart from a gently ironic fragment of 'God Save the Queen'; essentially, the *Nonsense Madrigals* are Ligeti's response to the fourteenth- and fifteenth-century Franco-Flemish music that he and his students had found so intriguing. And though there are no obvious medievalisms in the melodies or the harmony (in any case, there are no known six-part works from the fourteenth century!), all sorts of aspects of the medieval motet have been carried across: the simultaneous use of different but related texts, pairs of voices moving at different speeds (for example, in ratios of 2:3 or 3:4), and the use of a single slow moving line as a linking thread through the piece. Why nonsense rhymes? At one level, because of Ligeti's fascination with the playful use of language (and, in principle, composers can find words just as inspiring as 'meaning'), as well as the paradoxes and incongruities which are often a basic component of 'nonsense verse'. But for works inspired in part by the fourteenth-century avant garde, the use of 'irrational' texts is doubly appropriate; there can be few texts as quirky and obscure as those concocted by fourteenth-century *fumeurs* (possibly an early European group of opium smokers) such as Solage and Hasprois. A typical ballade by Hasprois, for example, begins: 'Since I am smoky, full of smoke/I have to smoke, for if I didn't smoke/Those who say that I'm a smoke-head/Would be proven wrong, by smoke!'

The medieval affiliations of the *Nonsense Madrigals* are particularly clear in the first piece, *Two Dreams and Little Bat*. The seemingly surreal title has a simple explanation: the two main texts, by William Rands, are 'The Dream Of A Girl Who Lived At Seven-Oaks' (upper voices) and 'The Dream Of A Boy Who Lived At Nine-Elms' (lower voices), with the two layers in a tempo ratio of 3:4. In the midst of this, the tenor sings Lewis Carroll's 'Twinkle, Twinkle, Little Bat' in long values', and just as Carroll's verse twists the familiar 'Twinkle, Twinkle, Little Star', so Ligeti's tenor part twists the tune of the nursery rhyme around, so that it is easier to recognize on paper than by ear.

Not all of the other madrigals are equally intricate, though none of them is exactly simple! *Cuckoo in the Pear-Tree* is like a fractured fourteenth-century caccia (a lively genre often involving pictorial elements); the *Alphabet* madrigal, whose text consists simply of the

Ligeti looks on as György Kurtág takes a master class during the International Bartók Seminar at Szombathely, Hungary, in 1990.

letters from A to Z, is predominantly in the calm, static *Lux aeterna* style, but extracts some Gesualdo-like moments of drama from the later letters. *Flying Robert* is a passacaglia whose placid repetitions serve as the backdrop for an increasingly agitated and virtuoso foreground, as the delinquent juvenile of Hoffman's cautionary tale ventures out into stormy weather, and is blown away for ever. Similarly in the fifth piece, a setting of Carroll's *Lobster Quadrille*, the mildly irritable 'Will you walk a little faster?' is repeated throughout the piece (here, the literal meaning of an ostinato – as something 'obstinate' – is perfectly represented), while varying degrees of porpoise-induced chaos erupt around it. The final piece, *A Long, Sad Tale*, was added a few years later, in 1993. Once again, there are two texts: the one that gives the piece its title comes from an early chapter of *Alice's Adventures In Wonderland*, while a second, more agitated layer consists of 'doublets' drawn from Carroll's *Original Games and Puzzles*, in which one word is transformed into another (normally with an opposite meaning) by changing one letter at a time, e.g. head – heal – teal – tell – tall – tail.

The biggest individual work of the early 1990s is the Violin Concerto, and like its predecessor for piano, it had a protracted genesis. Saschko Gawriloff, for whom it was written, had known Ligeti since the 1960s – he met him at the Darmstadt courses, and since Gawriloff was sitting at the leader's desk in the Cologne Radio Symphony, he got to talk with him whenever the orchestra was performing one of his works. More regular contact came in 1984, when Gawriloff was the violinist in the first performances of the Horn Trio. Talking to the composer, Gawriloff got the impression that he was on the look-out for a new commission, and proposed a violin concerto. It was true that Ligeti did not have the same first-hand knowledge of the violin that he had of the piano and the cello, but one only had to look at the violin parts of the Second String Quartet, or indeed the Horn Trio, to surmise that a Ligeti violin concerto had great potential. To Gawriloff's dismay, Ligeti dismissed the idea out of hand: 'No way. Out of the question. I just don't have the time.' Yet within a few days he phoned to say he had changed his mind; the project now appealed to him, but the time problem remained – the concerto would not be ready for a few years.

In fact, it took six years, and even then, only three movements of the eventual five were ready. Barely even three: Gawriloff got the last instalment of his solo part only a few days before the première, and the conductor Gary Bertini and the Cologne Radio Orchestra had to wait until two days before the performance to get the last of the parts. A première took place in November 1990, as part of a festival at the Cologne Philharmonic Hall somewhat arcanely entitled 'Encountering the Diaspora with Israel'. Kagel was in the audience, and according to Gawriloff, his response afterwards was: 'It's a good piece, but not so much for the soloist.' This coincided rather exactly with the violinist's own opinion – more than once he had thought of Beethoven's famous and abrasive response to his favourite violinist Schuppanzigh: 'What do I care for your wretched fiddle when the spirit comes over me!'

As it turned out, Ligeti was not satisfied either: he virtually threw out the first movement. And now Gawriloff, who had left Ligeti to his own devices first time round, felt emboldened to make a few requests, the most important of which represented a real innovation in relation to modern concertos: he asked to be allowed to write a cadenza for the fifth movement, based on materials from the rejected first movement. Ligeti agreed; the result comes right at the end of the work.

Constantin Floros has given an intriguing account of the various stages the concerto went through. For a long time, he says, Ligeti was undecided as to how many movements the concerto should have, and as late as March 1990 he was still toying with the idea of a kaleidoscopic form with as many as eight movements, all clearly polarized between fast and slow. In homing in on a five-movement form, he imagined two scherzos – one chromatic and muted, the other in 'Romanian polymodal' style. Yet he also wanted a contrast between a 'fluid' movement and a vigorous, 'metallic' one, as well as two slow set pieces: a lamento in the tradition of the Horn Trio, and a passacaglia. Floros presents two different drafts for a five-movement form; the first has mainly French titles, such as 'fluide' and 'résolute', while the second has Italian titles, and associates all but the first movement with a particular texture and/or melodic style (e.g. 'polyphonic', 'chromatic' etc.).

In its final version, the Violin Concerto takes Ligeti's fascination with different kinds of intonation to a new level. In doing so, it takes a few cues from the 'spectralist' composers who had been active in Paris since the late 1970s – Gérard Grisey, Tristan Murail and Horatiu Radulescu. These composers had looked at new ways of deriving melody and harmony from the natural overtone series: for example, an early piece by Grisey, *Partiels*, treats every instrument in the ensemble as if it were an overtone ('partial') of a low E, and many of Radulescu's works extrapolate their harmony from a theoretical 'fundamental' pitch which actually lies below the audible range. The result can feature familiar intervals – thirds, fourths, fifths and so forth – but is most notable for its introduction of a wide range of microtonal intervals, some of which are so small that one can barely distinguish between them.

Ligeti does not go to quite these lengths. However, in addition to all kinds of more *ad hoc* inflections of normal tuning, two of the orchestral strings, a violin and a viola, are retuned to match the 7th and 5th partials of the double bass. The result – a more 'scientific' version of the blurring already found in *Ramifications* – can be heard at the very beginning of the opening Praeludium, albeit only just: the solo violin and retuned viola enter on *ppppp* and *pppp* respectively. The continuous tremolo texture seems at first like a throwback to the works of the late 1960s, but here it serves a different function: instead of destroying any sense of pulse, it provides the quasi-African continuous fast pulsation on to which all kinds of conflicting rhythmic layers can be grafted.

The slow second movement (*Aria, Hoquetus, Chorale*), clearly reminiscent of the Piano Concerto's second movement, is Ligeti's 'Air

on the G String': the solo violin stays on its bottom string for the first
seventy-four bars! The tripartite title does not mean that there are
three sections (though that is also true), but that there are three
processes at work. The first is a slow, melancholy violin melody, very
obviously 'Hungarian' in style, that seems to be constantly repeating
the same phrases, but never actually does so for more than a few
notes; it gradually draws other instruments into its wake. The chorale
elements introduce all kinds of anarchic intonations – a nicely ironic
touch, when one considers the central role that chorale harmonization
plays in the teaching of traditional harmony. The brass parts
emphasize 'out of tune' partials, while the woodwind players exchange
their normal instruments for ocarinas, which are notoriously incapable
of sustaining a stable pitch.

The third and fourth movements are paradox pieces, slightly
reminiscent of the 'fractal' movement of the Piano Concerto. The
third is marked 'Presto fluido', but at first the 'fluido' aspect makes

The composer at his desk,
c. 1990, surrounded by
writing implements

the presto almost imperceptible: even though the upper strings are playing very fast descending scales, these act as the background for a leisurely, highly romantic violin melody that would not be out of place in the Szymanowski violin concertos, and the initial effect is that of a slow movement. Bit by bit, the wind instruments enter, with the horn taking the lead in 'bending' normal intonation, and though the tempo remains the same, the changes of timbre and articulation gradually make it clear that the underlying tempo is actually very fast. The fourth movement, a passacaglia, follows an analogous course, but viewed through the other end of the telescope. Here the framework is slow ('Lento intenso'): an ultra-smooth chorale over which all kinds of agitated, disparate materials are superimposed. As the level of unrest increases, the woodwind players exchange their 'stable' instruments for the wavering intonation of recorders and ocarinas (as in the Piano Concerto); like the previous movement, the final climax stops suddenly, 'as if torn off' – an old usage in a new context.

As the concerto proceeds, there is a growing sense of imminent catastrophe. Even if the final movement declines to produce a terminal débâcle – that kind of rhetorical pathos remains alien to Ligeti – all the elements deployed within its complex assemblage of disparate layers (including the return of the retuned orchestral soloists from the first movement) have a fatalistic air. Though one could not really describe the work as an 'anti-concerto', this is certainly an 'anti-finale': its scepticism about the possibility of grand resolutions is embodied in the decision to let the soloist write his/her own cadenza, and in the final perfunctory, derisive orchestral snorts that follow every attempt to write one.

The Etudes apart, Ligeti's latest work to date is a six-movement Viola Sonata, compiled over the course of four years and completed in 1994. The viola is not an instrument that Ligeti had been particularly drawn to in the past, though he found the slightly hoarse, acerbic sound of the low C string attractive: 'reminiscent of wood, earth and tannic acid'. But in 1990 he went to a WDR concert in Cologne given by Tabea Zimmermann, and found himself intrigued by the 'grainy, striking but always tender' sound of the G string as well. Two strings out of four were enough to stir him into thinking about a sonata, and the next year he wrote a short solo piece, *Loop*, as a contribution to the 90th-birthday celebrations of his first Western publisher, Alfred Schlee of Universal Edition. A couple of years later, he wrote another viola piece (*Facsar*) in memory of his former composition teacher Sándor Veress; then, the request for a première in Gütersloh in 1994 was sufficient incentive to write the remaining four movements, with the two already written becoming the second and third movements.

The first movement, *Hora lunga* ('Slow Dance'), is played entirely on the C string. Once again, it is an 'evocation' of the Romanian folk music that Ligeti heard in his childhood in Transylvania, but without exact quotation: it uses the same kind of 'near repetition' as the second movement of the Violin Concerto, and shares the same melancholy mood, which is intensified here by the use of 'natural' microtones – three degrees of lowering of the pitch corresponding to 'pure' major thirds and minor sevenths, as well as the 11th overtone. The whole of *Loop* is in double stops, one note of which is always an open string. Through the tempo remains constant, as does the metre (alternating bars of 10 and 8 semiquaver beats), the music seems to get faster and faster because more and more short values are introduced, making the constant changes of finger position increasingly hair-raising. Even so, the movement is to be played 'in the spirit of jazz – elegant and "relaxed"'. *Facsar*, the tribute to Veress, means something like 'twisting', but also, the composer says, 'the painful, twitching feeling one has in one's nose when one is about to cry'. The frantic 'Prestissimo con sordino' (dedicated to Klaus Klein) which constitutes the fourth movement of this sonata ends with the violist dramatically throwing the mute to the floor, and launching straight into a Lamento, again all in double stops, which is dedicated to Ligeti's long-time assistant Louise Duchesneau. Though the Balkan references of this movement may be most apparent to listeners, Ligeti also invokes influences from the more distant ethnic cultures of the Ivory Coast and Melanesia.

The final movement (dedicated, like the first, to Tabea Zimmermann) is a *Chaconne chromatique*. Typically, Ligeti warns listeners not to expect a sequel to Bach's epic chaconne in the Partita in D minor for solo violin. 'My sonata,' he says, 'is far more modest, a-historical, and can't cope with monumental forms. I use the word chaconne in its original sense: as a wild, exuberant dance in a strongly accented triple metre, with an ostinato bass line.'

In the next couple of years, two factors got in the way of the completion of further works. The first was a substantial revision of

Le Grand Macabre. Looking at the work from a distance of almost two decades, Ligeti found that, for his taste, it rested on too many cheap tricks, was dramatically flawed, and evaded the whole question of style that was facing him at the time. The process of revision did not even aim to reconcile the composer to his creation: it just aimed to fix up theatrical miscalculations, and to remove some instances of 'bad taste' that he now regretted (in terms of 'overkill' rather than prudishness), so that perhaps he would dislike his 'masterpiece' less.

The main thrust of the revision was to get rid of all the spoken elements, either by setting the words involved to music, or by getting rid of them altogether. Since the first scene has few of these, it was left almost untouched, whereas the second scene underwent major surgery. In the third scene, the ministers' alphabet of abuse was now set to music, but much of the subsequent dialogue disappeared, tightening the structure considerably. The new version of the final scene is mainly notable for a slight expansion of the ending.

Making the revision was enormously difficult: by the mid 1990s, Ligeti felt utterly remote from the Ligeti who had composed *Le Grand Macabre* in the mid 1970s. So he had to decide whether to risk the kind of stylistic schizophrenia that overtook Stravinsky's completion of *The Nightingale* (after a gap of only five years!), or to try to transplant himself back into his style of twenty years earlier. He opted for the latter solution, and describes the results as extremely disagreeable – a sort of extreme musical jet-lag. Getting back to his own current work afterwards was almost as difficult, but less unpleasant: at least he had a sense of returning home.

The eventual première of the revised version at the 1997 Salzburg Festival was also a mixed experience. By general consent, the musical performance, conducted by Esa-Pekka Salonen, was superb. The audience also responded enthusiastically to the bleak but glittering, post-atomic setting imposed by controversial producer Peter Sellars, in which Breughelland was replaced by Chernobyl, and which left no doubt that the world had indeed come to an end. But Ligeti loathed it, describing it as 'a scandal', and made no secret of his opinion in press interviews. 'I have to defend myself against this,' he said, 'because it's not just a matter of staging, it's a transformation of the piece's content … All of my piece is ambiguous, and he [Sellars] has taken this ambiguous piece and made it into a completely unambiguous story, a propaganda story with an obvious moral.' Sellars, with plenty of support marshalled behind him, was predictably unrepentant, and the same production went on to a five-day season at the Théâtre du Châtelet in Paris in February 1998.

The other obstacle to new composition, highly gratifying in its own way, was the Sony project to record a Complete Edition of Ligeti's works on CD to coincide with the composer's seventy-fifth birthday in 1998. The primary conductor for the series, Esa-Pekka Salonen, had the advantage of being not only an outstanding young artist, and a talented composer who had studied with leading Italian composers Niccolo Castiglioni and Franco Donatoni, but also a passionate Ligeti enthusiast. In 1992, Salonen had become principal conductor of the Los Angeles Philharmonic, and it was after hearing some of his performances there that Ligeti decided that he would be the man for a new series of recordings; since Salonen was exclusively contracted to Sony, they were the obvious company for Salonen and Ligeti to approach. Considerable financial and other support came from the philanthropist Vincent Meyer, the president of the London-based

Between recording sessions in December 1997 Ligeti discusses *Le Grand Macabre* with Esa-Pekka Salonen, the main conductor in Sony's Complete Works series.

A scene from Sellars's
controversial Salzburg
production of Le Grand
Macabre (1997); Sellars
chose a post-atomic
setting for his production of
the opera.

Philharmonia Orchestra, and also an important benefactor of the
Glyndebourne opera; in return, the series is dedicated to him.

The outcome was more than a recording project. Salonen wanted
the orchestra in question (the Philharmonic) to become familiar with
the works as concert repertoire, and accordingly devised a series of
concert programmes in which Ligeti's music would be performed
alongside more familiar twentieth-century works. For example,
Apparitions and *Lontano* were coupled with a Bartók piano concerto
and Skryabin's *Le Poème de l'extase*, while *Clocks and Clouds* and
Atmosphères shared a programme with Debussy's *Nocturnes* and Ravel's
Daphnis et Chloé.

As a matter of principle, Ligeti wanted to be closely involved in the
preparation of the performances, and so he was; at times, says Salonen,
it was almost as if Ligeti were doing the conducting. Seeing Ligeti at
a rehearsal, one has the impression of a composer who knows exactly
what he wants, and how to get it. Not that he is a tyrant; on the
contrary, he is a practised diplomat (it is only when he encounters an
unresponsive, uncommitted orchestra that he 'gets tough'). Fellow
Transylvanian Peter Eötvös, who has frequently conducted Ligeti's
works, describes him in this context as 'an unbelievably gifted actor –
in fact more like a director'. However, a few laudatory remarks at the
outset can be the prelude to twenty minutes or more of exact requests
involving the smallest details of intonation and balance. Everything he
says is aimed at making the music as effective as possible, and every
comment is something to which players can respond immediately.
From this one might easily infer that Ligeti's view of his pieces is a very
inflexible one. Not so, say the players of the Frankfurt-based Ensemble
Modern, who have often worked with him in recent years; yes, he
always knows exactly what he wants, but his view of a piece (or of what
he wants emphasized within it) may change from one occasion to
another. Though he does not revise works à la Boulez, he inwardly
reinterprets them. In fact, Salonen reveals that in the course of the
Sony project, some actual changes have been made, even to 'classics'
like *Aventures*. 'I am the composer,' says Ligeti, 'and I have the right
to change things.'

Apart from taking up a lot of time attending rehearsals and
recording sessions, the Sony project obliged Ligeti to take a definitive
view of what he wanted to include in the 'Ligeti canon'. Above all,

these decisions involved works from the Hungarian period, reaching as far back as his late teens. In some cases, minor revisions seemed called for, which took up more time; interesting as it is to hear the works of his juvenilia, it would be distressing to think that their rehabilitation might have got in the way of a promised Third String Quartet (for the Arditti Quartet), additions to the ongoing books of Etudes and, above all, the projected 'Alice' opera. However, there will undoubtedly be new works to look forward to; at the end of 1998, he was immersed in the composition of a horn concerto. Provisionally, this work will have the mosaic eight-movement format initially considered for the Violin Concerto, but as ever, this may be subject to change.

A few years ago, a German newspaper asked Ligeti what he would most like to be, and he replied: 'A very rich tramp.' In other words, while he welcomes the material comforts that go with being an established and much-performed major composer, he does not care much for the publicity and the forced image that accompanies it: if he has to be an actor, then he wants to choose the terms and conditions. Thus the flood of requests for interviews attaching to the Sony project and his 75th birthday, though gratifying at first, soon sent him into retreat. It is not that Ligeti has become a misanthropist, but time spent discussing finished works is time taken away from new ones. Furthermore, recurrent illness over recent years, coupled with a perfectionism that makes composing a slow process, has made time a precious commodity. So the recent acquisition of his musical 'estate' (autograph scores and sketches) by the Sacher Foundation in Basle had the welcome advantage of giving performers and scholars access to his 'composer's workshop' without him needing to be personally involved. And when it comes to composing, the scruffiest old clothes he can find will suit him best – not as a kind of symbolic hair shirt, but simply because they are comfortable, and do not get in the way. While he could no doubt afford a work desk with a huge computer screen, and the latest versions of notation programs such as Score, Finale or Sibelius, he personally finds the smell of newly sharpened, multi-coloured pencils more reassuring, and more inspiring.

Reaching a broad public is not a priority for Ligeti – the word 'élitist' is one he might disapprove of in social terms, but not at all in relation to art. His concern is always with the highest possible standard, the best possible achievement, and with the innate importance of art –

not as a source of messianic statements, which he detests, but as an expressive product of human intelligence and imagination. Such an approach does not court popularity, but does not exclude it either – the enormous popular success enjoyed by Haydn's late works at the time of their composition is proof enough of this. Approaching a new millennium in a period when commitment to concert halls and opera houses is at best unpredictable, it is impossible to predict the future of Ligeti's music, or indeed that of anyone else. But just now, it is thriving, and each new piece is eagerly awaited; even so, the exceptional position of his works in late-twentieth century composition has long since been a matter of established fact.

Classified List of Works

Like those of many contemporary composers, Ligeti's works often defy conventional classification: this listing inevitably involves some approximations in terms of genre. It is not comprehensive, at least as far as the works composed before 1956 are concerned. Inclusions of Ligeti's earliest compositions mainly reflect the contents of the Sony CD collection of Ligeti's Complete Works. This collection was produced in collaboration with the composer, and can be taken as representing Ligeti's definitive view on which of the surviving early works are worthy of retention. A fuller listing, including lost works, can be found in Ulrich Dibelius's *Ligeti: Eine Monographie in Essays*. Lost and uncompleted works are not listed below. Finally, details of first performance are given where known.

Opera

Le Grand Macabre, opera in two acts, libretto by Michael Meschke and György Ligeti, after *La Balade du Grand Macabre* by Michel de Ghelderode (1974–7, revised 1996). fp Stockholm, 12 April 1978 [concert version: *Scenes and Interludes from the Opera 'Le Grand Macabre'*. fp Berlin, 21 December 1978; arrangements (in collaboration with Elgar Howarth): *Mysteries of the Macabre,* for trumpet and piano (1988), version for trumpet or coloratura soprano and chamber ensemble (1991), version for trumpet or coloratura soprano and orchestra (1992); *Macabre Collage – Suite for Orchestra* (1991)]

Other Musico-Theatrical Works

Die Zukunft der Musik – eine kollektive Komposition ('The Future of Music – a Collective Composition'), for one protagonist and audience (1961). fp Alpbach, August 1961

Poème symphonique, 'musical ceremony' for 100 metronomes, ten performers and a conductor (1962). fp Hilversum, 13 September 1963

Rondeau, 'One-Man Theatre for an actor and tape', text by Ligeti (1976). fp Stuttgart, 26 February 1977

Vocal

Három Weöres-dal ('Three Weöres Songs'), for soprano and piano, text by Sándor Weöres (1947). fp (Nos. 1 & 2) Junsele, 23 March 1970

Négy lakodalmi tánc ('Four Wedding Dances'), for three female voices and piano, adaptations of Hungarian folksongs (1950). fp Budapest, 1952

Öt Arany-dal ('Five Arany Songs'), for soprano and piano, texts by János Arany (1952). fp 1952

Aventures, for soprano, contralto, baritone, and seven instrumentalists, phonetic text by Ligeti (1962). fp Hamburg, 4 April 1963

Nouvelles Aventures, for soprano, contralto, baritone, and seven instrumentalists, phonetic text by Ligeti (1962–5). fp Hamburg, 26 May 1966

Der Sommer ('Summer'), for soprano and piano, text by Friedrich Hölderlin (1989)

Choral
(unaccompanied unless otherwise stated)

Idegen Földön ('Far from Home'), for three-part female choir, texts by Bálint Balassa and from Hungarian and Slovak folk poetry (1945–6). fp Stockholm, 17 April 1971

Betlehemi királyok ('Kings of Bethlehem'), text by A. Joszef (1946)

Bujdosó ('The Fugitive'), for three-part mixed choir, text from Hungarian folk poetry (1946)

Húsvét ('Easter'), for two- and three-part children's choir, texts from Hungarian folk poetry (1946)

Magány ('Solitude'), for three-part mixed choir, text by Weöres (1946). fp Stuttgart, 18 May 1983

Magos kösziklának ('From a High Mountain Rock'), for three-part mixed choir, adaptation of a Hungarian folksong (1946)

Ha folyóviz volnék ('Like a Stream'), four-part canon, text from Hungarian translation of Slovakian folk poetry (1946). fp Budapest, 1954

Lakodalmas ('Wedding Dance'), for four-part mixed choir, arrangement of a Hungarian folksong (1950). fp Budapest, 1953

Haj, Ifjúság! ('Heigh, Youth!'), for four-part mixed choir, text: Hungarian traditional (1952). fp Budapest, 1952

Hortobágy, for four-part choir, adaptations of Hungarian folksongs (1952). fp Budapest, 1953

Kállai kettös ('Double-Dance from Kálló'), for four-part mixed choir, adaptations of Hungarian folksongs (1952). fp Budapest, 1952

Pletykázó asszonyok ('Gossiping Women'), four-part canon, text by Weöres (1952). fp Budapest, 1954

Inaktelki nóták ('Songs from Inaktelke'), for two-part mixed choir, adaptations of Hungarian folksongs (1953). fp Budapest, 1954

Pápainé ('Widow Pápai'), for eight-part mixed choir, text: traditional Hungarian ballad (1955). fp Stockholm, 16 May 1967

Éjszaka/Reggel ('Morning/Night'), two pieces for mixed choir, text by Weöres (1955). fp Stockholm, 16 March 1968

Mátraszentimrei dalók ('Songs from Mátraszentimre'), for two- and three-part children's choir, text adapted from Hungarian folksongs (1955). fp Saarbrücken, 9 June 1984

Requiem, for solo soprano and mezzo-soprano, two mixed choirs and orchestra (1965). fp Stockholm, 14 March 1965

Lux aeterna, for sixteen-part mixed choir (1966). fp Stuttgart, 2 November 1966

Clocks and Clouds, for twelve-part female choir and orchestra, phonetic text by Ligeti (1973). fp Graz, 15 October 1973

Drei Phantasien nach Friedrich Hölderlin ('Three Fantasies after Friedrich Hölderlin'), for sixteen-part mixed choir (1982). fp Stockholm, 26 September 1983

Magyar etüdök ('Hungarian Etudes'), for sixteen-part mixed choir, texts by Weöres (1983). fp (Nos. 1 & 2) Stuttgart, 18 May 1983; (No. 3) Metz, 17 November 1983

Nonsense Madrigals, for six-part choir, texts by W. B. Rands, Lewis Carroll and H. Hoffmann (in English translation) (1989–93). fp (Nos. 1–4) Berlin, 25 September 1988; (complete) London, 28 October 1989

Orchestral

Régi magyar társas táncok ('Salon Dances from Old Hungary'), for flute, clarinet and string orchestra (1949)

Román Koncert ('Romanian Concerto') (1951)

Apparitions (1959). fp Cologne, 19 June 1960

Atmosphères, for large orchestra without percussion (1961). fp Donaueschingen, 22 October 1961

Concerto for Cello and Orchestra (1966). fp Berlin, 19 April 1967

Lontano, for large orchestra (1967). fp Donaueschingen, 22 October 1967

Melodien (1971). fp Nuremberg, 10 December 1971

Double Concerto, for flute, oboe and orchestra (1972). fp Berlin, 16 September 1972

San Francisco Polyphony (1974). fp San Francisco, 8 January 1975

Concerto for Piano and Orchestra (1985–8). fp (provisional 3-movement version) Graz, 23 October 1986; (final version) Vienna, 29 February 1988

Concerto for Violin and Orchestra (1990–92). fp (provisional 3-movement version) Cologne, 3 November 1990; (final version) Cologne, 8 October 1992

Works for Chamber Orchestra

Fragment, for ten players (1961). fp Munich, 23 March 1962

Ramifications, for string orchestra or twelve solo strings (1969). fp (string orchestra) Berlin, 23 April 1969; (twelve strings) Saarbrücken, 10 October 1969

Chamber Concerto, for thirteen instruments (1969–70). fp Berlin, 1 October 1970

Chamber

Andante and Allegro, for string quartet (1950)

Baladä si joc ('Ballad and Dance'), for two violins (1950)

Six Bagatelles, for wind quintet, arrangements of *Musica ricercata*, Nos. 3, 5, 7, 8, 9, 10 (1953). fp (complete) Södertäjle, 6 October 1969

Sonata for solo cello (1949–53). fp Paris, 24 October 1983

String Quartet No. 1 (*Métamorphoses nocturnes*) (1954). fp Vienna, 8 May 1958

String Quartet No. 2 (1968). fp Baden-Baden, 14 December 1969

Ten Pieces for wind quintet (1968). fp Malmö, 20 January 1969

Hommage à Hilding Rosenberg, for violin and cello (1982)

Trio, for violin, horn, and piano (1982). fp Hamburg-Bergedorf, 7 August 1982

Sonata for Viola (1991–4). fp Gütersloh, 23 April 1994

Keyboard
(solo piano unless otherwise stated)

March, for piano duet (1942)

Allegro (1943)

Polyphonic Etude, for piano duet (1943)

Capriccios No. 1 and No. 2 (1947)

Invention (1948)

Három lakodalmas tánc, for piano duet (1950)

Sonatina (1950)

Ricercare, for organ (1951)

Musica ricercata (1951–3). fp Sundsvall, 18 November 1969

Chromatische Phantasie (1956)

Volumina, for organ (1961–2, revised 1966). fp Amsterdam, 10 May 1962; (revised version) Kiel, 8 March 1968

Trois Bagatelles (1961). fp Wiesbaden, 26 September 1962

Etude No. 1: Harmonies, for organ (1967). fp Hamburg, 14 October 1967

Continuum, for harpsichord (1969). fp Basle, October 1968

Etude No. 2: Coulée, for organ (1969). fp Graz, 19 October 1969

Three Pieces for Two Pianos: 1. 'Monument'; 2. 'Self-Portrait with Reich and Riley (and Chopin in the background)'; 3. 'Bewegung' (1976). fp Cologne, 15 May 1976

Hungarian Rock, for harpsichord (1978). fp Cologne, 20 May 1978

Passacaglia ungherese, for harpsichord (1978). fp Lund, 5 February 1979

Etudes, Book 1 (1984–5): *Désordre*. fp Bratislava, 15 April 1986; *Cordes vides* ('Open Strings'). fp Warsaw, 24 September 1985; *Touches bloquées* ('Blocked Keys'). fp Warsaw, 24 September 1985; *Fanfares*. fp Hamburg, 1 November 1985; *Arc-en-ciel* ('Rainbow'). fp Hamburg, 1 November 1985; *Automne à Varsovie*. fp Warsaw, 24 September 1985

Etudes, Book 2 (1988–93): *Galamb Borong*. fp Berlin, 23 September 1988; *Fém* ('Metal'). fp Berlin, 23 September 1988; *Vertige*. fp Gütersloh, 5 May 1990; *Der Zauberlehrling* ('The Sorcerer's Apprentice'); *En suspens* ('In Suspense'); *Entrelacs*; *L'Escalier du diable* ('The Devil's Staircase'); *Columna Infinitá*

Etudes, Book 3 (1995–): *White on White*; *For Irina*; *Etude No. 17*

Adaptations of Keyboard Works for Mechanical Instruments
(versions not by Ligeti, but made with his express consent and encouragement)

– For barrel organ (by Pierre Charial)
Capriccios 1 & 2: *Invention; Musica ricercata; Continuum; Hungarian Rock*

– For player piano(s) (by Jürgen Hocker)
Continuum; Monument-Self-Portrait-Bewegung; Etudes, Book 1 (Nos. 1, 4 & 6); *Etudes, Book 2* (complete)

Electronic Music

Glissandi (1-track, realized at WDR, Cologne) (1957)

Artikulation (4-track, realized at WDR, Cologne) (1958). fp Cologne, 25 March 1958

Pièce éléctronique No. 3 (planned 1958; realization started by Ligeti, but abandoned)

Further Reading

As noted in the Preface, Ligeti has been far better served in German than in English. The two main English sources are the monograph by Paul Griffiths and the volume of interviews listed immediately below. Readers interested in exploring the technical and aesthetic aspects of Ligeti's work in some detail should look out for a forthcoming book by Richard Steinitz, published by Faber Music, which has the composer's imprimatur.

Books in English

Ligeti, G. and others *Ligeti in Conversation* (London, Ernst Eulenberg, 1983)
Ligeti is the ideal interviewee, and though the four interviews don't extend much beyond *Le Grand Macabre*, they are an essential introduction to the composer's ideas.

Griffiths, P. *György Ligeti* (London, Robson Books, 1997)
Griffiths has long been a notable advocate of Ligeti's work. This is the updated version of a brief but important book that first appeared in 1983.

Griffiths, P. *Modern Music and After: Directions since 1945* (Oxford, Oxford University Press, 1995) This excellent summary of the last fifty years of Western classical music gives some prominence to Ligeti's work.

Friedemann, S. *An Introduction to the Early Works of György Ligeti* (Cologne, Studio–Schewe, 1996)
The most detailed examination to date of Ligeti's works prior to leaving Hungary.

English Versions of Ligeti's Major Articles

'Pierre Boulez: Decision and Automatism in Structure 1a', in *die reihe*, No. 4 (1960) [originally 'Pierre Boulez: Entscheidung und Automatik in der Structure Ia', in *die reihe*, No. 4 (1958)]
An important analysis in its own right, this was also the article that formulated Ligeti's scepticism about aspects of the young avant garde.

'Metamorphoses of Musical Form', in *die reihe*, No. 7 (1965) [originally 'Wandlungen der musikalischen Form', in *die reihe*, No. 7 (?1961)]
A classic statement of Ligeti's position at the time of his first masterpieces.

'On My Piano Concerto', in *Sonus*, ix/1 (1988) [originally in German]
Part of 'György Ligeti's Sixty-Fifth Birthday: A Celebration', which also includes Ligeti's notes on the early *Etudes*, and pages from the *Nonsense Rhymes*.

'States, Events, Transformations', in *Perspectives of New Music*, No. 31/1 (1993) [originally 'Zustände, Ereignisse, Wandlungen', *Bilder und Blätter*, ii (1960)]
Related to 'Metamorphoses of Musical Form', and dealing mainly with *Apparitions*, this important essay had to wait over three decades for translation.

Other Articles in English

Bernard, J. 'Inaudible Structures, Audible Music: Ligeti's Problem, and his Solution', in *Music Analysis*, vi, No. 3 (1987)
An important study of Ligeti's work in the 1960s.

Steinitz, R. 'The Dynamics of Disorder', in *Musical Times*, cxxxvii/May (1996)

Steinitz, R. 'Weeping and Wailing', in *Musical Times*, cxxxvii/August (1996)
These two articles offer fascinating insights into some of the Etudes.

Books and Articles in Other Languages

Though the following references will only be useful
to a minority of readers, they were important sources
of information for this book.

Burde, W. *Győrgy Ligeti: Eine Monographie* (Zürich,
Atlantis, 1993)
Burde's book is especially valuable for its biographical
information on the early years, and its discussion
of earlier works.

Dibelius, U. *Ligeti: Eine Monographie in Essays* (Mainz,
B. Schott's Söhne, 1994)
Dibelius astutely examines many different aspects
of Ligeti's work and thinking, and ends with
an excellent interview.

Floros, C. *Győrgy Ligeti: Jenseits von Avantgarde und
Postmoderne* (Vienna, Lafite, 1996)
The latest German monograph is particularly
informative about recent works, and contains several
colour plates of sketches, as well as childhood maps
of 'Kylwiria'.

Michel, P. *Győrgy Ligeti: Compositeur d'aujourd'hui*
(Paris, Minerve, 1986)
A good all-round book – biography, analyses and
some interviews.

Stürzbecher, U. *Werkstattgespräche mit Komponisten*
(Cologne, Gerig, 1971)
This includes a relatively early, wide-ranging interview
with Ligeti.

'Ligeti/Kurtág', *Contrechamps*, Nos. 12–13 (1990)
A double issue devoted to the two composers, with
contributions by both.

'Győrgy Ligeti 70th Birthday Issue', *Neue Zeitschrift für
Musik,* No. 154 (1993)
An excellent collection of articles – and an extended
interview on CD – including:

Ferguson, S. 'Tradition – Wirkung – Rezeption:
Anmerkungen zu Ligetis Klaviermusik'

Gawriloff, S. 'Ein Meisterwerk von Ligeti:
Marginalien zur Entstehung des Violonkonzerts'

Ligeti, G. 'Rhapsodische, unausgewogene Gedanken
über Musik, besonders über meine eigenen
Komposition'

Sabbe, H. 'Vorausblick in neue Vergangenheit: Ligeti
und die Tradition'

Selective Discography

There are two major components to the Ligeti discography. The first is a series of recordings on Wergo, initially issued on vinyl from the late 1960s onwards. In many cases the performers are the dedicatees and/or first performers of the work, and they recapture much of the excitement of those early performances. Unfortunately, some of the CD remastering shows signs of haste and carelessness (including the omission of the opening bars of *Continuum*). The other major contribution is the Complete Works series from Sony, seven volumes of which have appeared at the time of writing. This series, undertaken in collaboration with the composer, makes many works (especially early ones) available for the first time. The recording quality is, naturally, superior to that of the Wergo recordings, but in this author's view not all the performances are equally superior, though many are superb. In addition, there are many other individual CDs of Ligeti's works. Those selected below either offer outstanding performances, or else a particularly attractive combination of works.

In 1993 (i.e. prior to the appearance of the Sony series) Ligeti wrote an article for the *Neue Zeitschrift für Musik* which took a by no means uncritical view of his discography to that date. Performances which he praised highly are marked with an asterisk (*).

Wergo CDs

Six of them have been repackaged in two 3-CD sets. Special Edition 1 (WER 6901-2) comprises:

Musica Ricercata
Capriccios 1 & 2
Invention
Three Pieces for Two Pianos
Begoña Uriate, Hermann Mrongovius (pianos)
WER 60131-50

Continuum
Ten Pieces
Artikulation
Glissandi
Etudes for organ *
Volumina
Antoinette Vischer (harpsichord), Karl-Erik Welin (organ), Zsigmond Szathmáry (organ), Südwestfunk Wind Quintet
WER 60161-50

Chamber Concerto *
Ramifications
Lux Aeterna
Atmosphères *
Reihe Ensemble conducted by Friedrich Cerha; Südwestfunk Symphony Orchestra conducted by Ernest Bour; Saarland Radio Chamber Orchestra conducted by Antonio Janigro; Schola Cantorum Stuttgart conducted by Clytus Gottwald
WER 60162-50

Special Edition 2 (WER 6904-2) comprises:

String Quartets 1 * *& 2* *
Arditti Quartet
WER 60079-50

Horn Trio *
Passacaglia ungherese *
Hungarian Rock *
Continuum *
Three Pieces for Two Pianos *
Saschko Gawriloff (violin), Hermann Baumann (horn), Eckart Besch (piano), Elizabeth Chojnacka (harpsichord), Bruno Canino and Antonio Ballista (pianos)
WER 60100-50

Cello Concerto *
Lontano *
Double Concerto
San Francisco Polyphony
Siegfried Palm (cello), Hessian Radio Symphony
Orchestra conducted by Michael Gielen; SWF
Symphony Orchestra conducted by Ernest Bour;
Swedish Radio Symphony Orchestra conducted by
Elgar Howarth
WER 60163-50

Sony György Ligeti Edition

Vol. 1 String Quartets and Duets:
String Quartets 1 & 2
Hommage à Hilding Rosenberg
Balada si joc
Andante and Allegretto
Arditti Quartet
SONY SK 62306

Vol. 2 Choral Works, including:
Éjsaka
Reggel
Magány
Lux Aeterna
Three Fantasies after Hölderlin
Hungarian Etudes
London Sinfonietta Voices conducted by Terry
Edwards; with many of Ligeti's early choral works
SONY SK 62305

Vol. 3 Piano Music:
Etudes I-XV
Musica ricercata
Pierre-Laurent Aimard (piano)
SONY SK 62308

Vol. 4 Vocal Works:
Nonsense Madrigals
Mysteries of the Macabre
Aventures
Nouvelles Aventures
Der Sommer
Three Weöres Songs
Five Arany Songs
Four Wedding Dances
The King's Singers, Christiane Oelze (soprano), Phyllis
Bryn-Julson (soprano), Sibylle Ehlert (soprano), Eva
Wedin (soprano), Malena Ernman (mezzo-soprano),
Rose Taylor (contralto), Omar Ebrahim (baritone),
Pierre-Laurent Aimard & Irina Kataeva (pianos),
Philharmonia Orchestra conducted by Esa-Pekka
Salonen
SONY SK 62311

Vol. 5 Mechanical Music:
Poème symphonique
Continuum
Hungarian Rock, Capriccios 1 & 2, Invention (barrel
organ adaptations)
Etude XIV(a) (player piano version)
Etudes VII, IX. X, XI, XIII (adaptations)
Continuum
Françoise Terrioux (metronomes), Pierre Charial (barrel
organ), Jürgen Hocker (player pianos)
SONY SK 62310

Vol. 6 Keyboard Works:
Capriccios 1 & 2
Invention
Three Pieces for Two Pianos
Passacaglia ungherese
Hungarian Rock
Continuum
2 Etudes for organ
Ricercare
Volumina
Irina Kataeva (piano), Pierre-Laurent Aimard (piano),
Elisabeth Chojnacka (harpsichord), Zsigmond
Szathmáry (organ); with several early piano works
SONY SK 62307

Vol. 7 Chamber Music:
Horn Trio
Ten Pieces
Six Bagatelles
Sonata for Solo Viola
Saschko Gawriloff (violin), Marie-Luise Neunecker
(horn), Pierre-Laurent Aimard (piano), London Winds,
Tabea Zimmermann (viola)
SONY SK 62309

Le Grand Macabre (1997 version)
Laura Claycomb, Charlotte Hellekant, Jard van Nes,
Derek Lee Ragin, Graham Clark, Willard White, Frode
Olsen, London Sinfonietta Voices, Philharmonic
Orchestra conducted by Esa-Pekka Salonen
SONY SK 62312 (2 CDs)

Other Recordings

Aventures *
Nouvelles Aventures *
Requiem *
Gertie Charlent, Marie Thérèse Cahn, William
Pearson, Darmstadt International Chamber Ensemble
conducted by Bruno Maderna; Liliana Poli, Barbro
Ericson, Bavarian Radio Chorus, Hessian Radio
Symphony Orchestra conducted by Michael Gielen
WER 60045-50

Le Grand Macabre (original version) *
Dieter Weller, Penelope Walmsley-Clark, Olive
Fredricks, Peter Haage, ORF Chorus, Arnold
Schönberg Choir, Gumpoldskirchner Spatzen, ORF
Symphony Orchestra conducted by Elgar Howarth
WER 6170-2

Cello Concerto
Piano Concerto
Chamber Concerto
Miklós Perényi (cello), Ueli Wiget (piano), Ensemble
Modern conducted by Peter Eötvös
SONY SK 58945

Cello Concerto
Piano Concerto
Violin Concerto
Jean-Guihen Queyras (cello), Pierre-Laurent Aimard
(piano), Saschko Gawriloff (violin), Ensemble
InterContemporain conducted by Pierre Boulez
DG 439 808–2

String Quartet No. 2 *
Ramifications *
Chamber Concerto
La Salle Quartet, Ensemble InterContemporain
conducted by Pierre Boulez
DGG 423 244–2

Index

Photographic
Acknowledgements

Per B Adolphson: 2, 93, 128–9
AKG London: 20–21, 23, 25l, 34,
    47, 48, 53, 110, 119, 154
BFI, London: 15, 139b
© Cordon Art B. V., Baarn,
    Holland: 123
Corbis, London: 139t, 145, 204
DPA Bildarchiv, Frankfurt: 151
Andras Farkas: 18
Betty Freeman: 179, 213
Ines Gellrich: 186
The Gilbert and Lila Silverman
    Fluxus Collection Foundation,
    New York: 81, 82
Gisela Gronemeyer: 181
The Hulton Getty Picture
    Collection: 9
Interfoto, Budapest: 196–7
Internationales Musikinstitut,
    Darmstadt: 54, 65, 69, 73, 95,
    113, 132, 141, 172
Wolfgang Kaehler/Corbis: 143
The Lebrecht Collection, London:
    85 (Nigel Sutton), 101
By permission of György Ligeti: 13
Maria Austria, Maria Austria
    Institute, Amsterdam: 98
National Széchényi Library,
    Budapest: 29
The Estate of Ove Nordwall: 108
Performing Arts Library/Clive
    Barda: 164
Peters Edition, London: 91, 103
Popperfoto, Northampton: 37
Royal Opera Stockholm: 157,
    158–9, 161, 162, 168
The Science Photo Library,
    London: 193
Horst Tappe: 200
Peter Turnley/Corbis: 202

Universal Edition, Vienna: 78
Claudio Veress: 25r
Guy Vivien: 203, 210, 217
Ruth Walz: 166–7, 218–9
Westdeutscher Rundfunk,
    Cologne: 45, 55, 63
Adam Woolfitt/Corbis: 207